Changing
PACE

Sir Richard Hadlee

Changing PACE

A Memoir

Hodder Moa

National Library of New Zealand Cataloguing-in-Publication Data

Hadlee, Richard, 1951-

Changing pace : a memoir / Sir Richard Hadlee.

ISBN 978-1-86971-128-3

1. Hadlee, Richard, 1951-. 2. Cricket players—New Zealand—
Biography. 3. Cricket—New Zealand—History. I. Title.

796.358092—dc 22

A Hodder Moa Book

Published in 2009 by Hachette New Zealand Ltd
4 Whetu Place, Mairangi Bay
Auckland, New Zealand

Designed and produced by Hachette New Zealand Ltd
Printed by Everbest Printing Co. Ltd., China

To Mum and Dad
Thanks for all the wonderful love and support you have
given me in my life.

To my sons, Nicholas and Matthew
I am proud of the young men you have become.

To my wife, Dianne
My companion on life's journey.

Contents

Foreword

In sport, as in other fields of endeavour, the transition from young tyro to champion thoroughbred is an integral part of career development. In cricket, the youngster with tons of raw talent, but little knowledge of the art and craft, must serve those formative years often on natural ability and instinct alone. After honing those skills and harnessing the talent, there sometimes emerges a confident, polished performer who has got it together and can pace himself physically.

In R.J. Hadlee's case, I was lucky enough to witness that metamorphosis first hand. I first came into contact with Richard's bowling, his attitude to the game and his training habits back in 1976/77 when I was part of a very good Australian side that toured New Zealand. It included Ian and Greg Chappell, Doug Walters, Rod Marsh, Gary Gilmour, Max Walker and others.

In those days Richard commenced his long run in with a stuttering start, charged to the wicket like a bull at a red rag, and finally projected the ball at the batsman as fast as he could. He was very much the embryo fast bowler, with little or no subtlety.

During the tour, I chatted several times to the young Hadlee and we discussed a number of things such as fitness routines and food and drink intake. He agreed with me that meat pies, Coca-Cola and little physical fitness activity, apart from net sessions, was not the prescribed diet for him to reach the top, let alone stay there.

Richard has very kindly credited me with helping to start him along his pathway to success. And while I am the first to concede that my contribution to his total achievements was small, he at least listened and learned from that experience.

When I looked at R.J. Hadlee throughout the 1980s, I saw a complete athlete. His attention to detail ensured that he was well honed and he turned out to be the ultimate fast bowler. He was, without question, one of the top fast bowlers of all time — if not the best — a great example of the determination, skill and dedication that was required to master the art of fast bowling.

Richard, I've enjoyed (and sometimes not enjoyed!) some of those close encounters on the cricket field, and you have deserved all the successes you have had. Well done on a great playing career, congratulations on what you have done for New Zealand cricket and may our friendship be life long.

Dennis Lillee

Introduction

My autobiography, *Rhythm and Swing*, was released in 1989 and consequently did not include my last tour of England in 1990. During that tour I captured a wicket with the very last ball I bowled in international cricket, to end with a world record 431 test wickets during my 18-year test career. I also turned 39 as I retired from the international scene and was knighted for services to New Zealand cricket while still playing my last two tests.

This book tells the story of my life since that time, and if I thought things would slow down a little after retiring, I was wrong. Since then, I have had open heart surgery, my marriage has ended and a new relationship begun, I've written several cricketing books, I've been the chairman of selectors for New Zealand Cricket (NZC) and, along with my family, I've been through the emotional roller-coaster of my dad's decline and death in 2006.

This book describes those events and also explains many of the issues faced and decisions made by the selectors during my tenure on the panel. I outline what I think of the current group of players and what happened on our ill-fated 2003 World Cup campaign. I look at the emergence of the New Zealand Cricket Players' Association (CPA) and events of the players' strike in 2002 — a strike that was so destructive that many ex-players and older stalwarts of the game were reduced to tears. Dad said to me: 'The players have abused and betrayed our game — all for personal greed. They have held our game to ransom.'

My tenure as chairman of selectors came at a tumultuous time, with many issues and controversies that captured the public's and the media's imagination. I was attacked constantly by the *New Zealand Herald* and their sports writer Richard Boock, who 'bagged' me throughout my time as a selector. We had a tempestuous relationship and in this book I try to understand why Richard Boock took this view.

The book also contains many key thoughts regarding what motivated me as a player and how I was driven by personal goals and targets to be the best I could be. I recall the magic moments and my most memorable matches, and take a light-hearted look at myself and the fun I had in the commentary box. I examine my relationship with some of the media and there are personal thoughts on the state of the game today.

I would like to acknowledge the support of my wife, Dianne, who has assisted me in writing this book by editing my very raw manuscripts into readable form, Peter Marriott for providing my final career statistics and Dennis Lillee for his kind words. I valued the support and friendship of my co-selectors Ross Dykes, Brian McKechnie, Glenn Turner, Dion Nash and coaches Dave Trist, Denis Aberhart and John Bracewell. It has been a privilege to have been associated with NZC and the Black Caps.

For more information on Sir Richard Hadlee and
memorabilia items visit the website www.hadlee.co.nz

The Last Goodbye

As the saying goes, there are few sure things in life, except death and taxes. Over the years, I have attended a number of funerals and supported friends who have lost close family members, and although I could see their pain and felt for them in their grief, nothing prepared me for the depth of the raw emotional experience of Dad's death in September 2006.

Dad's impact on my life was, and remains, enormous. If it were not for his love of the game of cricket and the interest and dedication he showed in the early years when I played cricket with my brothers (on a pitch he prepared for us in the back yard and using his playing equipment) I may never have played the game to any great degree. Greater still was Dad's unconditional love, guidance, support and infinite wisdom. I will forever treasure my memories of him.

Walter Arnold Hadlee was born in 1915. He lived for cricket and the game gave him great joy and pleasure. He played test cricket for New Zealand, captaining the team on their successful tour of England in 1949. He later became a national selector, and was manager of the national team's tour to England in 1965, before becoming the Chairman and then President of the New Zealand Cricket Council (NZCC). He also held many honorary and life membership positions in cricket, such was his devotion and commitment to the game.

As an accountant he had an eye for detail and planning, and this was evident in the 1949 tour of England, which was a huge success. The team lost only one match and won nearly half of their 36 matches on tour. Importantly, they drew all four tests against England. This was a remarkable achievement in our cricketing history.

He believed in supporting charities and was a religious man, following the beliefs of the Methodist Church. He had extraordinary values, which he shared with many people, and was held in the highest regard around the world. He believed in fair play and sportsmanship. The spirit of the game was always uppermost in his mind. For him it was about knowing that he had done the right thing, and his ethics could never be questioned.

In the first test of the 1950/51 series against England at Christchurch, England opened the batting with Len Hutton and Cyril Washbrook. When Washbrook had scored 13, there was a stifled lbw appeal from the bowler, Fen Creswell, and umpire Tonkinson raised his finger. Dad was certain that he had heard a snick as the ball went from bat to pad. As Cyril walked slowly back to the pavilion he passed Dad at mid-off and Dad told him to wait a moment. Dad went over to Fen and asked if he thought Cyril had hit the ball. Fen replied: 'He did. I didn't mean to appeal.' Dad then asked the umpire if he could revoke the appeal and recall the batsman. It was agreed, and Cyril resumed his innings and went on to make 58. Dad said: 'Our consciences are clear.' Years later, when Dad and Cyril met, Cyril told him that he had never forgotten Dad's kind gesture and confirmed that he had in fact hit the ball.

Dad turned 91 on 4 June 2006. It was a normal celebration, with family members dropping around to Mum and Dad's home throughout the day to take Dad a card or gift and share a cup of tea and a chat. Mum and Dad were never happier than when they had family visiting and the faithful teapot was seldom empty. Dad always tried to ensure that we left laden with vegetables from his much loved garden.

People were continually amazed at how active Dad was. He was meticulous in answering his mail and having all his affairs in order. Even at 90 years of age Dad still mowed his own lawns, did odd jobs around the house, was

Tel: 061-980 2684

31 Briony Avenue,
Hale,
Altrincham
Cheshire
WA15 8PY.

June 14th 1990

Dear Walter.

Thank you for the message you sent to me by our Treasurer. I was delighted to receive it, and I am sorry there is no Test Match at Manchester to allow us to meet once again. I have told the story of how you brought me back after being given out L.B.W. I can assure you now that I did hit the ball.

I hope you have a very happy time during your visit to England.

Yours sincerely
Cyril Washbrook

Cyril Washbrook's letter to Dad.

actively involved with a number of organisations and regularly attended functions, which included speaking on occasions. He was also still playing bowls regularly and although the family felt that at times he was a hazard on the road, he had managed to retain his driver's licence, no doubt assisted by the fact that he had memorised the letters on the eye testing chart!

The day after his ninety-first birthday, Dad tripped over at home and broke his right hip. Tragically, this was the start of the final three months of his life. He had three metal pins inserted into his hip to hold the joint together and, initially, this was successful. We could see improvements in his mobility, especially as he pushed his walking frame to the elevators when family who had been visiting were leaving the hospital. Competitive as always, he would often put in a huge effort to ensure that he reached the lifts before we did.

During this time, Mum also had a fall at home and although nothing was broken, she needed to spend a few weeks in a nursing home to recuperate. We tried to keep Mum's situation from Dad as we knew he would be anxious for her, but when we realised that he would soon wonder why he couldn't reach her at home by phone, I went to tell him the news. As we had expected, he was devastated and inconsolable, blaming himself for not being at home to prevent her accident. Fortunately, we were able to take Mum to see Dad and they were able to spend time together and take stock of the situation. It was touching to watch them together, still very much in love, trying to comfort one another as they held hands.

Within a few weeks, they were both home again, although, unfortunately for Dad, his recovery had become slow and painful. X-rays showed that his hip bones were flaking away from around the pins and could no longer support his body. The result was constant pain. This distressed Dad greatly and his quality of life was severely compromised. He was given the option of having a total hip replacement operation, and was enthusiastic about the possibility of a good recovery and regaining his mobility. He talked about getting back behind the wheel of his car, and although the family knew that he would never drive again, we didn't tell him our thoughts as he was so motivated.

Prior to his operation, Dad was told of the risks associated with an operation at his age and although he was both concerned and disheartened by this knowledge, he was prepared to back the odds in an attempt to improve his quality of life. We were with Mum when Dad was returned to his room after the operation, which had apparently gone well. Dad was tired but chatted with us and drank a cup of tea. Assured that he was comfortable and was settling in to sleep, we left the hospital and took Mum home.

Sometime during the evening Dad suffered a stroke that immobilised his right side and took away his power of speech, leaving him unable to communicate except for the raising of his eyebrows, the odd smile and occasional wave of his left hand. For a man who was mentally alert and with a rich and wonderful memory, this was a tragedy beyond belief; he now had no way of telling us what he wanted or how he felt. I could not contain my emotions as I visited him like this and I know he saw the sadness and despair that I was experiencing, just as I could see and feel his. During this time in hospital, Mum spent up to eight hours a day sitting with him, chatting to him, reading him the paper and dozing with him as they held hands. It was very difficult to watch the shared love of a 66-year partnership in crisis.

For six agonising weeks we watched his health decline and his willpower weaken. His dignity was steadily being eroded — this was a slow and relentless degradation of a man who until then had had all his faculties intact. Dad believed that a strong handshake could determine the strength and character of a person, and each day when I left him I would hold his left hand and he enjoyed showing me the strength of his grip.

This ritual ended the day before his death, when he had no response at all in his hand. Unknown to me at that time, it was my last goodbye — the end of an innings of a lifetime was only hours away. On the morning of Friday, 29 September 2006, I was driving Mum to the hospital to see Dad, when I received the call that he had gone. With tears rolling down my face I passed on the news to Mum and we continued on, lost in our own sadness.

Within minutes the family were together to say goodbye to Dad. Although I had a deep sense of relief that his suffering had ended, it was more than I could bear to see him lying in his bed and Mum so devastated. The family spent the morning together at the hospital and it was a precious time during which we gained comfort and strength from one another. Within an hour of Dad's passing, although neither the family nor the hospital had released any information, the news of his death was on the radio and television news in New Zealand and Australia.

It had been difficult to maintain privacy during Dad's illness as reports of his condition had been in the media and many people, obviously well intentioned, would ask after him whenever I was in public. Even walking the dog, strangers would stop me and ask after Dad, and I constantly struggled with my emotions as I had to respond. The family unanimously decided to have a private family funeral service where we could say our goodbyes to Dad, and then hold a public memorial service a couple of weeks later.

During Dad's illness, I had been suffering from a heart condition. My heartbeat would kick out of rhythm and, instead of beating solidly, one chamber would fibrillate or flutter. Apparently, this was caused by my body releasing adrenalin as a response to the stress I was feeling. This condition could result in complications when the heart kicked back into its normal rhythm if the blood, not moving as the heart fibrillated, had formed clots. Although this problem was not directly caused by the congenital heart condition I had been born with, it was indirectly related to it by some scar tissue that I had as a result of the operation to correct the original disorder.

On 3 October 2006, a day that dawned cold and raining, the family gathered in St John's Methodist Church, where Mum and Dad had been parishioners for 60 years. Seated in a circle around a flower-laden casket, we said goodbye to our much loved dad, father-in-law, grandfather and husband, in an emotional service, with many sharing personal memories and speaking confidently, while I wept openly and struggled to express some heartfelt thoughts. I stumbled my way through a few brief words: 'It is time to say thank you to you, Dad. Thank you for your love, kindness, generosity, advice, support, and for just being there. You were everything expected of a father. We had some wonderful times. You will be missed. Rest in peace.'

During the next few weeks the family received hundreds of cards and letters expressing condolences and sympathies. With his extensive contributions to sport, business, church life and numerous charities, acknowledgments were received from all around the world. The common themes in the messages we received were of dignity, humility and compassion, and all spoke of their respect for a man who always took the time to give to others.

We held a memorial service for Dad in the Christchurch Boys' High School Auditorium in October 2006. It was a grand occasion, attended by approximately 800 people, to celebrate a life of achievement and success and to give many of his friends and associates the opportunity to pay their respects. There were several speakers, including long-time family friend, former cricket commentator Iain Gallaway, and the president of New Zealand Cricket, Don Neely, who was brilliant, as ever, in his research and delivery. The speakers and musicians — who included my brother Dayle and the former CEO of New Zealand Cricket, Chris Doig — all contributed to a fitting and, for me, very emotional service and I was very moved to see a number of my former team-mates in attendance as well. Although most had come from out of town to support me, they also had their own memories of Dad and the effect he had on their lives.

Years on, I have come to terms with Dad not being here but there are still some wonderful memories that will never be forgotten. Sometimes it is just the little things that are missed, of looking out the office window and visualising him driving up to our home and shuffling out of his car with yet another bag of vegetables, a huge grin on his face.

Much of my life had taken me away from Christchurch and family, but over the last 11 years of his life I had become a lot closer to him and Mum. They only lived a couple of kilometres away, and were often with us for dinner or to watch a game of rugby on our big screen. These were special times, and while life goes on, it will be a lot emptier without him, such was his impact on my life.

A fitting epitaph for Walter Arnold Hadlee CBE and OBE, known as Wal, Dad, Grandpa, W.A. and 'Skipper' (a name given to him during the 1949 tour of England and for the rest of his life by team members): 'And when the Great Scorer comes, to write against your name, it matters not that you won or lost, but how you played the game.'

Reflections

My ancestry is Scottish and English: Mum, née Monro, is of Scottish descent, and Dad came from an English heritage. My grandfather was named John Hadlee and my father, Walter, was named after an uncle who served in the First World War. Over time, the names Richard, John and Robert have often appeared as Christian names in our family — I am named Richard John, two of my brothers are named Dayle Robert and Martin John and one of my sons is named Nicholas John. But of course there are other names in our family too: my other brothers are named Barry George and Christopher Wallace, while my second son is named Matthew James.

For my first 39 years — until I retired from playing internationally — cricket was a major part of my life. I was raised in a cricketing family, with Dad having played for and captained New Zealand, as well as having major roles in cricket administration. My older brothers, Barry and Dayle, also played for New Zealand. As a baby I was regularly taken to Dad's club and provincial matches. Mum was there too of course, providing the team morning and afternoon teas and lunch while keeping an ever watchful eye on the Hadlee boys, who would all be at the cricket.

Around the age of seven or eight, I began playing cricket in the back yard with my brothers. We had all the correct cricket gear and plenty of encouragement to play the game. Mum also played an essential role in those cricket matches. Again, we were always fed and watered, and first aid was often administered by her capable hands. Mum also gave me my first introduction to match referees, as our brotherly encounters were always highly competitive. I'm not sure that I liked some of her decisions, but it provided me with many opportunities to practise my appealing and eventually taught me to accept decisions. After all, if I did not accept her decision there was the chance that I might go without my evening meal.

On rainy days I would play imaginary test matches in the garage. I would put a cricket ball in a sock, attach a rope to the sock and the other end to the rafters so that I had a ball on a string. I would sneak into Dad's cricket bag and put on his Canterbury or New Zealand cap, along with the big baggy pads and gloves. I would hit that ball again and again — I would always score a hundred and never get out. It only took 25 hits to score a hundred! At cricket grounds I had noted that when someone had scored a hundred, they would take their cap off and raise their bat to the crowd, so, of course, I did likewise. All the time I was playing in the garage, I was unaware that Mum and Dad would sometimes watch from a window upstairs. It must have looked quite amusing, I imagine.

In the first two houses we lived in, Dad made sure that we had a cricket pitch in the back yard — one was a concrete pitch and the other a grass pitch. On a fine day, there were times when I would cut and roll the pitch to pretend that I was the groundsman preparing a test match pitch. In those days I was a skinny little fellow and my hand was not big enough to hold and control a real cricket ball, so I used to bowl a golf ball and tried to hit one wicket. If the ball missed the wicket, which happened quite often, the golf ball would bounce back from the side wall of the brick garage and I would dive and catch it with one hand, as though I were the wicketkeeper, someone at first slip or as if it were a caught-and-bowled dismissal. I always got 20 wickets and never lost a test match. I lived in a dream world, a wonderful land of make believe.

At night I would take a scorebook to bed and score an imaginary test match with the heroes of that time. As a selector, I picked myself, scored the odd hundred and captured a few five-wicket bags. Of course, New

Zealand never lost a match. I would also do cricket commentaries, with Mum and Dad often listening outside the door. Without knowing it, I was preparing myself for the future and reality — I did go on to play for cricket for New Zealand, create three world records, coach young fast bowlers, become a television and radio commentator, and a national selector.

During this time, whenever a first-class match was being played at Lancaster Park in Christchurch, I used to gather up empty bottles from the spectators on the embankment and collect the refund of two pence from the shop to buy an ice cream or some sweets. I used to compete against myself to see how many bottles I could collect in a day. I was never too embarrassed to ask spectators if they had finished or wanted their empty bottles. I had a nice little business going.

At around 12 or 13 years of age, I used to sell programmes to the spectators at Lancaster Park. At 16, along with seven or eight other youngsters, I helped operate the gigantic scoreboard on the embankment at the ground. I often looked out from the scoreboard area over the playing arena, saying to myself: 'Wouldn't it be nice to be out there playing a real game of cricket for my province or country?' Five years later, at the age of 21, that land of make believe that I had lived in became a reality and I played my first match for Canterbury, followed a year later by my first match for New Zealand.

At school I played cricket, rugby and soccer. I recall once playing Lyttelton at the Lyttelton Domain, not far from the port, when I was about nine years old. When we were five metres from the Lyttelton line, someone from the touchline, it could have been Dad, yelled out: 'Pick the ball up, attack the line and score a try.' I was the nearest to the ball so I picked it up and ran for the line. I didn't know what the word 'attack' meant, but I ran and ran. In fact I ran 90 metres, and touched down under my own posts at the other end! It appeared that 14 other players in my team did not know what the word 'attack' meant either, because they all followed me and cheered me on. I guess rugby was never going to be my game and although I did play some rugby in high school, I had a slight build and was only a very timid winger and soon switched to playing goalkeeper in soccer.

My early years at school were at Elmwood and Fendalton Primary, followed by Heaton Intermediate School. I used to ride a three-wheeled chain-driven tricycle to Elmwood, shooting along the footpath ringing my bell and sometimes swerving wildly to avoid cars that were backing out of driveways.

I vividly remember having to leave Fendalton School when they changed from being a full primary school to one that only went to the end of standard four (now called year six). I then had to go to an intermediate school for my final two years of primary education before going to high school. That meant I did not play in the annual Fathers v Sons cricket match that had been a traditional feature of the final year at school for those in standard six. That really disappointed me.

I also recall Fendalton's athletics carnival when I competed in the 220-yard race for the Tosswell Cup. The first year I competed, I sprinted from the outset in an effort to beat the school champion, Graeme Gemmell. By the time I had gone 150 yards I started to tire, and with 20 yards to go my legs had given way and I was well beaten into fourth place. I had not trained and I paid the price. The following year I prepared myself better, paced myself and won the Cup. It was my first trophy and was a proud moment — and a lesson learned.

The two years I had at Heaton Intermediate were nothing too spectacular for me. One occasion I recall distinctly was a general knowledge test in which we were asked: 'Who was the captain of the New Zealand Cricket team in 1949?' I knew the answer to that question and wrote down 'Dad', but was marked as being incorrect. I wasn't too happy about that — it was all a matter of interpretation! I also had my first experience of making a fool of myself in the classroom when I had to read aloud to the class. I said: 'The Maoris were singing the Treaty of Waitangi . . . ' instead of 'signing' the Treaty. Perhaps an easy mistake to make, but from that point on reading was never a popular pastime.

We lived in Wairarapa Terrace until 1958 when we moved to 41 Fendalton Road. It was tucked away down a long, tree-lined shingle drive that led to a very large back section on which stood a large, two-storeyed, white, wooden house, a separate brick double garage and a separate green shed. The shed was a playhouse for me and friends and was good enough to be used as a sleep-out. Like many young boys I played 'Cowboys and Indians' in the back yard and used the shed as a base for the 'cavalry'. I decided to name the shed 'The Triple Trigger Club' and painted the name on the door. I was admiring my artistic touch when one of my brothers noticed that I had misspelt the name — The Tipple Trigger Club did not have the same appeal or meaning but it remained on the door for years — perhaps there was something wrong with my eyes after all.

There were always jobs to do around the house — every week I cut the lawns, which were extensive, and I helped with the gardening and raked the leaves in autumn. On Friday nights I used to make the supper and the cheese toasties, or 'mousetraps' as they were called. As bedtime was about 8.30 pm, I would time the production of these delicacies to more or less happen at that time, so that I could walk into the living room with the supper tray for seven people and then watch James Garner in the television series 'Maverick' — something that probably explains my continued interest in western movies.

I learned to drive when living on Fendalton Road. Mum had a Ford Anglia with a floor gear change and I could get through three gears down our long drive before stopping and reversing all the way back. Somehow it seemed to take less time to get back to the house than going forward. With a shingle drive and courtyard in front of the house, I could do a few wheelies, much to Mum's disgust. I would then have to get the rake and smooth out the skid marks in the shingle.

Along with kicking a football and playing 'test' cricket matches and practising in the back yard, trout fishing and boating on the Wairarapa Stream that ran past our section were the order of the day. Around the age of 14, sport really took off for me. I could not get enough. One minute I would be hitting a cricket ball and then I'd be bowling it, next I'd be kicking a soccer ball, then a rugby ball, and because Dad had also played representative hockey, I would find his hockey stick and have a game by whacking the ball into the side of the brick garage where there was an imaginary goal.

In 1965 I was selected for the Canterbury Primary Schools XI to compete at the South Island cricket tournament in Ashburton. We finished second, behind Otago. It was a memorable tournament for me because I captured 15 wickets for 56 runs and scored a few runs as well, reaching 20-odd on several occasions. At the conclusion of the tournament, back in Christchurch at Hagley Park, I was presented with the ball (mounted) with which I took 5/14 against Central Otago. That was the first cricket trophy I had ever won.

Later that year I was asked to fill in as a replacement player for the High School Old Boys' Presidents team (the over 40-year-olds). At 14 years of age it was easy to feel intimidated and out of place playing against men. But that was short-lived. Playing against Riccarton I had a field day — I scored 43 not out in 30 minutes and then went on to capture five wickets in one over, including a hat-trick. We scored 92 but bowled them out so cheaply and quickly that it was decided Riccarton should bat again. I had nine wickets in the match, seven in the first innings and two in the second innings. I was able to hold my own in a different league.

Between 1965 and 1969 my secondary school education was at Christchurch Boys' High School. I had five great years at CBHS, playing cricket and soccer for the first elevens, and captaining both the cricket and soccer teams in my last year. I was a goalkeeper in the soccer team and that experience helped me to become reasonably proficient when I fielded in the gully position in cricket. However, my academic record at school was only average. Needing a pass mark of 200 points in my four best subjects, I failed my School Certificate by five marks in 1967, but sat it again the following year, passing it with flying colours. I hadn't put a lot of effort into studying first time round and I learned a valuable lesson: if I coasted along aimlessly, I would pay the price. Failure was not a nice option — it was embarrassing, degrading and disappointing. Planning, preparing, implementing and achieving became a major part of my life's philosophy. The rewards of success were there to be enjoyed.

In my last year at high school, I was a prefect. That was my first experience of having a position of real responsibility and, hopefully, respect among my peers. I was able to enforce the school rules and impose penalties for those who chose to cross the line. Discipline became important to me but I believe I was fair and listened to reason without being dictated to by those who offended.

I managed to avoid the senior school dance, as well as most other situations involving girls. Such encounters were well outside the comfort zone for a shy lad raised in a family with four brothers. 'Womanhood' was not a subject much discussed around our dinner table. Even our dog, a little Maltese terrier, was a male, and I guess it was Dad who had named him 'Randy'.

At CBHS I was taught by three former All Blacks — Pat Vincent, Tony Steele and John Graham. Mr Graham taught me English, History and the meaning of the word 'procrastination'. After I had turned in a late assignment he said, 'You are a procrastinator, Hadlee.' I had to ask him what that meant. He replied, 'You keep delaying things.' From that point on I was determined to be reliable, punctual and well organised.

John Graham taught me to speak with clear diction, to use words in their proper context and to use tenses correctly. One day at school he asked me to demonstrate the different tenses of a verb. I thought that cricket would be a very good way of illustrating the matter.

'I was a good cricketer — that is the past tense, sir.'

'Very good, Hadlee.'

'I will be a good cricketer — that is the future tense, sir.'

'Excellent, Hadlee, you are learning fast,' he said.

'I am a good cricketer . . . '

At which point he interrupted with a smile and said, 'I am sorry, Hadlee, that's *pretence*.'

While I was in the fourth form (14 years old) at CBHS, part of the school sports events was a bowling competition. I felt I had a reasonable chance of winning that, so I entered. I felt a little nervous and apprehensive but it was a chance to win a sports award for cricket at school and impress the First XI coach, who was watching. I let rip and bowled as fast as I could but unfortunately my line and length suffered considerably and after six balls

I was eliminated from the competition, which disappointed me. Someone pointed out to me that it wasn't in fact a fast-bowling competition but a competition for accuracy. On reflection I did myself no favours by trying to bowl too fast, as the ball ended up in the right-hand corner of the net on six consecutive occasions. Common sense suggested I could not expect to win anything if I bowled like that. At that point, I thought I would give bowling away and concentrate more on my batting. Thankfully, the advice from school coaches was to keep bowling.

My first real bollocking in cricket came in 1966 when, at 15 years of age, I was asked to be twelfth man for the school First XI. I had no experience of the twelfth man role, as teams I had previously played in had only ever had 11 players. Robert Anderson (who later opened the batting for New Zealand in 1978) was captain. For some reason I was asked to go on to the field of play and I still had my size 12 black school shoes on instead of my boots. Robert tore a strip off me and told me that it was not good enough and that I needed to be better prepared to do the twelfth man job properly. From that point on the lesson had been learned.

When I was 16 my cricket career nearly ended before it got started. I was cutting the lawns at home and noticed that the blades of the mower had caught some flax-like grass. My first reaction was to pull the grass out, so I put the mower in neutral. Just as I touched the flax, the engine coughed, the blades moved and my right index finger was cut down through the nail and into the skin. Blood poured from the wound and I was lucky not to have lost the finger. My right index finger later became a very important part of my bowling technique. If I had severely damaged or lost my finger in that accident, I would never have played cricket again. I was lucky to get another chance.

In 1969 I was in my final year at school and I was captain of the First XI. The annual match against the Canterbury Supporters Club took place on the number one pitch, which ran between the school's war memorial shrine at one end and the main school steps at the other end. The CSC team had several first-class cricketers, as well as a few club and social cricketers. Dad was captain. This was my moment to forget about the

Fathers v Sons match that I missed at Fendalton School and play against Dad in a real match.

The CSC team made 131 in the 30-over match. Going into the last over we needed six runs to win the match but we managed to score only five. Everyone came off the field thinking a tied match was a very good result. But as I walked out onto the field to thank the opposition I put my hand out and shook Dad's hand.

'Thanks for the game, Dad. We enjoyed the match and are well pleased with the win.'

'What do you mean "win"? The match is tied.'

'We checked the scorebook and there was a mistake,' I said. 'It turned out we only needed five from the last over — and we got them.'

I could see that Dad was somewhat bemused. He said, 'The result may go down as a win in the school magazine but in the CSC's records, the result is a tie.'

To this day I still maintain that we had a win, but I was never that great at maths at school. In fact, I gave it up after the third form when it was no longer compulsory. History was a better subject for me . . .

As a youngster I enjoyed sport. I was nothing special or different from anyone else. I just played, had fun and tried to win. I did not like losing but I learnt how to lose, and that made me appreciate winning. Unless you learn the feeling of both, it is difficult to grow from the experience. I always acknowledged the victor because I expected the same courtesy when I had been successful.

Although Easter 1968 is now remembered for the tragic sinking of the inter-island ferry, the *Wahine*, and the subsequent sad loss of lives, I was unaware of the seriousness of those events as they unfolded and that Easter was, in fact, a memorable occasion for me. The weather around the country was atrocious but it did not prevent the annual cricket match at Patearoa in Central Otago being played. Iain Gallaway, a sporting stalwart and rugby and cricket commentator from Dunedin, and Dad would find a team each — from Dunedin and Christchurch respectively — to play one another. This tradition had been going for years. Patearoa is a little farming village in the Central Otago area near Ranfurly consisting of a pub and a few other small amenities. Teams would stay at the local pub and have a good time with a beer or two, but as I was still under the drinking age, it was inappropriate for me to stay there. I was billeted out and stayed on a farm — an enjoyable experience.

Over the Easter period we played several games around the Central Otago area. It was a big occasion for me, and, being a Hadlee, expectations were high. It was not as though I was brought into the team to make up the numbers — I wanted to do well and not embarrass myself or anyone else. I played in all the games and by the time I had returned home, I had not captured a wicket or scored a run. A year or two later I returned to Patearoa and I got to stay at the pub only to realise that most of us bunked in one room, which was rather crowded. I was allowed to sample a wee beer with the lads but more importantly I was able to capture a wicket and score a run or two.

In early 1970 I was selected for the Canterbury Colts cricket team to tour Northern NSW country to play against the Australian Emus team for the Boomerang Trophy. Mum and Dad paid about $700 for me to go on this two-week tour — my first overseas experience. This was a lot of money at that time, but Mum and Dad always seemed to sacrifice something and find the money for any of the boys to go on trips and play cricket. What fantastic parents they were. All the players had to finance their own trip to make the team — in simple terms, no money, no trip.

Although I had the money, I nearly didn't make the trip because of a breach of discipline that happened when playing for the Lancaster Park senior team. At the end of the day's play, I went back to the club rooms at Lancaster Park and had some social beers and downed a few jugs — it was in fact my first experience of sampling and then drinking the brown liquid in a public place. After a couple of hours, I was drunk and completely forgot to notify Mum and Dad that I would be late home for dinner. They were becoming concerned. Dad sent out a search party to find me and bring me home. In the meantime I had been dropped back at Hagley Park, at about 9.00 pm, to pick up my bicycle. In the fading light, my older brother Barry found me riding my bike home with my cricket gear bag over the handle bars, whistling, as happy as Larry, and my legs going like the clappers, with the bike wobbling from one side of the road to the other. If the police had seen me, no doubt I would have been stopped and would have had to explain to Mum and Dad that I was in trouble with the law, drunk-in-charge of a pushbike!

Of course, Mum and Dad soon observed the state I was in, and Dad did not approve, saying: 'If this is the way you want to carry on, the tour is off.' I would have been bitterly disappointed if I hadn't been allowed to go, but the lesson was learned — don't get caught by your parents if you've had a few too many beers!

The tour itself was a great opportunity and introduced me to both Sydney and hotel life for the first time — although bars were off limits. The team then travelled to Dungog (the home of Australian great Doug Walters), Armidale, Taree, Coffs Harbour, Gunnedah, Tamworth and Narrabri to play matches. Helped by the inclement weather, we just managed to draw the 'test' match at Narrabri to retain the Boomerang Trophy. The most memorable match for me was at Taree. The pitch soil was black-looking and had plenty of pace and bounce. I made the Australian newspapers for the first time when they noted that at one stage I held the figures of 4-5 off three overs and finished with 4-27 off eight overs.

After leaving school, I embarked on a career as a trainee manager for Woolworths, an experience that helped me to develop an eye for detail. But after three years, I found it increasingly more and more difficult to meet the expectations of a sporting and a business career simultaneously, so I made the decision to move on.

In 1970 I joined the Rangers Football Club in the Southern League competition. I played in goal for three seasons. It was a time that I enjoyed very much but there were several downsides, especially on cold winter nights when we had to train at Rangers Park. I would stand in goal whether it rained, hailed or snowed for an hour behind our defence as we played the second team — naturally enough I did not have too much work to do until the coach decided it would be a better idea if I stood behind the second team defence facing the first team attack — that way I would have more work to do. The coach was right.

I recall playing a match against Invercargill Thistle at their ground, which was very muddy. We lost the match 2-1 and a couple of days later a newspaper report mentioning our match said that Rangers had the better of the game but it was the defensive lapse of their goalkeeper Richard Hadlee that cost his team the match. From that point on I was known as 'DL' (Defensive Lapse Hadlee) at the club.

I had a year or two off soccer to concentrate on my cricket but returned to the game to play for Woolston. The club was trying to qualify for the National League playoffs and I was asked to play in the remaining four games of the season. The highlight for me was defeating my old club, Rangers, at Burwood Park, 2-nil. We lost the other three games and I had conceded 21 goals, although I thought that I had played quite well. I had a theory — if the ball got past me, it had got past 10 other players first. I then decided to give soccer up completely and concentrate solely on cricket, which turned out to be a wise choice, even though some soccer judges felt that I had enough goalkeeping potential to go on to represent New Zealand.

Before my first-class career began, I played club cricket for Lancaster Park. It was thought that when I left CBHS I would join the High School Old Boys club, the same as Dad and my older brothers had done. I did not think that I would make the senior grade team as there were several quality pace bowlers in the team, including my brother Dayle. I thought my best opportunity to play senior cricket was to go to a club where there was a shortage of new-ball bowlers. For three seasons the club and I enjoyed some notable successes. I thoroughly enjoyed my time there — they were wonderful guys to play with. As I was the only genuine pace bowler in the team I was nicknamed 'Hoss' which was short for hostile Hadlee. Many years later Australian commentator Bill Lawry called me 'Hurricane' Hadlee after I destroyed the Aussies at the Gabba in 1985. Those nicknames were very flattering, especially as there had been some wonderful fast bowlers given nicknames, such as Frank 'Typhoon' Tyson and Fred 'Fiery' Trueman. But the nickname that stuck with me was the first ever given to me, 'Paddles', bestowed on me by my woodwork teacher, Arch Lamb, in 1963 at Heaton Street Immediate School because of my feet, which were large for a boy of my age.

> My nickname 'Paddles' originated from the size of my large feet when I was aged 11 at Heaton Street Intermediate School. My woodwork teacher, Arch Lamb, gave me the name and it has stuck with me for life. When I walk, my feet are usually positioned at a ten to two position on a clock. Glenn Turner, who had captained me for several years, was now in the commentary box describing a piece of play relating to my bowling and the way I was walking. When New Zealand played Pakistan at McLean Park, Napier in 1979, I was bowling from my long run up in hot conditions when the television cameras panned in on my feet. 'And there is Paddles Hadlee — he has bowled a long spell this afternoon — he is getting very tired indeed at the moment — his feet are positioned at quarter to three.'
>
> On the ill-fated tour of India and Pakistan in 1976, I was violently ill, vomited and collapsed on the fine leg boundary during the third test against India at Madras. The match had been in progress for two overs and I was dragged from the field by two of my team-mates with my feet positioned at 5.30.

Eventually, I left Lancaster Park and joined High School Old Boys, playing senior grade for 17 years and later for the Presidents Grade off and on for a further 13 years.

My first first-class match came in 1971/72 when I was selected to play for Canterbury against Auckland at Lancaster Park. Dayle had accidentally got his big toe caught up in a lawn mower which ended his first-class season and I was his replacement for the remaining three matches of the season. I probably owe my early selection to Mum, who had to tell the Canterbury selectors about Dayle's misfortune, and, noting their dilemma, told them not to worry as she had another son just like Dayle at home!

Graham Dowling, a New Zealand test player and the captain of the Canterbury provincial team, asked me to bowl the first over and I had a very nervous start to the match. The first ball I bowled was a full toss and the New Zealand test opening batsman at the time, Terry Jarvis, hit it straight back past me for four runs. Ross Morgan was my first victim — bowled. I ended the game with three wickets for 57 from 12 overs (eight-ball overs) in the first innings and hit the winning runs, so it was a nice start to my first-class career.

A hat-trick followed two games later at Trafalgar Park, Nelson against Central Districts. Getting a hat-trick is a bowling triumph and rare. New Zealand test wicketkeeper Ken Wadsworth was the first victim, out lbw, followed by former All Black Blair Furlong, who was bowled, and then John Howell, the last man, entered the fray. John was in so much of a hurry to get to the wicket that he forgot to put his abdominal protector or box on. No wonder he missed a straight one and had his middle stump knocked backwards! Great delight for me.

In 1972 I was selected to play for the New Zealand B team in the Coca-Cola knockout competition in Australia. At the same time the national team was playing in the West Indies but we had a reasonable team to play against Victoria in the semi-final at the famous MCG in Melbourne. They had a powerful team that included test players Bill Lawry, Keith Stackpole, Ian Redpath, Paul Sheahan, Max Walker and Ross Duncan. Jimmy Higgs and Richie Robinson, also in the team, later went on to play for Australia. We lost the 40-over match by 76 runs, but several things stood out — the ground entry price was a dollar, the Man of the Match award was won by our own Rodney Redmond, who scored 69, and he won $50. Things are a bit different today.

The team talk that we had prior to the match was led by our captain Ross Morgan. Ross said: 'If these Aussies nick the ball they don't walk. We will have to get a crane to lift them off the field.' As it turned out, I found the outside edge of Bill Lawry's bat and he was caught behind by wicketkeeper Maurice Ryan for 24 — and Bill walked.

Prior to the semi-final encounter I met a very generous Australian. We were playing a practice match against the Victorian Combined University XI and after bowling the second ball of my second over I split my left bowling boot — a severe six-inch tear. I had no other boots to continue bowling, let alone play against Victoria in a couple of days' time. I left the field of play and David Trist completed my over. Noticing that I was in a predicament, Jimmy Higgs came up to me and offered me a pair of his boots from the back of his car. They fitted quite well and I was very relieved. I came back onto the field to complete my bowling spell and was rewarded with 3-18 off eight overs. When Higgs came out to bat I could see that he was a genuine number 11 — he carried a bat with him to the crease only because he knew he had to. I did not have the heart to get him out — it was as though I owed him a favour — but he eventually ran himself out for four, his highest score of the season.

During the 1972/73 season I was selected to play my first test, which was against Pakistan at the Basin Reserve in Wellington. Again I bowled the first ball of the match. It was another full toss and Sadiq Mohammad hit it behind square leg for four runs, although I have since been told it only went for three. It was another nervous start in the next phase of my career. In those days we bowled eight-ball overs and I got 2/84 from 18 overs in the first innings and 0/28 from seven overs in the second innings. I scored 46 with the bat in our first innings. I thought I had done not too badly, but it appeared that it wasn't good enough for the selectors. I was twelfth man for the next two test matches.

In my early international years winning a test match was rare. Kiwis tended to have a self-defeating mentality, telling ourselves things like: 'How could we, amateur cricketers, beat the professionals from England, the mentally tough and intimidating Australians, and the blistering pace and skilful batting of the West Indians?'

Most of us played club cricket on Saturdays, five or six first-class matches for our provinces and then we were supposedly test players. When we beat the Australians at Lancaster Park in 1974 at Christchurch for the first time in our history, it was almost a national holiday. Each player was given a $100 bonus cheque for the win and we all thought that we were rich! Then, in 1978, at the Basin Reserve in Wellington, we defeated England for the first time. After something like 50 years and 50 tests of trying, we finally did it. Another major milestone in New Zealand cricket history had been achieved.

To further my playing career and learn how to play in foreign conditions I spent four months playing for Tasmania in the Sheffield Shield competition during the 1979/80 season. Tasmania was allowed two overseas players then — Brian Davison from Rhodesia (later Zimbabwe) and I were employed to bolster the team. The team did not enjoy much success — we were too immature as a group, we lacked experience and too much was expected of Davo and me. Personally, my bowling statistics were very average — 13 wickets at 30-odd and a batting average of around 30 did not satisfy the Tasmanian supporters and some of the players.

The truth is that it was not a lack of effort on my part but the dreadful number of catches that were dropped. We invariably bowled only once per match because we were usually bowled out twice for around 250 and the opposition would score 400 to 500. The only consolation for me was that I was the first Tasmanian player to capture five wickets in a first-class match — I got five wickets against Queensland, and Davo scored a hundred, batting without a helmet against Jeff Thomson, who was still a very swift bowler then.

I returned home for the test series against the West Indies — a series we won — and I picked up 18 wickets in the three matches. An ankle injury suffered during that series meant that I was unable to return to Australia for the final two matches of the season and that created more controversy with the locals, who suspected me of not caring about honouring my contract. Whenever I returned to Tassie with the New Zealand team, the locals made their feelings very clear about my contributions, or lack of them, by waving banners: 'Welcome to Hadlee's holiday isle'.

Despite all the flak that came my way, I still had an enjoyable time playing for the Riverside Cricket Club and I still have friends there today.

The benchmark of any sporting team or sportsperson is to perform on foreign soil when the conditions and everything else are against you. New Zealand cricket successes offshore were poor. Finally, in 1983, we beat England in England for the first time (at Headingley) but lost the series. In 1985/86 we beat Australia in Australia for the first time with a marvellous win at the Gabba — we won the series 2-1. Then, in 1986, we won our first test series in England. It was a great time to be playing. There were also some successes in Sri Lanka and India during the 80s.

I experienced some wonderful moments. My first test century was against the might of the formidable West Indies at Lancaster Park in the 1980/81 series. Michael Holding, Andy Roberts, Joel Garner and Colin Croft formed one of the most lethal four-pronged fast-bowling combinations in test history. It was a very controversial and bitter series and I would have to say that when I scored that hundred, the West Indians weren't focused, weren't trying very hard and all wanted to go home, citing poor umpiring decisions continually going against them. They had a point too.

Of all the test innings I played, my best was against England at Lancaster Park in 1983. I was going through a low period in my life and there was some doubt as to whether I would be fit enough to play in that series, but I did. I scored 99 before I was caught behind by the wicketkeeper, Bob Taylor, from the bowling of Bob Willis. I batted for 111 balls and played very positively. Following that innings I was often asked whether I was disappointed in not scoring a century. The obvious answer was 'yes', but I was comforted by the fact that England scored only 82 and 93 in both innings and we won the match by an innings and 132. Perhaps my 99 was worth 150 in the context of the match, which was over in 12 hours of play — one of the shortest games in test history.

From 1978, I spent 10 seasons at Nottinghamshire playing county cricket and it was the greatest cricketing experience that I ever had. To learn to play cricket as a professional six days a week for six months a year taught me to get into good habits, disciplines and routines — it fine-tuned me as a player and that benefited not only Notts cricket but also New

Zealand cricket. During that time Notts won two county championships (1981 and 1987), and we appeared in three one-day finals at Lord's, winning the Natwest Trophy in 1987, my last season with the club. It was a wonderful way to end my playing association with a club that I have the utmost respect for. Since that time I have been accorded the honour of being made an Honorary Vice President. This was a nice gesture from some wonderful people at the club.

Perhaps my greatest individual achievement was performing the 'double' in English county cricket — scoring 1000 first-class runs and capturing 100 first-class wickets in the same season. It had not been done for 17 years and with fewer games being played per season many felt that it would never be achieved again. In 1981 I had had a great year for Notts, capturing over 100 wickets and scoring about 800 runs. Ken Taylor, the Notts manager, told me that I should have a go at the double. I had to ask him what he meant. I set about having a go at this target in 1982 but injury curtailed my season. In 1983 New Zealand toured England, so there was no opportunity to play the 24 County matches I would need. But I became very serious about this goal in 1984 and I plotted and planned it down to the smallest of details. I banked on playing 20 matches, so the simple equation meant that I had to score 50 runs and capture five wickets every game. If I had a bad match or a game was rained out, those statistics would naturally change.

As the season progressed the wicket tally was on budget but I was always behind on my run tally. When we played against Middlesex at Lord's, we bowled them out cheaply but were soon also struggling with the bat at 17/4. Clive Rice, the Notts captain, said to me, 'Paddles, go out there and score a double hundred.'

I replied, 'Ricey, my highest score is 130-odd, we have just bowled them out cheaply on a frisky pitch, and they have one of the best bowling attacks in the game, with West Indian fast bowler Wayne Daniel, England fast bowler Norman Cowans and the two best spinners in county cricket, John Emburey and Phil Edmonds. What's more, we've lost our top order and are 17 for 4, you are out for a duck, we are in the shit, and you're telling me to go out there and score a double century!'

He calmly replied that I should just go out there and do it. I had 20 minutes to bat before tea and I played positively, making 20-odd before the break. I had a start and it would be up to me to carry on and take advantage of the opportunity. I ended up scoring 210 not out, which got me back on track and ahead of budget. Ricey had put a thought in my mind that I had never considered before: 'Can I go beyond what I think I am capable of achieving?'

The coveted and rare 'double' was finally achieved with several games to spare. It was planned, implemented and fulfilled.

Perfection is something that sportspeople should aspire to. We may not get there, but the closest I came was when we played the Australians at the Gabba, Brisbane, in 1985/86. Conditions were perfect for fast swing bowling — a heavy atmosphere and a pitch that had some juice in it. We caught nearly everything that was offered behind the wicket and I captured 9/52 in the first innings, a career best, and then took a further six wickets in the second innings — two New Zealand records had been broken: best bowling performance in an innings and in a match. I featured on the scorecard 10 times during the first innings when I caught Geoff Lawson to give Vaughan Brown his first test wicket. It was a special moment, only bettered when we won the test match, the first we had ever won on Australian soil.

I have often been asked whether I thought about dropping the catch to give myself a chance of capturing all 10 wickets and repeating the feat of English off spin bowler Jim Laker. The answer is, as it always has been, an emphatic 'No'. When the ball went up in the air the natural thing to do was to catch it. It was important for the team and extremely important for Vaughan Brown to launch his test career with his first wicket. There was no time to think about any personal goals.

During that series, which we won 2-1, I took 33 wickets at 12 runs apiece, the most by a New Zealand bowler in a three-match series. I was voted Player of the Series and I won an Alfa Romeo car. Rightly or wrongly, I kept it, after having previously won two cars and putting the money into a team fund. On each of those occasions I was not given the car *per se*, but the cash equivalent. In Australia, on this occasion, I was given the keys to the actual car to keep. My feeling was that I had earned it, had deserved it and there was little difference between that and keeping a gold tray and set of six gold goblets or a television set for being named Man of the Match or Man of the Series. On all those occasions where a player had been given an object as his award he had been allowed to keep the spoils, but cash awards were always divided among the players. However, my decision to keep the car created some controversy, and although a team vote eventually allowed me to keep the car there was nonetheless some bitterness and ill feeling. Perhaps even today there are some who do not forget and may still carry some baggage about the controversy.

Capturing my 300th test wicket in 1986 at the Basin Reserve, Wellington, was a special moment — Australian captain Allan Border was given out lbw by umpire Fred Goodall. There had been a lot hype and expectation as to when I would reach this major milestone, including sweepstakes and speculation on radio as to when it would happen and who would be the victim. When Border was dismissed, I was one of an elite band of six bowlers who had reached 300 test wickets, with Fred Trueman, Lance Gibbs, Dennis Lillee, Bob Willis and Ian Botham all being part of the exclusive '300 wicket club'.

Statistics always motivated me and I liked to view every ball as a potential wicket-taker, although of course I knew that that never happened. I had captured a couple of first-class hat-tricks and on several occasions, like a lot of bowlers, had taken two wickets in two balls. But it wasn't as though I was constantly delving into the record books to check it all out. There was no need: I always knew where I was with the number of test wickets I had taken because the media kept telling me as I was knocking off targets.

But I set myself targets and it was good to achieve them. Capturing my 1000th first-class wicket was a major milestone and certainly one that I wanted to achieve. Pakistan batsman Salim Malik was caught by Lance Cairns at mid-on at the Basin Reserve, Wellington in 1985. Dare I say it, off another full toss! Perhaps there was some justice in capturing a wicket with an average delivery when most of those balls usually got hit to the boundary for four runs. On 12 November 1988, at Chinnaswamy Stadium, Bangalore, India, I became the leading wicket-taker in the history of test cricket when Arun Lal became my 374th victim. He was caught at slip by Chris Kuggeleijn for 6, and I had surpassed Ian Botham's record.

On 4 February 1990, on my home ground of Lancaster Park, Christchurch, and in front of my family, Indian batsman Sanjay Manjrekar became my 400th test wicket when he was bowled for 4. I was the first bowler to break the 400 wicket barrier. For me, it was my Everest — the feeling could not have been better and the game stopped momentarily as I was presented with 400 roses to mark the occasion.

Records will always be broken — they are a temporary benchmark for someone else to aspire to. Five years later, Indian all-rounder Kapil Dev equalled my world record of 431 test wickets at Bangalore and later broke it at Ahmedabad when Hashan Tillakaratne was caught by the wicketkeeper down the leg side. Perhaps in jest, someone said that even the umpire appealed for the caught behind decision on that day. It would have been a moving moment and a great thrill for Kapil and his team-mates to be part of cricket history and I wrote to congratulate him, as I did to Courtney Walsh when he joined Kapil and me with 400 or more test wickets in March 1999. Courtney went on to be the first bowler to capture 500 test wickets, ending his career with 519 wickets — a remarkable performance, surpassed only by the incredible career performances of Shane Warne, who became the first bowler to capture 600 and then 700 test wickets, and Sri Lankan off-spin bowler Muttiah Muralitharan who surpassed Warne's record of 708 in 2007.

The 1990 tour of England was my last test series. I had played in the home series against India, and at the conclusion of that series we played a one-off test match — which we won — against Australia at the Basin Reserve in Wellington. I had made it very clear that I would be retiring from the international scene and I was unsure whether I wanted to go to England and finish it all off there. However, team-mate Ian Smith convinced me that it was a fitting way to end my career.

From a playing point of view the tour was not too spectacular but it was meaningful for me in different ways. Chris Lewis, the England fast bowler, broke a bone in my right hand during the one-day international at the Oval. While I was still able to bowl during the tour, batting was a problem for several weeks. My last test was at Edgbaston, Birmingham and on 9 July 1990 I bowled my last ball in test cricket to England's number 11 batsman, Devon Malcolm, who was given out lbw for nought. It was also my last bag of five wickets.

Devon Malcolm was a character — he was a very useful fast bowler but he couldn't bat to save himself. He faced only six balls in the whole match — all of which I bowled to him — and was out twice for a pair of ducks. At the end of the match he came into our dressing room and asked me to sign his run chart, which I duly did, with a rather large smile on my face — there was plenty of room to sign my name. Someone said that I had wasted too much energy in bowling the six balls to Dev because he should have been dismissed twice in two balls.

We had a chance of victory in that match but were bowled out, so in some ways I ended my career on a low. I was, however, relieved. The decision had been made and I realised that it was all over and I would wake up the next day knowing that I would not have to train and go through all the aches and pains associated with fast bowling. My cricket gearbag was emptied — I kept my New Zealand cap, floppy hat, sweater, bat and boots. All the rest was given away to a memorabilia collector.

As a cricketer I was highly motivated. I was criticised from time to time for being single-minded and, at times, selfish. But I make no apologies for playing the game the way I did. Cricket, more than any other team game, is an individual game. It is the skill of the bowler against the skill of the batsman, with the fielders playing a supporting role. When I look at many of the world's superstars, most of them have been controversial characters in one way or another and perhaps at times have been perceived as unpopular. There were times when I may not have been very popular, but I learned very quickly that if I did not toughen up mentally and play the game hard, being a nice guy generally meant you came second.

My job was simply to bowl a ball and get a batsman out, and if I could destroy his confidence, or even his career, then I had done my job. If I was getting wickets and scoring runs, then I was making a significant contribution to the team. If I was winning Man of the Match awards, the team was probably winning the match and sharing in the delights of victory and its financial gains.

By the time I had finished my last tour of England I had been knighted for services to New Zealand cricket and I had three world records — most test wickets, most five-wicket bags in a test innings (36 times) and most 10-wickets-in-a-match (nine times). I had captured 431 test wickets and I was striking at five wickets a test, which was up there with some of the best in the game. As far as statistics were concerned, I had rounded off my career almost to the decimal point — Devon Malcolm's wicket was a bonus! I had been honoured in New Zealand with the New Zealand Sportsman of the Year Award in 1980 and 1986, Sportsman of the Decade in 1987, and I shared an award with one of New Zealand's greatest athletes, John Walker, in 1987 — New Zealand Sportsman of the last 25 years.

The Hadlee family has received a number of wonderful tributes. The Hadlee Stand at AMI Stadium, Lancaster Park is very meaningful. Dad, Barry, Dayle and I all had fond memories of the ground, and we had served Canterbury and New Zealand cricket for many years. As a final tribute to the family, in 2004 NZC and Cricket Australia announced that the annual one-day series between New Zealand and Australia would be called the Chappell-Hadlee Trophy. Dad, the statesman of the family, who had served NZC in so many ways for many years, was particularly pleased to have Dayle and Barry also recognised for their contribution to cricket. Hopefully this trophy will become as prized as the Bledisloe Cup is in rugby between the two nations.

In 2009, the Hadlee family had completed 71 years of consecutive involvement with New Zealand cricket. I doubt whether any family in any sport, anywhere in the world, has a record like that. Our commitment to New Zealand sport can never be challenged.

In July 2008, Nottingham University presented me with an honorary doctorate for services to Nottingham and world cricket. That award gave me some extra letters to add after my name. I am now formally known as Sir Richard Hadlee, [Kt Bach, 1990], MBE, Hon. DLitt.

In November 2008, I was awarded the Bert Sutcliffe Medal for Services to New Zealand Cricket — a lovely gesture. And, in 2009, it was announced that I was to be one of the 55 inaugural inductees into the ICC Hall of Fame. Thousands of test cricketers have represented their countries over a 120-year period and to be included in the elite company of such greats as W.G. Grace, Sir Jack Hobbs, Sir Donald Bradman, Sydney Barnes, Harold Larwood, Keith Miller and Sir Garfield Sobers is very special.

Arise, Sir Richard

In 1990, on my last tour of England, New Zealand was playing Worcestershire when I received a surprise phone call at the team hotel from the New Zealand High Commissioner, Bryce Harland, who was based in London. He was phoning on behalf of the New Zealand Government to see whether I would accept a knighthood for services to New Zealand cricket. I was absolutely stunned but managed to reply that I would be very honoured to accept. The High Commissioner advised that I would receive an official letter in due course, but was not to tell anyone except family and the closest of friends as the announcement was going to be made in six weeks' time as part of the Queen's Birthday Honours in New Zealand. I could not believe this was happening and seriously considered that some of my team-mates were playing a practical joke on me. When the official notification finally arrived, I began to discard the practical joke theory as I didn't think my fellow players would be clever enough to organise such an official-looking piece of correspondence.

The first test of the tour was to be played at Trent Bridge, which had been my home ground for 10 years when I played county cricket for Nottinghamshire. I would have loved to have walked onto that ground known as Sir Richard, but the six weeks had not lapsed. It would have been special because Sir Garfield Sobers was also a former Notts player — two cricket knights from the same club was unbelievable. The test ended in a draw following bad weather and as it happened I scored a duck, so it may have been a little embarrassing being known as Sir Richard on that occasion.

By the time of the second test at Lord's, the announcement had been made. I was now officially Sir Richard but had not yet been invested. I was going to be invested back in New Zealand some months later by the Governor-General, Sir Paul Reeves, and not by the Queen, who awards honours personally on only a couple of occasions a year in England. I was 38 years old and all of a sudden had become the only cricketer to be knighted for cricket while still playing the game at an international level. This created a small problem at Lord's, the home of cricket: how would my name appear on the scorecard or on the scoreboard, and how would I be introduced over the public address system when I batted or bowled? They had no history or protocols to work from, as previous cricketers had been knighted after they had retired. Would I be Sir Richard or Sir R.J. Hadlee, or Sir Richard Hadlee?

The decision was duly made and I appeared on the scorecard as *Sir Richard Hadlee, Canterbury.* We fielded first in the match and my captain, John Wright, gave me the honour of leading the team onto the field. The public address system announced me as: 'Ladies and gentlemen, Sir Richard Hadlee.' There was a standing ovation, which made me feel 10 feet tall, yet also very humble.

I was now in an elite group of cricketers who had been knighted for services to cricket. There was the greatest of all cricketers, Sir Donald Bradman, and several other greats, Sir Garfield Sobers, Sir Leonard Hutton, Sir Jack Hobbs, Sir Frank Worrell, Sir Learie Constantine, Sir Everton Weekes, Sir George 'Gubby' Allen, Sir Colin Cowdrey (later named Lord Cowdrey) and Sir Pelham 'Plum' Warner. There were also some outstanding players of more recent vintage, including Sir Vivian Richards, Sir Alec Bedser and Sir Ian Botham.

Apart from the usual pressure of people's expectations of me, I now put myself under even greater pressure to perform and live up to the reputation of what an award like this actually meant — I felt I needed to be almost invincible and produce a magical performance. I was relieved when I got a few wickets (3/133), but more importantly I scored 86 in the

(20p) **LORD'S** ⓂⒸⒸ **GROUND** (20p)

CORNHILL INSURANCE TEST SERIES
ENGLAND v. NEW ZEALAND
THURS., FRI., SAT., MON. & TUES., JUNE 21, 22, 23, 25 & 26, 1990   (5-day Match)

ENGLAND		First Innings		Second Innings	
†1 G. A. Gooch	Essex	c and b Bracewell	85	b Hadlee	37
2 M. A. Atherton	Lancashire	b Morrison	0	c Bracewell b Jones	54
3 A. J. Stewart	Surrey	l b w b Hadlee	54	c sub b Bracewell	42
4 A. J. Lamb	Northamptonshire	l b w b Snedden	39	not out	84
5 R. A. Smith	Hampshire	c Bracewell b Morrison	64	hit wicket b Bracewell	0
6 N. H. Fairbrother	Lancashire	c Morrison b Bracewell	2	not out	33
*7 R. C. Russell	Gloucestershire	b Hadlee	13	----------	
8 P. A. J. DeFreitas	Lancashire	c Franklin b Morrison	38	----------	
9 G. C. Small	Warwickshire	b Morrison	3	Innings closed	
10 E. E. Hemmings	Notts.	b Hadlee	0	----------	
11 D. E. Malcolm	Derbyshire	not out	0	----------	
		B , l-b 13, w 1, n-b 22,	36	B 8, l-b 8, w , n-b 6,	22
		Total	334	Total	272

FALL OF THE WICKETS

1—3 2—151 3—178 4—216 5—226 6—255 7—319 8—322 9—332 10—334

1—68 2—135 3—171 4—175 5— 6— 7— 8— 9— 10—

ANALYSIS OF BOWLING

Name	1st Innings						2nd Innings					
	O.	M.	R.	W.	Wd.	N-b	O.	M.	R.	W	Wd.	N-b
Sir Richard Hadlee	29	5	113	3	...	10	13	2	32	1	...	3
Morrison	18.4	4	64	4	...	7	16	0	81	0	...	3
Snedden	21	4	72	1	1	5	...	...	...	...	...	...
Bracewell	21	3	72	2	...	...	34	13	85	2	...	...
Jones	...	...	...	...	...	...	12	3	40	1	...	...
Rutherford	...	...	...	...	...	...	3	0	18	0	...	...

NEW ZEALAND		First Innings		Second Innings	
1 T. J. Franklin	Auckland	c Russell b Malcolm	101	----------	
†2 J. G. Wright	Auckland	c Stewart b Small	98	----------	
3 A. H. Jones	Wellington	c Stewart b Malcolm	49	----------	
4 M. D. Crowe	Central Districts	c Russell b Hemmings	1	----------	
5 M. J. Greatbatch	C. Districts	b Malcolm	47	----------	
6 K. R. Rutherford	Otago	c Fairbrother b Malcolm	0	----------	
7 Sir Richard Hadlee	Canterbury	b Hemmings	86	----------	
8 J. G. Bracewell	Auckland	run out	4	----------	
*9 I. D. S. Smith	Auckland	c Small b Malcolm	27	----------	
10 M. C. Snedden	Auckland	not out	13	----------	
11 D. K. Morrison	Auckland	not out	2	----------	
		B 12, l-b 15, w 2, n-b 5,	34	B , l-b , w , n-b ,	
		Total	‡462	Total	

‡ Innings closed

FALL OF THE WICKETS

1—185 2—278 3—281 4—284 5—285 6—408 7—415 8—425 9—448 10—

1— 2— 3— 4— 5— 6— 7— 8— 9— 10—

ANALYSIS OF BOWLING

Name	1st Innings						2nd Innings					
	O.	M.	R.	W.	Wd.	N-b	O.	M.	R.	W.	Wd.	N-b
Malcolm	43	14	94	5	...	1	...	...	...	...	...	...
Small	35	4	127	1	1	...	...	...	...	...	...	...
DeFreitas	35.4	1	122	0	...	4	...	...	...	...	...	...
Hemmings	30	13	67	2	...	...	...	...	...	...	...	...
Gooch	13	7	25	0	1	...	...	...	...	...	...	...
Atherton	1	1	0	0	...	...	...	...	...	...	...	...

Umpires—M. J. Kitchen & D. R. Shepherd   Scorers—E. Solomon & P. N. Culpan

† Captain   * Wicket-keeper

Play begins each day at 11.00   Luncheon Interval 1.00—1.40

Tea Interval 3.40—4.00 (may be varied according to state of game)

Stumps drawn 1st, 2nd, 3rd & 4th days at 6.00, or after 90 overs have been bowled, whichever is the later - 5th day at 6.00, or after a minimum of 75 overs for playing time other than the last hour, when Law of Cricket 17.6 and 17.7 shall apply (20 overs). (In the event of play being suspended on any of the first four days for any reason other than normal intervals, the timing for cessation of play on that day will be extended by an amount of time equal to the aggregate time lost prior to 6.00. However, play shall not continue on any of the first four days after 7.00). The captains may agree to stop play at 5.30 on the 5th day if there is no prospect of a result.

New Zealand won the toss and elected to field

Match Drawn

The Lord's scoreboard which listed me as *Sir Richard Hadlee, Canterbury.*

first innings. It would have been almost too much to have scored a century — that would have been fairytale stuff. I had a chance, but I was bowled by former Notts team-mate, off-spinner Eddie Hemmings — good bowling from Eddie, no doubt, but it was also a poor shot on my part. I should have had more patience and made the situation count.

In 1991, I received notification that the investiture ceremony would be held at Government House in Wellington. I was allowed to take my wife and two other people to the ceremony. We decided to take two very close friends to witness the occasion. To this day, I do not know why we did not take my mum and dad. I do not have many regrets in my life, but this was a major blunder. Without question, they should have been part of the occasion — they deserved that. Whatever it was that determined our decision, it was wrong.

The ceremony was very straightforward. On that day many other notable New Zealanders received their awards for outstanding service to the community and sport. Before the knights were called in to be officially invested, there was a protocol to be learned — how to kneel on the cushioned stool. We had a practice run in the waiting room and were advised to place our left knee on the cushion, with our right leg on the floor next to the stool. So what did I do when it was my turn to be dubbed? I got my knees mixed up, placing my right knee on the cushion. I felt very awkward, and uncomfortable, with nowhere for my left knee to go. I was somewhat embarrassed, but no doubt not too many people were aware of the situation or confusion. Sir Paul Reeves, the Governor-General of New Zealand, tapped me first on one shoulder and then the other with his sword and simply said, 'Arise, Sir Richard.' It was now official.

Being known as Sir Richard is something that is difficult to explain but it has a significant importance. I learnt that the objectives of the Imperial Society of Knights Bachelor — the most ancient title of honour known in England, with its origins going back to the Saxon times in the sixth century — were to uphold the dignity and the standing of the Knight Bachelor rank and to carry out charitable works, which included supporting the society's London chapel, the Priory Church of St Bartholomew the Great.

A knight was expected to possess dignity, honesty, integrity, humility, chivalry and to support mankind. My wife, Dianne, tells me that chivalry means helping out with the dishes and that three out of six isn't too bad. I also find it amusing, mildly, when some people do not know how to address me. The correct way is to call me Sir Richard, but I am often called Sir Hadlee, which sounds quite strange. Even the Australians are very polite and receptive these days, although I have been called many different names by them in the past!

From 1996, Knights of the New Zealand Order of Merit replaced Knights Bachelor. Those who received the new accolade were not given the title Sir or Dame, which was a shame because it is a special title to have. However, I was pleased to hear in 2009 that the National Government was looking to reinstate knighthoods and damehoods to fully recognise worldwide those who have been outstanding achievers.

Being known as Sir Richard Hadlee has changed my life. Although it has opened some doors, more importantly I have been asked to be a figurehead or patron of many different organisations. It has also allowed me to be involved with a number of different charities, including the Zipper Kidz Club (part of Heart Children NZ), the Sir Richard Hadlee Sports Trust and others. There is an expectation that as a knight you will be available and be involved with the many different things that allow people to live with dignity and have a good quality of life. And that is as it should be, it is part of the knight's doctrine after all.

When I played cricket in Australia, the crowds gave me heaps of flak. However, they did motivate me, whereas they could have destroyed me. To prove a point, I captured more test wickets against Australia than any other team I played against. Greg Chappell advised me not to react: 'The crowds do respect you. It is their way of saying that they rate you, otherwise they would not bother to target you.' That comment sounded rather peculiar.

There was an incident at Geelong, not far from Melbourne, when we played Victoria Country. Peter Oxlade, a left-handed opening batsman, had batted all day without a helmet and crawled his way to 96 not out. He had bored the pants off everyone. I was given the ball to bowl the last few overs of the day and I bounced him several times only to cut him above the eye with the last ball of the day. As we left the field of play, a youngster ran up to me and said, 'You're a mongrel, Hadlee.' I chased this youngster, who was probably 10 years old, and gave him a stern talking to, saying, 'If you were older and yelled abuse like that to someone, they will probably smack you one.' Next morning helicopters were flying over the ground — news crews from Channel Nine, Channel Seven and Channel Ten wanted to interview me on the incident. Rather foolishly I let go to prove a point: 'I would have to question the education system here in Australia and the parenting in this country when guests are abused by youngsters. I am sure your Prime Minister, Bob Hawke, will not be very happy with this sort of carry on.' Whilst I felt that I made my point, the only problem I had was that we had to play some one-day matches at the SCG and the MCG. As expected, I was subjected to more abuse and flying missiles with the chant: 'Hadlee is a wanker.' Perhaps I had asked for that sort of retaliation and backlash!

My Most Memorable Games

Having played so many games of cricket in different forms, selecting my 10 most memorable matches is a difficult task. To omit from my top 10 matches the world record wicket-taking match against India at Bangalore in 1988 and the 400th test wicket match against India at Lancaster Park in Christchurch in 1990 highlights my dilemma. Some matches are remembered for historical reasons, others for personal achievement and some because they had a huge effect on my career. I have played test matches, one-day internationals, first-class and one-day games, club games, single and double wicket competitions, charity and exhibition matches. The following are my 10 most remembered matches in order of importance.

New Zealand v Australia at the Gabba, Brisbane, Australia, 1985

New Zealand's 22nd test victory.

I am sure that all those players who participated in this test would say that it was the greatest win in our history. If ever there was a perfect test match, this was it. We won the toss and bowled Australia out for 179 in helpful atmospheric and pitch conditions; we secured a first innings lead of 374 on a good batting pitch that had flattened out; and then we had to work hard to bowl them out again to win by an innings and 41 runs on the fifth day. It was significant because it was our first test win in Australia, our first win over Australia by an innings and it helped set up our first test series win in Australia (2-1). It could not have been better.

Personally, it was my greatest test performance, with New Zealand records galore: my best bowling performance of 9/52 and 6/71, a total of 15 wickets in the match, and a cameo 54 with the bat. Add that to Martin Crowe's career best innings of 188 (at the time, he subsequently scored 299 against Sri Lanka) and John Reid's 108 and it was a complete and comprehensive performance, with everyone chipping in with either some useful runs, a crucial wicket or a catch.

Just prior to the first test an important bowling change took place at practice that was to change my game and performances. Glenn Turner, the coach, had noticed at practice and in the build-up games that I was bowling too wide of the crease and this was limiting my ability to get lbw decisions. Together we worked out where the umpire should stand in order to not interfere with my action and my delivery point, as in the last few matches the position of the umpire had forced me wider, changing my angle of delivery and reducing my effectiveness. The results were spectacular: I could get closer to the stumps, be more 'side on' at delivery and bowl wicket to wicket with extra swing, seam and cut. That gave me three chances of getting the batsman out: bowled, lbw and caught behind the wicket. From that point on I became more effective and my career took off to another level.

When I had captured eight wickets in a row in the first innings, Vaughan Brown enticed Geoff Lawson to sweep the ball, only to sky it to midwicket and I ran from mid-on to catch it. People often asked me whether I thought about dropping it so that I could go on and get all 10 wickets in an innings, a rare feat. The answer to that was quite simple — if the ball is in the air, you catch it. I came back to capture the last wicket to feature on the scorecard 10 times, nine as a wicket taker and once for taking a catch. Max Walker, the former Australian medium-pace bowler, was in the Channel Nine commentary box as I led the players from the field and said: 'This was one of the all-time great bowling performances. No intimidation, no bouncers, just sheer skill.' I must admit to feeling very satisfied on that occasion.

I ended up with 33 wickets in the series at an average of 12.00, another New Zealand record, for most wickets in a three-match series. It was a series to remember.

New Zealand v England at the Basin Reserve, Wellington, New Zealand, 1978
New Zealand's 10th test victory.

Previous encounters with England had always gone their way and while there were some drawn matches we did not know how to beat these professionals; we could put ourselves in match-winning situations but couldn't finish them off, and that frustrated many of us.

England lost their captain, Mike Brearley, to injury in Australia and the 1977/78 England team arrived in New Zealand with a new captain, Geoffrey Boycott. The England team had also lost several of their star players to Kerry Packer's World Series Cricket, including Derek Underwood, Alan Knott, Tony Greig and John Snow, but they still had some hardened professionals. Their pace attack included Bob Willis, Mike Hendrick, Chris Old and the exciting Ian Botham, equal to if not better than most teams in the world at the time. Boycott was a run machine and anchorman for others to support. They were a capable team, one that many thought good enough to beat us convincingly.

Mark Burgess took over the captaincy for the first time and both teams were evenly matched over the first few days. We made 228, a small lead of 13 runs on the first innings, but then collapsed in the second innings to be bowled out for 123, leaving England an easy 137 for victory.

Between innings Richard Collinge and I had talked about needing a sensation to give us a chance. I recall walking down the steps to the field and some of the spectators saying: 'Typical New Zealand. You've done it again: thrown away another game.' That made me angry. We needed support, not humiliation.

We also truly did need something special to happen — and it took only four balls, as Richard Collinge dismissed Boycott for a duck. Richard then proceeded to quickly dismiss Geoff Miller and Derek Randall. I hit Brian Rose on the forearm and he retired hurt for 5, having to go to hospital for an X-ray. I then had Graham Roope caught behind by Warren Lees, and England was 18/4 and we were on a roll. The big fella and I bowled unchanged for two hours as the adrenaline started to flow and every time we got a wicket the siren outside the ground would rev up to create a wonderful atmosphere. The crowd livened up and began clapping, chanting and cheering as they sensed something special happening.

Botham then mistimed a hook from my bowling and Stephen Boock took an easy catch behind square on the leg side. Next ball, Boocky ran out Bob Taylor with a direct hit and England were reeling at 38/6. Old was soon lbw, Hendrick was dismissed caught at the wicket, and at stumps England were incredibly 54/8, still 83 short of victory and with a day's play left.

That two-hour session was one of the most dramatic in New Zealand's history, with sustained hostile and intimidating bowling on a pitch that was uneven in bounce and a little unpredictable — batting was not easy, and that explained why we had been bowled out cheaply in our second innings.

The next morning, rain delayed the start of play to 12.30 pm but it didn't take too long to remove Edmonds and Willis to win by 72 runs. I had 6/26 and Richard 3/35 from 26.3 overs between us. We had done the almost impossible — won from a losing position to secure our first test match victory against England. It had taken 48 years.

This was an important breakthrough in our history. All the major teams had now been beaten — West Indies, South Africa, Australia, India, Pakistan and now England. Geoff Boycott summed up the feeling from England's point of view: 'England lost the first test in Wellington because we batted lamentably against some superb fast bowling from Richard Hadlee and could not make 136 to win the game. We were bowled out in the second innings for 64, which was quite pathetic.' Boycott became the first England captain to lose to New Zealand, something that does not sit too comfortably with him.

New Zealand v West Indies at Carisbrook, Dunedin, New Zealand, 1980
New Zealand's 11th test victory.

The 1980 tour of New Zealand by the West Indies was much anticipated, yet we were not expected to be very competitive. The Windies arrived in New Zealand after hammering the Australians and we were rebuilding as a team under the fresh captaincy of Geoff Howarth. As the tour progressed it developed into one of the most controversial series in the history of cricket, with the Windies showing some remarkable ill discipline.

Against the odds, we won the first and only one-dayer at Christchurch in a close encounter and then we went to Carisbrook, Dunedin, for the first test, winning that match by one wicket. That was the start of it all. Michael Holding kicked the stumps out of the ground when his appeal for a caught behind against John Parker was declined. In the second test, at Christchurch, Colin Croft deliberately ran into and bowled over umpire Fred Goodall with a shoulder charge when his appeal against me for a caught behind was turned down. The Windies were so incensed and frustrated with poor decision-making during the series that they decided to strike during the second test and play was held up for about 15 minutes while attempts were made to resolve issues. They wanted to go home. It is true that decisions certainly went against them and I can understand their frustration, but they were still the leading team in world cricket at that time and should have set a better example. We went on to win the series 1-nil.

Despite the Windies' attitude, the first test was a magnificent game of cricket, easily the match with the most emotion. It was a close game, full of highs and lows, and was eventually decided by a leg bye as Stephen

Boock and Gary Troup scampered through for a single to win the match by one wicket.

After bowling the Windies out for 140, we secured a handy lead of 109 on the first innings. We knocked them over again relatively cheaply in the second innings for 212 and I had 11 wickets in the match, including seven lbws, a world record at the time. It showed that if a bowler bowled straight and pitched the ball up on our pitches, which were uneven in bounce, success could happen — and more so because the Windies had come from the bouncier wickets in Australia. Their batsmen struggled to adapt to the lower bounce of our pitches and most were creasebound, much to a fast bowler's delight.

We now needed only 104 to win. Many teams in the world would back themselves to win comfortably but the Windies had a formidable fast bowling attack, with Michael Holding, Colin Croft and Joel Garner looking to cause our batting line-up problems. When we were 54/7 it was clear that they had found that magical length and had all but won the game. I thought we had blown it after all the good work we had done. We were all bitterly disappointed at that stage, and when I was dismissed for 17 we were 73/8 and hopes of victory were almost shattered. Then there was a nice partnership of 27 between Lance Cairns and Gary Troup before Lance was out with the score at 100. The real drama unfolded as Boock and Troup thankfully survived the Windies' lethal pace attack and then took us to victory.

The significance of the win was huge in the history of our game. We were basically still a team of amateur players with only four professional players — Geoff Howarth, John Wright, John Parker and me — in the side. We had brought back to New Zealand an attitude of how we should prepare as players and as a team and we developed a simple theme of 'WIN'. It was amazing that throughout the series, whenever someone mentioned the word 'win', something tended to happen.

The victory gave us much needed self-esteem and the confidence that we could not only compete against the best team in the world but also beat them. That was the start of a remarkable era in the history of our game

— during the next 10 years we didn't lose a test series at home and beat everyone in test matches, winning and drawing test series. All of a sudden we were a team that had huge expectations and excellent crowd support. This team became part of the 'Glorious 80s'. Cricket in New Zealand was on a real high.

New Zealand v England at Lancaster Park, Christchurch, New Zealand, 1984
New Zealand's 17th test victory.

This was one of the most extraordinary test matches that I played in. The game was over in only 12 hours and one minute of actual playing time. Such was the comprehensive nature of the win that it was hard to believe that England could be bowled out twice for under a hundred in both innings and we had won by an innings and 132 runs in such a short time.

The England team criticised the pitch for its uneven bounce, but we made 307 in the first innings. They bowled poorly it is true, but they did not apply themselves when they batted and our seam attack exploited the conditions, giving them very little to hit. They were dismissed by run outs, or not playing a shot to a swinging ball, by lbws when shouldering arms, or by being caught on the boundary, and it is difficult to blame a pitch for those sorts of dismissals. England simply did not work hard enough and they were dismissed for 82 and 93.

There was some doubt as to whether I was going to be fit enough to play in this match. I was recovering from a low period in my life after suffering from food poisoning. Other things were also going on in my life that worried me and many of those close to me. The NZCC was advised that there was a distinct possibility that I would not play. But at that point another big change took place in my life. Grahame and Doreen Felton, motivational experts, took a major interest in me and such was their impact that during the next seven years my cricket career and life changed forever. They helped me set goals and get focused on the job, eliminating all the negative self-doubts that inhibit performance. I was able to plot and plan many of the successes that I was able to enjoy in years to come.

Somehow I managed to get fit in time for this series but I had a lot to do quickly. Although my performance in the first test was not too spectacular we managed to draw the match with some fighting batting.

By the time the second test arrived, I felt that I was ready to fire. I had had a good blow-out in Wellington during the first test and could feel that that had helped me get my game together and that now there was a chance of making a significant contribution. It is called 'being in the zone'. I scored 99 in our first innings. I felt that it was my best test batting innings, even though I had scored more runs on other occasions. I timed the ball very well, I tried to dominate their attack by being positive, and I played sensibly until I nicked one to wicketkeeper Bob Taylor, from Bob Willis, to miss out on my second test hundred. My only comforting thought was that I had made 99 and England could not muster that in either innings. A five-wicket bag in the second innings and eight wickets in the match made me feel that I was back on track and ready to continue my playing career.

Nottinghamshire v Middlesex at Lord's,
London, England, 1984

18th championship match of the season.

I was desperately keen to achieve the coveted double of scoring 1000 runs and capturing 100 wickets in the same first-class season. The game at Lord's against Mike Gatting's Middlesex team was an ideal opportunity to achieve something special in my career and I was determined and ready to perform. There were no signs of anything extraordinary about to happen after bowling Middlesex out for 152, even though I had four wickets. We then slumped to 17/4 and Clive Rice, our captain, told me to go out and score a double hundred. I was somewhat bemused at this advice, especially as my previous best was well short of that total and we were in desperate trouble against one of the best bowling attacks on the county scene — fast bowlers Wayne Daniel and Norman Cowans, and spinners John Emburey and Phil Edmonds.

As I walked to the wicket I was fuming, feeling that we had thrown away all the good work our bowlers had done. I said to umpire David Shepherd: 'If I am still here at the break (tea was 20 minutes away) I will have 20 runs.' I intended to play positively. I then proceeded to hit West Indian fast bowler Wayne Daniel for 18 runs from one of his overs and at tea I was 26 not out. At stumps we were 195/5 and I was 127 not out, so it had definitely been my day.

Next day, runs kept flowing from my bat at a brisk pace, but I was running out of partners. When we were 287/9 I was 184 not out and had virtually no hope of reaching 200. We still needed another 13 runs to reach 300 to capture a much needed bonus point when our number 11 batsman, Peter Such, strode, somewhat reluctantly, to the wicket. He had taken more wickets during the season than runs scored.

To Suchie's credit, though, he hung in there and we added a further 57 for the tenth wicket, and he reached a career best 16. I had never seen Suchie hit a boundary but when Cowans bowled one down the leg side, he nipped it behind square to the rope. Then he followed that up with another four as he poked one between the wicketkeeper and first slip. He was battered and bruised from the fast bowling of Wayne Daniel, Norman Cowans and Nellie Williams because on numerous occasions he turned his back on the ball and took it on the backside, but I admired his guts as he helped me through to my only double century — 210 not out.

The runs scored were highly significant in my search for the 1000 runs I needed to complete the batting half of the double — it took me to 880 runs for the season. Now there were still six matches left to score the remaining 120 runs I needed to reach 1000 runs. I also had to get 12 more wickets to reach a 100 wickets for the season. I was well on target; in fact, I was ahead of budget. From a personal point of view this was a great moment in my career because I went beyond what I thought I was capable of achieving.

This was a valuable lesson learned — Ricey had put a thought in my mind that I had never considered before.

Nottinghamshire v Northamptonshire at Lord's, London, England, 1987
Natwest 60-over Final.

I had been at the club since 1978 and we had appeared in two previous Lord's finals, in 1982 and 1985, both without success. I had my testimonial year in 1986 and I said to the club that I would be back in 1987 but I would not leave the club until we had won a one-day title. I had put myself under enormous pressure because I had planned to finish my professional life at the club in 1987. This would allow me to play out my career in the test arena for another three years.

We had played well enough to reach the final and we came up against Northants, who were firm favourites to win as they had been an efficient and successful one-day team for several years. As usual, there was a sell-out crowd, but rain delayed the start of play and the match was reduced to 50 overs. Rain later intervened during the day but we restricted Northants to 228/3, which was an obtainable score, especially with a batting line-up that included five England players in Chris Broad, Tim Robinson, Derek Randall, Bruce French and Eddie Hemmings, as well as Clive Rice and me. We were an experienced team — but, then, we had faltered in the past.

There were delays during the day and when bad light ended the day's play we were precariously placed at 57/4 off 21 overs and had to return to Lord's on Monday to restart the match. This was the first time in 25 years that a one-day final had stretched over two days, but it gave us time to gather our thoughts and plan our strategies.

The headline in the papers that capped Saturday's play read 'Notts need a miracle to stop Northants now'. On Monday rain again delayed the start of play until 1.30 pm. A small crowd of about 2000 people, including eight Notts supporters who had travelled from Trent Bridge, braved the weather, hoping to see a positive result in the match. We still needed to score a further 171 runs from 29 overs with six wickets in hand.

I came to the wicket at 84/5, knowing that I had to do something, otherwise we could end up embarrassing ourselves. I played sedately at first, picking up some singles, but the scoring rate was growing to 8.5 runs per over. With the required run rate soon over 10 runs an over I decided that we had reached the point of no return and needed to take some risks. I had to have a go at the off-spinner Richard Williams. In the forty-fourth over I slogged him to the midwicket boundary, where Allan Lamb dropped me and the ball went over the boundary for six. The next ball was skied to long off, where Robert Bailey, perhaps blinded by the sun that had just appeared, dropped me and we ran two. The third ball was again hit to Lamb for a single. West Indian fast bowler Winston Davis was brought back to the crease and bowled tidily but conceded seven runs. A Duncan Wild over then went for 11. David Capel, who had not bowled since Saturday, when his five overs had cost only 10 runs, was brought on to bowl — he went for 10 and all of a sudden we needed 16 runs from the final two overs with four wickets in hand.

In the fiftieth and final over we needed eight to win. French was run out when attempting a single from the first ball of the over — the ball hit my feet and went straight to the bowler, who ran Bruce out. I had the strike and proceeded to hit the next ball to the long off boundary for six, clearing the boundary by 20 metres. I stood there with my hands upraised, with most people thinking that I was signalling six, but what I was doing was signalling victory to my team-mates on the balcony. Nothing was going to stop me now, with four balls left to score two runs. The next ball went behind square on the leg side for four to end the match and I had finished with 70 not out from 61 balls to be named Man of the Match and help secure an elusive one-day title for the club. This was a moment to savour for me and the club — at last a one-day title. There was also great joy and relief for all those associated with Trent Bridge and Notts cricket. This was something we deserved.

My playing career at Notts was now complete. That season we also went on to win the County Championship — it was a double for Notts. I was also only three wickets short of capturing 100 wickets for the season, having already scored over 1000 runs — I had nearly completed the 'double' again. What a year!

New Zealand v Australia at Lancaster Park, Christchurch, New Zealand, 1974
New Zealand's 8th test victory.

It had been a long time, 28 years in fact, since we had last played an official test match between New Zealand and Australia. That ill-fated match, in 1946, had been captained by my father and at the time had been deemed to be an unofficial test match, much to the delight of Dad and the team, but in 1948 the ICC had decided otherwise and the match became official. New Zealand had been bowled out for 42 and 54 at the Basin Reserve in Wellington to lose to Bill Brown's Australians by an innings and three runs.

For years thereafter Australia sent their B teams to New Zealand. Obviously, the Australian Cricket Board did not regard New Zealand as worthy opponents. This attitude annoyed many players, and no doubt the New Zealand Cricket Council (NZCC) at the time. We needed more exposure to Australian cricket and respect from our neighbours. In my view, they should have helped develop our game more than they did, by exposing our amateur players to the level of play required to be competitive in international competition and for the benefit of world cricket. As a cricket nation we were taking too long to get our total game together, even though we had tasted seven rare victories. We certainly had some talented players but winning was not a habit and there were times when a drawn match or series was considered as good as a victory.

The first 1974 test in Wellington was a runs spree and became a boring draw. Lancaster Park, Christchurch, was the scene for the second test and a magic moment in our cricketing history. It was a fantastic contest over five days on a pitch that did not change too much. The highest score of the match was 259, scored by the Australians in their second innings, and the lowest score was 223, also scored by the Australians. Somewhere in between we were consistent with 255 and 230/5, with Glenn Turner being the national hero as he scored a century in each innings.

At 23 years of age I was somewhat overawed to be playing against the Australians, but I came away with seven wickets — not that I had bowled well. In the first innings I dismissed the Australian captain rather fortuitously — it was a slower ball that ended up being a rank long hop. Ian Chappell had time to take at least two swings at the ball, perhaps have time for a cup of tea and a sandwich, and hit it anywhere around the ground, but he missed and the leg bail fell off, much to my surprise and delight.

However, the wicket that gave me the most satisfaction in the match was the dismissal of Greg Chappell in the second innings. We had a lead of 32 on the first innings and Richard Collinge had dismissed Keith Stackpole and Ian Chappell to have the Aussies at 26/2. Bowling from the southern end, and with good pace and rhythm, Greg flashed at a ball just outside the off stump, edged it and Jeremy Coney took a sharp catch at first slip. The whole moment appeared to be in slow motion. I could hear the large crowd in the Number Five stand erupt. Australia was now 33/3, and we were on top.

We were left 228 for victory on the fifth day and managed it without too much fuss, Ken Wadsworth stroking a ball from Greg Chappell through the covers for four runs to secure an historic win by five wickets. There was immense satisfaction within the team and such was the magnitude of the win that people in New Zealand thought we should have a national holiday to celebrate. After the win, and while we were still in the dressing room, NZCC gave us each a $100 bonus, which, coupled with the match fee of $100, meant that we were 'rich'.

More important than the money, though, was the feeling of finally getting a win over Australia and what it did for New Zealand as a nation. Even though I was to experience many more team wins, that immense feeling of satisfaction was never replicated — and the celebrations continued for some time. The Australians now had to show us more respect as a cricketing nation, and in the years that followed we were to experience many more test wins against our neighbours.

Nottinghamshire v Glamorgan at Trent Bridge, Nottingham, England, 1981

When I joined Notts County Cricket Club in 1978 the club had been struggling for years to be competitive. It appeared that the biggest challenge of the season for the club was to win the local derby against Derbyshire to get off the bottom of the county championship table. In those days, pitches at Trent Bridge were white featherbeds, ideal for batsmen to get their quota of 1000 runs in a season to secure a contract for the following season.

In 1981 we started the season well, winning matches. We had an inspirational captain in South African Clive Rice, who led from the front with his all-round skills; I was fit and capturing wickets and other players were also contributing consistently throughout the season. It was a big season for me with over 100 wickets and nearly 800 runs.

We were winning tosses at Trent Bridge and we inserted opposition and continually bowled them out on sporting pitches. We won something like nine of the 10 matches played at home. There was a directive from the TCCB (Test and County Cricket Board) to all counties to prepare result pitches. We certainly did that. Generally, visiting teams were bowled out for around 150/180, we scored nearly 300, bowled them out again and then scored the winning runs if we had not already won by an innings.

Going into the last match of the season we had a slender points lead over Sussex. To be assured of the county championship title we needed to not only win the match but also earn some bonus points. The game itself was against lowly rated Glamorgan, but that included class act

Javed Miandad, who had tormented New Zealand teams of the past. The match was a low-scoring affair, with both teams struggling to score runs. However, we did the business and won in convincing style by 10 wickets. We had picked up enough points to head off Sussex's challenge and won the title by three points.

It was the first time in 52 years that we had won the three-day Schweppes County Championship. The scenes at Trent Bridge were very memorable and emotional. Thousands of supporters gathered on the ground cheering and clapping as the team stood on the balcony taking the accolades. Reg Simpson, a former Notts and England player, came into our dressing room shedding tears, such was his emotion at what we had achieved. The players were extremely happy and proud — there was plenty of shaking of hands and hugging. We had done something very special and although I was not there at the time because I was back in New Zealand, the Club eventually accepted the trophy from Prince Philip at Buckingham Palace.

Nottinghamshire v Lancashire, at Trent Bridge, Nottingham, England, 1980
Sunday League 40-over match.

This was the last game of the season. I had made up my mind to finish my three-year contract with the club and not return. I had played only seven of the 24 county championship matches because of a chronic ankle injury that had not responded to treatment and I was being paid to do a job I could not complete. I felt embarrassed, degraded and disappointed — this was not my idea of giving service and value to my employer — so I needed to move on in my life.

The Sunday League competition allows bowlers to complete a maximum of eight overs but more importantly to bowl from a limited run-up of only 15 yards. A white line was drawn on the ground and bowlers had to start their run-ups either inside or on the line.

The next two-hour session changed my life in cricket. Bowling first, we dismissed Lancashire for a paltry 114 in 39.4 overs and I left the field having captured 6/12, the best bowling return for a Notts player in the Sunday League competition and the best figures of the season for all teams. We won the match convincingly by six wickets. It was a great result, but was followed by an emotionally charged moment.

I was standing on the balcony waving my goodbyes to the fans who had gathered below. Beside me was my captain and great friend Clive Rice and next to him were two legendary Notts figures, Harold Larwood and Bill Voce. Clive and I were the players of today and Harold and Bill the symbols of the past. Moments later, the chairman of the club, John Heatley, came into the dressing room and took me unawares by saying: 'We want you back next year even if you bowl off two paces.' I was shocked at his comment but he had opened the door for me to reconsider my future and I gave him an undertaking that I would let the club know within several months. For me this was an extraordinary vote of confidence by the club.

I returned to Christchurch and saw my physiotherapist, who treated my ankle injury. He inserted orthotics into my shoes and I had a brace made to support my left ankle while bowling. My ankle problem was never totally cured but it was manageable, much to my relief, and I could play, even if there was some small discomfort at times in years to follow. Months later I confirmed with the club that I would return, provided I could bowl from a Sunday League run-up so that there was less strain on my body and hopefully that would allow me to play for an extended period. This was a defining moment in my career — it gave me an extra seven years at the club and in that time we won two county championships and appeared in three Lord's finals, winning the Natwest 60-over competition in 1984 and in 1987. I completed the coveted double by capturing 100 first-class wickets and scoring 1000 first-class runs in that time. Internationally, I was able to play for 10 more years, even though the short run-up was controversial in New Zealand for a brief time before it was accepted after some good performances. From a shortened run-up, my remodelled action contributed to better performances and in years to come world records followed.

New Zealand v India at the Basin Reserve,
Wellington, New Zealand, 1976
New Zealand's 9th test victory.

This was a pivotal moment in my career. I was still an amateur player, working five days a week, playing club cricket at weekends and practising two nights a week. I was still learning my trade. I was in and out of the national team but still trying to cement my place as an international cricketer. During the season I had not performed that well for Canterbury. I was still coming back from an injured shoulder that had kept me out of the game for 12 months and it was frustrating me. I had bursitis of the shoulder, an inflammation under the scapula which had not responded to various types of treatment — rest, ice, massage, applying heat liniments, and other mechanical treatments. Someone sent me some horse liniment to try but again my injury did not respond. Other potions arrived in the mail but none were successful. I could not even lift my shoulder to comb my hair, such was the pain and discomfort I was in. In the end, with five or six treatments, acupuncture cured the problem. At least I was on the field of play, trying to regain my fitness and form.

The test team to play India was announced and I was in the squad of 13 but did not play in the first test, which was a heavy loss. In the second test I had been less than impressive with 0/74 in the first innings from 12 eight-ball overs and 1/74 from 14 overs in the second innings. I had been smacked all over the park and my confidence and performance levels were at an all-time low.

By the time I got to Wellington for the third and final test, I was resigned to the fact that I was not going to play. There was no way the selectors could justify my inclusion, but just before the toss I was advised that I would play and much to everyone's surprise, Hedley Howarth, our left-arm spinner, was omitted. For the first time in my experience we went into a match with a four-pronged seam attack and no recognised spinner — was this one of the biggest gambles taken by a New Zealand selection panel?

From my point of view, the good thing that came out of my late call-up was that I did not have time to think about my situation and go through all the self-doubt and worry about playing and how I would bowl. Within minutes, I was on the field, expecting to open the bowling and share the new ball with Richard Collinge. I was almost about to measure out my run-up but Glenn Turner, the captain, did not have the confidence to use me with the new ball. He decided to open the bowling with Collinge and Lance Cairns, followed with my brother Dayle at first change. I had been banished to the boundary where I had plenty of time to reflect on my position in the team and wait until it was my turn to bowl at the crease. Was this a master stroke by the selectors and Glenn to get the best out of me?

When I was given the ball India was 40/0, with Sunil Gavaskar and Dilip Vengsarkar at the crease. Very quickly, Gavaskar edged the ball to wicketkeeper Ken Wadsworth, much to my relief. That wicket was very important to my confidence. I kept telling myself that I was good enough to be playing at this level and that every ball was a potential wicket-taker. I tried to be as consistent as I could, attacking and probing the off stump, waiting for the batsman to make a mistake — Ken had taken three catches from my bowling. My usual method of bowling was to bowl as fast as I could, but this attitude to bowling was not necessarily the right approach at international level, especially if accuracy was lacking. After 14 overs I had 4/35 and India was dismissed for 220. Boy, did I feel relieved!

We had a lead of 134 runs on the first innings. Glenn still opted for Collinge, Cairns and Dayle to bowl ahead of me in the second innings. When I came on to bowl I started well and after 8.3 overs I had 7/23, hitting the stumps three times. I had come from the depths of despair to being a New Zealand record holder — the best bowling figures in a test innings and most wickets in a test match. I had learned more about bowling in that match than I had in my previous three years. India was dismissed for 81 and we had won by an innings and 33 runs.

This was truly a remarkable match for me and the tour to India and Pakistan that followed some months later proved to be successful with another 25 wickets in the six tests. After the tour was over, even though we lost 2-0 in both countries, I had bowled well enough for Glenn Turner to say that I had come of age. My career started to gather momentum and I never looked back.

During Pakistan's tour of New Zealand in 1985, our champion batsman, Martin Crowe, was going through a period of self-doubt. He was waking up in the mornings not knowing whether he should shave, have breakfast, or which bat he should use during the match. He gave all the indications that he was likely to fail during the day.

I said to him, 'Hogan (his nickname), you will shave, you will have bacon and eggs for breakfast and you will use your favourite bat.'

On the first morning of the second test at Eden Park, Auckland, he arrived in the dressing room and taped a chart to the wall above his seat. It used my nickname 'Paddles' as a reminder, and said:

'Listen here, Hogan, this is a test match, now is the time'.

- P   Pride of performance
- A   Aims and application
- D   Desire to do well
- D   Dedication to the job
- L   Be one of the lads
- E   Enjoy the game
- S   Success and winning

I must admit to being a little choked up: it was a great compliment. I then watched him produce a delightful innings of 84, until he was caught off the handle of the bat at short leg, from the bowling of Abdul Qadir. At Dunedin for the third test, he added 'Hogan' to his wall chart:

- H   Hundreds
- O   Organisation and be prepared
- G   Guts
- A   Aims
- N   Play natural game

During that test he scored very well, with 57 and 84. The transformation of Martin Crowe during the three tests was very pleasing. He went on to average 59, having scored 295 runs, and we won the series against Pakistan for the first time in New Zealand.

While all this had been going on, Stephen Boock, our left-arm spinner and number 11 batsman, had noticed Crowe's motivational chart and the success that he had enjoyed. During the third test Boocky was sent in as nightwatchman and survived. Next morning he arrived at the ground with his own chart using his own nickname, 'Boocky', as a source of inspiration for any possible success that may follow:

B   Block
O   'ook'
O   On drive
C   Cut
K   Kill the . . .
Y   Yahoo

'Boocky' continued his batting and was out hooking ('ookin'), so Frank Cameron, the chairman of selectors and our manager, very quickly deleted 'ook' from his chart and replaced it with 'off drive'.

Boocky averaged 5 for the series.

The Testimonial Year

In March 1990 a galaxy of cricket stars arrived in New Zealand to participate in my testimonial matches. Never before had the New Zealand public been treated to seeing the world's leading players along with New Zealand's best. Sunil Gavaskar, the world's highest run-scorer in test cricket, led a very competitive team that included Kapil Dev, Allan Border, Alvin Kallicharan, Derek Randall, Aravinda de Silva, Abdul Qadir, Terry Alderman, Michael Holding, Tom Moody, Greg Matthews, Ravi Ratnayake and Franklyn Stephenson. Local wicketkeepers Lee Germon and Adam Parore were given the opportunity to play and rub shoulders with the world superstars.

I was hoping that my great friend, Notts captain and team-mate, and South African, Clive Rice would be able to play in the World XI. Sadly, however, IMG (International Management Group Ltd) — the company involved in organising and promoting the event — advised me that, for political reasons, I should not invite him. South Africa at the time was still under apartheid rule and IMG feared a backlash towards the event.

My XI included players that I had played with and most of the current test team at that time — John Wright, Andrew Jones, Jeff Crowe, Mark Greatbatch, Ian Smith, Martin Snedden, Lance Cairns, Ewen Chatfield, John Bracewell, Stephen Boock, Paul McEwan and Danny Morrison.

The players were all paid a match fee and they competed for $35,000 in prize money to ensure that the games were competitive. Allan Border donated his two match fees back to me, saying, 'This is your benefit season mate. One day you may come and play for me.' Several years later I was at the Gabba in Brisbane to play in his match.

The World XI won the series 3-1, with three of the matches being closely fought: the first match was won by the World XI on the last ball of the match by six wickets; they won the second match by five wickets in the last over; and the third match by five runs. My XI took revenge in the last match and had a conclusive six wicket win with 15 overs to spare.

With the support of the Canterbury Cricket Association and the New Zealand Cricket Council the four matches were played at Lancaster Park, Christchurch; the Basin Reserve, Wellington; Seddon Park, Hamilton; and Eden Park, Auckland. The games were the focus of the Testimonial series but they also created other serious fundraising opportunities. Dinners were held in Christchurch, Wellington and Auckland, merchandising opportunities were created and the sale of a testimonial brochure almost guaranteed an income that would secure my future.

Testimonial or Benefit seasons are very much a part of English county cricket. After 10 years' service a county will usually grant a player a fundraising year to ensure there is life after cricket and retirement is comfortable. The net proceeds tend to vary from county to county but in my time at Notts a beneficiary could receive £40,000 to £50,000, while a player in London (Middlesex or Surrey) might receive anything from £100,000 to £200,000. Today it is not uncommon for a player to receive £500,000 plus (NZ$1,500,000).

In New Zealand it was rare for provinces to reward players in that way but the Canterbury Cricket Association wanted to recognise my 18-year contribution to the game and gave me the opportunity to organise some events. IMG felt that I should have a national testimonial year, allowing me to raise funds outside my province. In England it was frowned upon to go outside your county as it could cause a possible conflict with other beneficiaries, but the rarity of testimonial matches in New Zealand meant that it was less of an issue here. The New Zealand Cricket Council readily

Waiting for my first bat and ball to arrive.

Ready for school with my brothers (from left to right):
me, Dayle, Martin and Barry.

The Christchurch Under 5 Stone C team with me as captain holding the ball.

'Stick 'em up big brother!' Barry is not amused. Westerns are still my favourite movies.

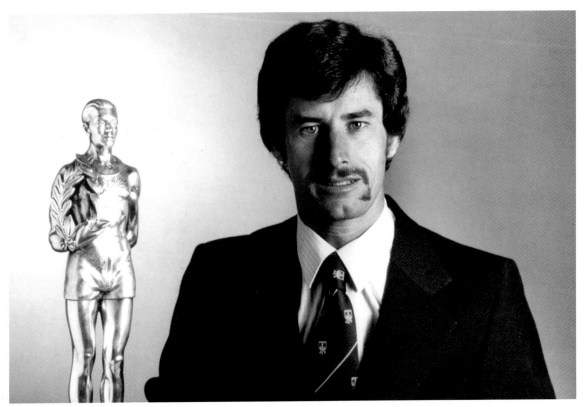

Winner of the New Zealand Sportsman-of-the-Year Trophy in 1980 and 1986 (also Sportsperson-of-the-Decade and last 25 years in 1987).

A three-ball duck for Australian Test batsman Dean Jones at Adelaide in 1987 — caught Ian Smith, bowled Hadlee 0.

Australia retains the Trans Tasman Trophy as Australian number 11 batsman, Mike Whitney, survives my last over and the last ball of the third test match at the MCG in 1987.

Bowling in English County Cricket — seam up was my specialty. Umpire Barry Duddleston looks on.

On the way to scoring a century in a Sunday League match against Gloucestershire at Cheltenham, England.

On the balcony at Trent Bridge with my team-mate and great friend Clive Rice and England and Notts legendary fast bowlers Bill Voce and Harold Larwood, 1980.

India's Sanjay Manjrekar becomes my 400th test wicket, bowled for 4 at Lancaster Park, Christchurch in 1990. To mark the occasion I am presented with 400 roses from Roger Bhatnagar, my niece Jamie Provan and Mel Brown.

England captain Graham Gooch, out lbw to the first ball of the Trent Bridge Test, Nottingham, 1990.

gave their support to a national campaign and the four matches, for which I was very grateful.

I formed a committee with local friends and businessmen in Christchurch who were willing to provide their time and expertise to ensure that the event was efficient and organised, calling ourselves the Richard Hadlee Testimonial Committee (RHTC). IMG became the professional event organisers and, at their request, Baldwin Boyle and Associates were appointed the public relations company to promote the event. There were high expectations from everyone and an early budget prepared by IMG suggested a projected income of around $1,400,000, with costs of around $1,000,000, to leave a nice profit of around $400,000. Although it sounded good, I thought it was a little *too* good to be true.

IMG secured two massive sponsorships totalling $300,000 to ensure the four matches would go ahead. Dominion Breweries (DB) had the naming rights for the series and TV3, who were new to the New Zealand television market and saw an opportunity to be involved with sport for the first time, won the broadcasting rights for live television coverage of the games. Feedback from IMG was that TVNZ (the normal broadcaster of cricket in New Zealand at that time) was interested, but indicated that they would not guarantee coverage of all four games and that they may have also been reluctant to pay anything for the broadcasting rights. All systems appeared to be a go but before a ball had been bowled a series of problems began that steadily eroded, and almost sabotaged, the event and ended up testing emotions and having a huge effect on the financial outcome.

First, DB, the major sponsors, wanted exclusive liquor rights for their products at all four venues, but that could not be guaranteed as Lion Breweries had rights at two of the venues. Thankfully, DB finally soldiered on without reducing their sponsorship fee, but it caused a lot of concern as we would have had to cancel the whole event if they had withdrawn their sponsorship.

Then we received letters from two regional cricket associations informing us that the series would have an impact on the testimonial seasons already granted to two players, Martin Snedden in Auckland and Evan Gray in Wellington, and that accordingly they sought compensation, which together came to around $35,000. We had to factor that in.

IMG made the decision to print the brochures before all the advertising had been sold to cover the costs of the printing, therefore we faced a potential loss of $56,000 before the first brochure was sold — and at the end of the series 4500 brochures were left unsold. In addition, there were disputes with some of the brochure advertisers, who refused to pay for some of their bills, saying that they had not placed the advertising. But commission was paid for those advertisements nonetheless.

We had trouble with the merchandising too. Around 3000 ties were made but the series ended with 450 left unsold. There was supposed to be a tie advertisement in the brochure with a mail order coupon to assist and promote sales, but that didn't happen. Then the proposed documentary video of my career that we had hoped to produce was never made and the budgeted revenue from that source melted away as well. Overall the merchandising sales organised by IMG, who employed an independent person, were well below expectation, and once again this eroded our income.

Nor was the income from attendance as good as hoped. The sale of corporate hospitality packages at the grounds was well below expectations and the net gate receipts were disappointing, even though some good crowds turned up for the matches. Cold weather in Christchurch had a huge effect, with 8000 people attending when 12,000 to 15,000 had been expected. Auckland had the biggest crowd, of around 18,000 people, but up to 3000 of those had free admission as they were members, and this meant that there was less revenue than expected. Wellington and Hamilton had good crowds but the overall gate receipt from all venues was $174,020 when the budget had been set at $600,000.

In the second match of the series, which was played in Wellington, I suffered a groin injury while batting and although I played the remaining matches as a batsman, I was unable to bowl. This may have had some impact on crowd numbers.

Then the running costs at the venues blew out. The Victory Park Board, who controlled Lancaster Park, generously halved their ground rent but the Auckland Cricket Association wanted 25 per cent of the gross gate plus $25,000-30,000 for the match day running costs. The Eden Park Trust did, however, refund $5000. The RHTC had been under the impression that additional ground signage rights sold would produce additional revenue for the fund. But this turned out not to be the case.

With the exception of Christchurch, the dinner venues were too small, holding a maximum of 250 people. We could have filled larger venues, but at least the three dinners broke even.

The RHTC had also always been under the impression from IMG that Mazda would provide a car for each venue for a spectator to win, something that would encourage more people to turn up to the games. Mazda, we understood, would also pay the fund $15,000 to be involved with the event. In the words of IMG, there appeared to be some 'shagging around' from Mazda and there was a late change of sponsor to Nissan. There was a car promotion in the end but it was totally different from that first indicated — one car was made available and to my knowledge no fee was paid to the fund.

Then we had some difficulty from some of the players. In accordance with the New Zealand tax laws all players had 20 per cent of their match fees deducted to cover withholding tax. This annoyed one or two of the overseas players, who threatened to withdraw their services from the last match at Auckland. Thankfully, all players participated, but there were question marks over their playing effort on the day as my XI had the biggest win of the four-match series, with 15 overs to spare. The RHTC fund paid the additional taxes to keep those players happy, once again reducing the net gain to the fund. Then we found that some players did not pay for their phone charges, drinks and meals at the hotels, leaving the RHTC fund to pay those additional costs, and that amounted to several thousand dollars. There were several other cost overruns, with additional hotel, travel and player expenses incurred because some of the overseas players were only available for a couple of games and fresh players had to be brought in and accommodated.

At one stage the Testimonial was heading for a big financial loss and the RHTC was greatly concerned. They had worked very hard to ensure that there would be a positive result, but so many aspects relating to the running of the event were out of their control. In fact, they were devastated at the potential disaster, which would leave Karen and me liable for the shortfall. If the RHTC had to pay dollar for dollar for all the costs that were incurred there was a potential $60,000 loss. However, both IMG and Baldwin Boyle reduced their fees and the brochure printers gave the RHTC a credit, which meant that a loss was avoided.

On 31 March 1992, two years later, an audited set of financial statements was lodged with the tax department to finalise the 1990 Testimonial season and officially declare the amount raised. The final figure was $44,186.33 and although it wasn't the end-of-career bonus originally hoped for, there was some relief for all involved.

After 10 years' loyal service to a club or provincial team, a player is generally awarded a Benefit or Testimonial season to raise funds for his future and allow the public to say 'Thank you' for the contribution he has made. Invariably, there are benefit cricket matches and players from all over the country, and at times from around the world, will play in these tribute matches. It is always standard practice to make sure that the beneficiary gets off the mark when he bats and his team wins the match, even if it is off the last ball. Some games are contrived to make it go to the last ball, but there are times when the result can go wrong.

All the players understand 'the rules' so generally there is no confusion.

However, I played in a benefit match in England for Mike Hendrick, a former England fast bowler and No. 11 batsman. Hendo fancied his batting in these games, even though his average in first-class cricket was about 5!

My captain, Clive Rice, said to me, 'You'd better let him have one Paddles.'

'Are you sure, Ricey?' I questioned.

'Yes, let him have one,' came the reply.

The next ball I bounced Hendo and the ball whizzed past his nose.

'What the hell are you doing Richard?' Hendo yelled.

'Ricey told me to give you one,' I replied.

Clive very quickly came over to me and said, 'Paddles, I meant let him have one run to get off the mark, not a bouncer!'

If only captains would make their instructions a little more clear! Hendo ended up scoring 6 before he skied one and was caught, but as he departed he passed me and said, 'I see you were bowling with a Duke-made ball Paddles. I could see the crown on the ball as it passed my nose.'

Cheeky bugger, but I guess he had the last laugh as he had surpassed his normal batting average!

A View from the Commentary Box

When I retired from playing international cricket in 1990, it did not take too long to get into the commentary box and start talking about the game. It was a great privilege to have the opportunity to tour the world for 10 years and commentate in England, Australia, India, Pakistan, South Africa and New Zealand. At 39, I found it easier to talk about the game than play it — at least there were no more aches and pains.

In 1990 I became the Bank of New Zealand Cricket Ambassador which involved general promotional work, as well as television and radio commentary. I soon found that the demands of both forms of commentary were very different. A radio commentator needs to paint the picture before his eyes for the listeners, so they feel as though they are at the ground watching the action unfold. The television commentator has the pictures on the screen already telling the story, so he needs to add information likely to be of interest to the viewer. In this regard, as an ex-player, I was looking to share my appreciation of the tactical and psychological aspects of the game and the specific situation.

But I first needed to learn the basic etiquette that both forms of commentary required. These were often simple things such as not talking over my co-commentator, which is surprisingly easy to do, and always referring to the players by their surnames — calling players by their first names or nicknames conveys a too friendly, 'matey' approach that comes across as being unprofessional. It was important to project an attitude of impartiality. I also learnt that it does not pay to criticise the umpires. It is better to explain why the umpire made a particular decision and to always recall that an umpire only had one chance to get the decision right, whereas we commentators may get to view the television replay several times, and from different angles, before making a judgment and expressing an opinion. This, to me, was part of being as fair and constructive as possible when analysing the game. There is no need to be controversial for the sake of being controversial. Both umpires and players will accept criticism if it is fair and constructive. Say what you think and believe in, but any criticism should also propose solutions to the problem.

I tended to enjoy radio more than television because you could develop a theme without the constant interference of commercial breaks at the ends of the overs. It was like having a telephone conversation with millions of people listening and feeling part of the action. We had a picture to paint and a story to tell.

It is surprising how, for such fleeting stuff, some pieces of commentary stay with you. My favourite piece of radio commentary took place in Australia when the South Africans toured there in the late 1950s. A test was being played at the Adelaide Oval and Charles Fortune, a South African commentator who liked to use a lot words, was explaining to the listeners exactly what was happening:

'And Lindwall bowls to Tayfield, who pushes the ball back to the bowler. What a magnificent ground the Adelaide Oval is, surely one of the best cricket grounds in the world. The outfield is in magnificent condition: lush, green and very flat. It is like a bowling green out there. The Bradman Stand dominates the western side of the ground and the Victor Richardson Gates look resplendent on the eastern side of the ground. I can see St Peter's Cathedral in the background. The River Torrens meanders peacefully along behind the main gates. The scoreboard situated on the hill gives us all the information that we need to know to keep us up-to-date with the state of play. Twenty-three thousand spectators are jam-packed into the ground today. The crowds on the grassy hill are enjoying the spectacle. Several youngsters are playing cricket with a tennis ball near the embankment. The seagulls are basking in the sunshine, picking up scraps left over by the spectators from lunch . . . oh . . . by the way, the scorer has just advised me that that was Lindwall's first hat-trick in Australia.'

Television commentary demanded most of the same basic skills as radio commentary but it was also fundamentally different. There was no need to describe the obvious because the viewer could see what was happening. Instead, the aim was to embellish the picture with constructive and interesting comment. For this reason it was important to always watch your own television screen and not the ground in front of you, as that was the picture the viewers would see and to start pontificating about something offscreen could sound very odd and be confusing for viewers. Television commentary is much more about teamwork because there are so many different people involved. The director, producer, statistician, camera crew and those who get the replays to air, all have roles to play and must be respected. I always considered it of vital importance to relate to my fellow commentators and establish a rapport with them. I felt that conversations that drew on the experience of my colleagues and allowed them to offer their expert knowledge or to recall and relate anecdotes were likely to be of interest to viewers — a batsman and a bowler commentating together can offer differing points of view and give a more complete idea of the intricacies of the game.

My greatest challenge in the television commentary box was when I was working with the Channel Nine commentary team in Australia in the early 1990s. To survive in the box with Richie Benaud, Bill Lawry, Ian Chappell and Tony Greig could be daunting. They were all former captains and had a wealth of cricket knowledge and experience as players, and in the box I was a lone voice from New Zealand — although when challenged I felt I could hold my own and come back at them. They were always keen to bait the overseas commentator and to this end were, let's say, very supportive of their own players. If an Australian misfielded the ball, there was a bump in the outfield, or if he dropped a catch, it was a difficult chance. On the other hand, if the touring team fielder missed a ball, it was poor fielding or he had dropped a 'dolly'. To be fair, though, I think that they are among the best and most entertaining commentators in the world, and the new breed of commentator, former players such as Mark Nicholas, Michael Slater, Ian Healy and Mark Taylor, are making a big and successful impact.

The game of cricket, more than any other sport, lends itself to the commentator being caught out, as it were. The game is described in an extraordinary way, has its own bag of terms and expressions, and can often sound like some sort of code or lingo of its own. John Emburey, the English off-spinner, was once described as bowling with two short legs, one of which was wearing a helmet, something that seems perfectly acceptable if you know the game but must sound decidedly odd if you don't. Players can bowl maidens over, make a glance to fine leg, even have a slash outside off stump, and there are an endless number of misunderstandings possible when commentators are referring to bats and balls. One slip I made of that sort came when I was commentating with Richie Benaud during New Zealand's tour of England in the early 1990s. The third test was being played at Old Trafford and the pitch was on the frisky side, allowing New Zealand's two opening bowlers, Chris Pringle and Dion Nash, to make life distinctly uncomfortable for Michael Atherton, the England captain. So much so, in fact, that Nash got the ball to bounce a little higher than normal and Atherton was struck in the groin. Atherton's reaction indicated that he was in serious trouble as his eyes started to roll and he went down on his knees, taking some time to recover. A five-and-a-half-ounce leather projectile bowled at 85 miles per hour into the groin can do that to you. As Atherton, ashen-faced, took his time to get his breath back and recover, the television monitor showed a slow-motion replay of the incident and, watching the bounce Nash had extracted from the pitch, I said: 'That ball bounced.' Richie turned, looked at me and said with a small, wry smile: 'Which one, Richard?'

Some other television commentators have also had their moments when informing viewers what was happening. Ian Chappell, the former Australian captain, had a habit of hitching his box after he had played a shot at the ball.

Chappell duly played and missed, and the camera moved in on the batsman, but the commentator clearly wasn't watching the screen as he said: 'Well, it's been a good pitch and only two balls have moved all day.'

There is ample room for comedy. For some reason, though, it seems that it is radio commentators who find themselves in more trouble than television commentators. It may be because of the importance of describing the scene with absolute accuracy on the radio to enable listeners to picture what is happening at the ground. Alan Gibson was describing an incoming batsman in 1995, when Lancashire were playing Hampshire at Aigburth and the fourth wicket had fallen for a small total: 'The next batsman is Leo Harrison. He has been in these situations before and saved his team on many occasions. Hampshire tend to rely on him and as he walks to the wicket he looks confident. It is his typical swashbuckling walk to the crease. What a great servant he has been to Hampshire this year. It must be a comforting sight to his captain to see this familiar figure joining him at the crease.' Then there came a moment's silence as his co-commentator informed him that it was in fact Colin Ingleby-Mackenzie who was walking out to bat.

Sometimes, feeling the pressure to say something, anything, to fill in the silence, can lead to some rather elliptical comments, such as when Imran Munshi described the fog rolling into an East London ground to Sanjay Manjrekar: 'It's fog. It is coming from the sea area — that is where the coastline is.' And then there was Trevor Quirk sharing his knowledge of the game's history during a test between the West Indies and South Africa at Bridgetown, Barbados: 'And there is the George Headley Stand — it is named after George Headley.'

It is even possible to simply describe the action in the most minimal terms and not realise quite what you have said until you've said it, as in what is arguably the most famous cricketing faux pas, delivered by Brian Johnston (who has delivered many memorable lines in his time) during the 1976 test between England and the West Indies at The Oval, who in giving a very brief summary of the players involved said; 'The batsman's Holding, the bowler's Willey.' Trevor Quirk also showed how easy it is to not quite say what you mean to, during a tense Benson and Hedges one-day match, when he said: 'Alan Kourie, Transvaal's slow left-arm spin bowler, looks very calm at present, but inside his chest beats a heart.' Brian Johnston played cricket in his own right. When he was playing for the Lord's Taverners Club, at the end of the day's play, 'Blob', his dog, would walk onto the field, pick up Brian's wicketkeeping gloves and waddle back to the pavilion. Other members of the team very quickly nicknamed Blob 'Larwood', because he had four short legs and his balls swung both ways.

There are also some interesting terms used by commentators. I recall once talking to Tony Cozier, the West Indian commentator, on live television, about the performances of the West Indian all-rounder Winston Benjamin during the 1995 New Zealand tour.

He said: 'Winston is a "daisy" player.'

'What does that mean?' I asked.

'Well,' Tony replied, 'he's the type of player whose performances depend on the mood he's in at the time. Some days he does, some days he doesn't.'

I always tried to interact with my co-commentators, to develop a conversation on air that viewers and listeners could eavesdrop on, as it were. But sometimes my co-commentators didn't quite come to the party. I recall one such afternoon during New Zealand's 1994/95 tour of South Africa. I was a television commentator for TV3 in New Zealand and we were covering the third and final test in Durban, with the series locked at one-all. One of my roles was to inform viewers back in New Zealand about some interesting South African history between balls. Robin Jackman, a former Surrey and England fast bowler, joined me in the commentary box as I started to enlighten the viewers.

'Durban is in Natal and is, in fact, named after D'Urban, who was the former Cape Governor. About a million people live here. In the 1860s indentured Indian labourers were brought to Natal to work the sugar plantations. Interestingly enough, Mahatma Gandhi arrived in Natal in 1893. History records that he was refused the right to sit in the first-class section of a train — he was relegated to second class because of the apartheid (racial separation) policy.'

Jacko nodded and then opened his mouth to speak, clearly, so I thought, to support and embellish what I was saying about Gandhi. He said: 'I wonder if he got a refund.'

Taken aback a little, I responded: 'He probably would today in the new South Africa.' I continued with the history lesson: 'KwaZulu-Natal is the homeland of the Zulus. Many Zulu battles were fought in Natal, with the most famous battle being at Isandhlwana where 20,000 Zulus destroyed and killed 1300 British soldiers in two hours. Four thousand Zulus then marched on Rorke's Drift, where a small garrison of just over 100 British soldiers remained defiant. Rorke's Drift is only 200 kilometres from Durban — about two hours by car.'

Jacko chimed in again: 'They didn't have cars in those days, Richard. It would have taken them about a week to walk from Durban to Rorke's Drift.'

I continued to describe the next few deliveries and was then fed some information from our director that I shared with the viewers: 'I've just been told that a local fisherman has told our cameraman that the weather is going to change and bad light will stop play within three hours.'

Jacko, who seemed to just be following his own line of thought that afternoon, responded with: 'I didn't know that fishermen needed bad light to fish.'

I had to give up and stick to what was going on out in the middle: 'The New Zealand bowlers are bowling well. South Africa is struggling at 122/5 in reply to New Zealand's 185 in the first innings — the game is well poised.'

One of my favourite commentators is England's John Arlott, who had some unique ways of getting the point across to listeners. Some Arlottisms include:

'It is rather suitable that umpires should dress like dentists, since one of their tasks is to draw stumps.'

'A constable is using a helmet to cover the streaker's confusion.'

'As the train withdraws from the Warwick Road end, so does Boycott, caught Marsh, bowled Lillee, no score.'

'There is Johnny Douglas, who said that he wanted to score four more runs in an hour than the number of trains that passed through the Warwick Road station. The trains win by nine.'

Worcester was playing a televised Sunday League match when the cameras panned in on Ivan Johnson, a six-foot tall player from the Bahamas, one of the few black players in the team and sporting, at that time, a very large and distinctive afro hairdo. Arlott said, 'There is the figure of Ivan Johnson fielding at fine leg. He is easily recognised by his sleeves buttoned at the wrist.'

Hampshire's medium-pace bowler, Jim Rice, was bowling to Somerset's Viv Richards. Richards stroked the ball out into the covers, where it was fielded by likeable Irishman, Andy Murtagh. Or as Arlott described the action: 'Rice bowls, Paddy fields.'

Arlott once described my run-up to the wicket when bowling: 'Here is Richard Hadlee, rather tall and lean-looking. As he moves in to bowl there is a bit of a stutter in his run. A bit like Groucho Marx stalking a barmaid.'

Commentators all have their personalities and I find that I appreciate those whose wit is dry. One of my favourite lines occurred when my brother Dayle, who was having an off day, was bowling quite poorly to Middlesex and England's number three batsman, Clive Radley. When describing the play all the listeners could hear was this nice piece of rhyme: 'And sadly, Hadlee bowls badly to Radley.' Christopher Martin-Jenkins is a delightful man, a wonderful commentator and an accomplished writer. He has a great knack of being able to put things succinctly, for example when he said: 'England have been bowled out by the West Indies for 210. They faced 267 balls and survived all but 10 of them.' Fred Trueman, describing Jerry Coney, a gentle, medium-pace bowler, once said: 'Coney runs in to bowl, rather, he walks in to bowl. He has bowled the ball so slowly, that by the time the ball reaches the other end the batsman has played himself out of form.' And for quiet understatement it is hard to go past: 'Surrey started cautiously and only three runs were scored in the first hour's play. Clarke was the more aggressive of the two batsmen.' Another favourite of mine was the commentator who said: 'So 67 runs are required from 11 overs and we don't need a calculator to tell us that the asking run rate per over is 6.0909 recurring.' New Zealand was playing England at the Oval, London in 1983. Jeff and Martin Crowe had both had a disappointing match. Umpire Harold 'Dickie' Bird had to make a decision and gave one of the Crowes out lbw, or as the commentator observed: 'At the Oval here today, both Crowes scored ducks and one was given out by a bird.' Such small observations from the commentator can bring a touch of humour to the game, and I certainly greatly enjoy that sort of creative commentary.

We have had several very good commentators here in New Zealand as well. One of my favourites was Iain Gallaway, widely known as one of New Zealand's best cricket and rugby radio commentators. He had a smooth voice and a ready charm that made for easy listening. He was an avid Otago supporter, and when he was in the commentary box at Carisbrook, Dunedin, his opening line would always be: 'Welcome to Carisbrook, where there is not a cloud in the sky.' Whether it was raining or not, Iain was proud of the Otago weather and playing conditions. When Iain released his autobiography, it was appropriately titled 'Not a Cloud in the Sky'.

Iain was always very precise with what he wanted to say and when he wanted to say it, he was always articulate and spoke with immaculate diction. However, like all commentators, he too slipped up at times: 'Welcome back to Carisbrook, where there is not a cloud in the sky. That was a lovely shot by Richard Hoskin, who has driven the ball through the covers for four. What a magnificent shot, and the cloud craps.' I am sure the *crowd clapped* on that occasion when they heard that comment on the radio!

Another fine New Zealand commentator is Jeremy Coney, also a gifted and very talented after-dinner speaker. He was a very fine middle-order batsman, who captained New Zealand in the mid-1980s. He once described his bowling during the 1983 World Cup in England by saying: 'My bowling is just like autumn leaves — it just keeps fluttering down and the batsmen do not know whether to hit me for four, six, or treat me with respect.' He has now become a successful radio commentator, enjoyed by many for his wit, humour and commentary on the game.

Jeremy works very well with Bryan Waddle, who was commentating on his hundredth test match at Wellington, when New Zealand played South Africa in the third and final test in 1999. New Zealand were in some difficulty as the South Africans had piled on the runs to be 392/3, and a deflated New Zealand team looked ragged in the field. New Zealand, at that point, had captured a total of nine wickets in the entire three-match series. Jeremy was in the box as Chris Harris delivered yet another ball with very little success and described the event by saying: 'There is Chris Harris, bowling another ball. It comes out of his hand like an inexperienced gynaecologist — a rather slow delivery.'

Commentators will always have their moments but they are an important and, at times, colourful part of the game. Commentary gave me a new perspective on the game. As a player out in the middle, the focus was simply on the job of scoring runs, capturing wickets and trying to win matches. Commentating, though, is about the whole overview of the match and explaining what is happening, what players are thinking, and speculating about possible outcomes. Somehow, commentating for me required more thinking than in actually playing the game. There was a need to enlighten millions of listeners and viewers all around the world, all of whom had different loyalties towards teams and players. There was a need to 'win them over', even if they disagreed with my comments.

As a former player, there is one trap in commentating which is easy to fall into, and that is becoming too judgmental and losing empathy with the current players. Sometimes you forget that there are things going on within a team that you don't know about.

> During my 10 years of English county cricket I came across some wonderful umpires, including the legendary Dickie Bird. Ray Julian was also a popular umpire, who took great delight in keeping his personal tally of victims. He would count the lbws, caught behinds, stumpings and run outs.
>
> One day at Trent Bridge I went into the umpire's room to select the ball I wanted to bowl with. Ray asked me, 'What end are you going to bowl from today, Paddles?'
>
> I replied, 'I'll wait until I get out in the middle and see which way the wind is blowing.'

'I think you should bowl from the Ratcliffe Road end,' said Ray.

As I walked onto the field there was Ray with his handkerchief in the air blowing in the wind, to give me an indication as to the end I should be bowling from. Not surprisingly, Ray took his position at the Ratcliffe Road end, giving me a clear indication that he wanted me to bowl from that end. I was advised that as he walked onto the field he said to his colleague Jack Hampshire, 'I think I will get a few more today with the way Paddles has been bowling this year. I need five more to get to a hundred for the season — if Paddles can keep bowling straight, there are at least four lbws and a caught behind.'

I went on to capture 6/38, leaving Ray one short of a hundred for the season, but he got that in the first over when we batted.

A Night to Remember

The heart problem I experienced in 1991 was the greatest 'test' I was ever involved in. It required all the inner strength and positive mental attitude I had learned in cricket and also taught me the previously largely unknown ability of putting my fate in the hands of others. So much was out of my direct control. I was floundering in unknown waters, where my skills with a 156-gram cricket ball were irrelevant. More than this, though, was that I had never before passed on the responsibility for myself to anyone else and I found this aspect of my situation both intimidating and frightening. I was a fit and energetic sportsman, one who had achieved some major milestones in the history of world and New Zealand cricket, and in everything I had ever done, although playing the game in a team with others, I was highly self-reliant.

All of a sudden I was faced with a major health problem and I found myself asking how that could be happening at 39 years of age, within only six months of retiring from playing the game, when I had achieved so much on the sporting field. Like many people, I had a feeling of invincibility with regard to myself. It was other people who suffered life-threatening problems. This cannot have been happening to me.

I learned for the first time that I suffered from a congenital heart problem known as Wolff-Parkinson-White Syndrome — in layman's terms, an irregular and racing heartbeat. All through my playing career, when my heart had raced, or I had had chest pain or difficulty breathing, in ignorance I had assumed that it was an effect of the physical exertion I was putting my body under. Generally, I responded well to pressure and all the travelling, training and playing was always just another day at the office. I enjoyed being busy when I wasn't playing cricket, even if it was just pottering around the house when I was home.

At the time, I was living on an 8-acre working property, slowly trying to make a flower growing business successful. My role was to keep the place clean and tidy by doing all the maintenance work while my wife, Karen, and her sister, Janice, worked the flower side of the business. I had also been employed by the Bank of New Zealand as their cricket ambassador when I retired from the game. This was an ideal relationship for both the bank and me as they were the major sponsor of New Zealand Cricket. It was an exciting and challenging role that I enjoyed because it kept me close to the game. I worked for the BNZ for between 100 and 120 days a year in public relations and promotional work with clients, staff, charities and school visits, and I was busy coaching, speaking and presenting prizes and awards.

The cricket-related duties accounted for half my bank time and consequently I was often away from home, leaving Karen and Janice to run the business. When I arrived home from a BNZ job, I invariably did a circuit of the house and the property to see what needed to be done, and it was not uncommon for me to get off the plane, drive home, and get straight on a tractor or a mower or use a spray pack. It was not unusual to be working until nine at night.

Part of my role with the BNZ was to host bank clients at international cricket matches, do some television and radio commentary work and help ensure that our sponsorship was working. I attended all New Zealand's test and one-day matches around the country. In 1991, New Zealand was due to play Sri Lanka at Dunedin in a one-day international. I was staying at the Southern Cross Hotel and during breakfast I felt a little strange and noted that my heart was racing a little too fast, but I was not overly concerned. Although I enjoy my food, I did not eat very much as I wasn't hungry.

I arrived at the ground around 10.00 am. I had a few small jobs to check up on in the Referee's Room where the Bank was to host about 100 guests at lunchtime. When I got there, my heartbeat had still not regulated. I just assumed that I was suffering from a little too much stress at the thought of the busy day ahead, meeting people, making small talk, doing three sessions each of radio and television commentary, running the media conference, presenting the Man of the Match award on live television and the usual post-match socialising. It was going to be my usual 10-hour day at the cricket.

At about 10.30, half an hour before the game was due to start, I made my way to the radio commentary box at the southern end of the ground and climbed the ladder up to the three-man box to prepare for my opening stint behind the microphone. By the time I had got into the box, I was very unwell. I asked Bryan Waddle, the Radio New Zealand commentator, if someone could fill in for me. At that point, all I wanted to do was lie down on the floor of the box and rest, but I decided to leave the box and sat down to the left of the sightscreen, waiting for the match to start. I thought that if I sat down for a while my heartbeat would regulate and everything would be back to normal.

Iain Gallaway, the doyen of cricket radio commentary, came and sat next to me and asked if I was all right. I told him that I felt awful. I felt dizzy, my heart was beating very fast and I needed to lie down. We walked, rather slowly, around the back of the main stand to the players' tunnel, where I sat down out of the sight of the public. Several times while we were walking, I felt as though I was about to fall over and I knew something was going on that I had never experienced before.

Local cricket enthusiast and administrator Dr John Heslop stood next to me and then escorted me to the first aid room. John did a quick check to try to find out what my problem was. Within minutes, an ambulance had arrived. Unknown to me at the time, John was very concerned, knowing that without equipment there was little he could do for me. I recall former New Zealand wicketkeeper Warren Lees being asked to stroke my legs and hands. I never did find out why he did that, and I must add that it wasn't a common occurrence to touch one's old team-mates in such a way. I knew I was going numb around the mouth, I had a tingling sensation in my fingers and my heart was racing very quickly. I was hyperventilating and wanting more air. I guessed then that I was having a heart attack.

The ambulance arrived and I was placed on a stretcher and then put in the ambulance, where the medical team went to work. I was given oxygen, injected with something and plugged into a machine. All I could see were red numbers going up and down on the machine that was monitoring my heartbeat. The numbers were alternating very erratically between 60 and 300 beats a minute. I was told later that the heart cannot pump blood that quickly without something fatal happening. A normal heartbeat rhythm at rest is about 70 to 80 beats a minute. I didn't know that then, but I knew that I was in real trouble and there was nothing I could do. When I arrived at the hospital, I was admitted to emergency immediately. I was conscious and watched them cut off my tie to get to my chest. It was a cricket tie, one of my favorites, and I never saw it again.

I was then moved into another room where I was again plugged into a machine. One of the doctors told me that there were two things they could do to slow my heart down and get it to regulate. I asked what they were. They could either give me an injection or use some electric plates to stop my heart and then shock it to restart. I thanked him and told him that the injection sounded just fine! The next thing I recall was searing pain in my chest and the doctor asking me how I felt. Now, I know — because I've been told — that I am pretty much a 'woosy' when it comes to pain and being unwell but this was out of my league. The pain in my chest was so intense that I asked what had happened. Apparently, I had gone into cardiac arrest and lost consciousness, despite the injection, and the emergency team had administered shock treatment to resuscitate me.

Fortunately, now that I was awake again I was able to see the cricket on the television and could watch New Zealand comprehensively beating the Sri Lankans. The win made me feel a lot better, but I was incredibly tired. In the meantime, Karen and my oldest son, Nicholas, who was nine years old at the time, had flown down to Dunedin from Christchurch.

I was allowed to leave the hospital the following day and was put on medication to keep my heartbeat regulated. I was physically weak and emotionally drained and the drugs were having some initial side effects, including drowsiness and dizziness. Getting through each day and the days to come would not be easy, especially with the medication that I was on and would need to be on for possibly a long time.

Somehow my experience had attracted a lot of media interest and speculation. However, we managed to avoid the television cameras and get back to Christchurch, where I took things easy for a few days. When I visited my cardiac surgeon, Dr Ian Crozier, in Christchurch for tests, he told me that I simply had two options. I could either stay on drugs for life, with possible side effects, or I could have open heart surgery, with around a 90 per cent chance of fixing the problem. The decision was mine to make. Although I did take some time to think about the dilemma I was in, the decision was quite simple. I wanted quality of life and the drug choice was not going to achieve that. Surgery was the only option.

I had numerous tests to determine how bad my heartbeat rhythm was, and although manageable it was still irregular. I was now faced with the mental anguish of self-doubt and of going into the unknown of open heart surgery. What was heart surgery all about? What did they do? Did it hurt? Would I survive? What would happen to my family if I died? How would they cope? For me, as for others in similar situations, these thoughts and concerns became all-consuming.

I returned to work as the BNZ ambassador, continuing my cricket-related activities with our sponsorship for a couple of weeks to end the international season. They were tough days to get through because of the constant feeling of tiredness caused by the drugs I needed to take. I recall being in the Carlton Hotel in Auckland and taking the lift back to my room on the twentieth floor after breakfast. From there I looked down, over the railing, and viewed the foyer below. I felt as though I could have jumped off the balcony and flown, such was the effect the medication was having on me. Luckily, I was able to gather my senses and pull back, but it gave me an insight into how drugs can make people do some crazy things when their body and mind are out of control.

My fortieth birthday fell a few days before I was due to depart for Auckland for my operation. A surprise party on the Saturday night had been organised. I was sitting in the living room, watching television, contemplating a nice quiet evening. The doorbell rang once and some friends arrived in fancy dress, followed by more doorbell ringing and then more friends, and, in all, about 30 people turned up for a 'Hearty Knight' party. They were dressed up as a doctor, surgeon, nurse, the fairy godmother, nun, priest, skeleton, butcher and an undertaker, all looking forward to some good fun. I changed into a knight's outfit that had been secretly hired for me and joined into the spirit of things. It was certainly a 'Knight to Remember' with a lot of stories told, plenty to eat and drink and, by all accounts, it was a lot of fun. However, when it was time to have the speeches, the tone became rather more sombre. Naturally, I thanked everyone for coming and for their support and concern, but at the back of my mind, I was wondering whether I would see them again. Emotions started to run high at that point. On reflection, I was saddened that there were no members of my family present — possibly an oversight as there had been so much going on at the time.

Being an organised person, I checked to see that all the insurance policies were paid up, the bills were paid, the property was tidy and that everything was up to date. Within a day, I was having a final look around the property and saying goodbye to the kids, Nicholas and Matthew. I told the boys that I would be seeing them again in 10 days' time and tried to reassure them that everything was going to be fine. They were difficult words to say because, again, I did not know whether I would in fact see them again and I wasn't good at expressing my emotions at that time in my life.

Next day, I met my surgeon, Clive Robinson, in Auckland and I tried to convince him that I was really feeling great and questioned whether I actually needed to go through with the operation at all! Clive took my ECG (electrocardiograph) and told me that the condition of my heart had in fact worsened. I remember that he was smiling at me as he told me that I would be getting operated on in three days' time and that there was no turning back now. I knew then that there was definitely no turning back and I was comforted by the fact that Clive had a 95 per cent success rate in correcting the problem, but, more importantly, he had had no fatalities. I'm not a gambling person but I had to back the odds that appeared to be in my favour and put my life in the hands of professionals. I was very grateful that I had become ill while in New Zealand and not in some other obscure place in the cricketing world where I may not be around to tell my story.

The hospital staff were very good as they settled me in to the routines of life prior to surgery. They were a much needed calming influence. I decided to ring a couple of my cricketing mates to let them know that I was in Auckland to have the surgery and that I would like to see them during the next few days if they had the time. Jeff Crowe, Ian Smith and John Wright came to cheer me up. Chopper and Wrighty saw me the day prior to surgery and on a couple of other occasions after surgery. I greatly appreciated their visits.

During the next few days they would have seen me in various states of health, from being a fit-looking 12-and-a-half stone to a washed out 10-and-a-half stone by the time I had gone through the process of surgery and recovery. Smithy saw me after the operation and I later learned that he'd said it was one of the most difficult things he had done. He had been used to seeing me running in and bowling when I had been fit and well, and all of a sudden, he was seeing me flat out on my back, pale, weak, pathetic, anaemic, with bones showing through my skin. It scared him, apparently, and to tell the truth I wasn't too happy about it either!

On 9 July 1990 I had bowled my last ball in test cricket, taking a wicket with it and ending up with a world record 431 test wickets, now, exactly a year to the day later, I was undergoing heart surgery. Somehow, all my cricketing achievements meant very little as I was about to endure the greatest test of my life, with the outcome entirely in the hands of other people and beyond my control. As I understood it, the procedure was supposed to be simple enough. Clive had to cut into my chest, get behind to the back of my heart, find the problem, make an incision to cut the pathway where the heartbeat rhythm was short-circuiting and then sew me up again. Clive was pleased with the operation and how well it went. Naturally enough, I did not know anything about the operation.

I also do not recall too much of when I was in intensive care recovering on a life support machine for two days, because I was well sedated, but I do recall that once, as the staff removed some of the tubes in my body, I vomited all over the place. No doubt I was not a pretty sight.

The surgeon thought I was recovering well, even though I was tired, frail and in some pain. My chest was sore but that was to be expected as the sternum had been cut open, clamped, wired up and then stitched up again. I had to take a lot of pills and I was hugging a pillow all the time (and for the next five weeks) because I did not want to cough or sneeze as it caused extreme pain. Under the circumstances, I was feeling really good and I had my first meal, which tasted great, and I even sampled a glass of red wine, thinking that all the self-doubt I had experienced was nonsense and that this whole process was a breeze.

From the next day onwards, the staff got me up a couple of times a day to walk around the wards to get me mobile. Pretty rapidly, my body reacted to all that I had been through. Apparently, I suffered the usual post-operative depression. I could not eat, and I was being weaned off some of the painkillers. Over the next few days some aspects of the depression I experienced were quite weird but very real. Wherever I looked, all I could see were rats and bloodied red teeth. I was hallucinating and becoming increasingly aggressive towards Karen and anyone else I came into contact with. I didn't want to see anyone, let alone talk to people.

Mum and Dad were in Australia during the time I was in Auckland. They were obviously very concerned and phoned me on several occasions to see how I was going. I guess they would have had mixed messages and different ideas on how things were really going.

In the meantime, my red blood cell count was very low, and consequently not enough oxygen was getting to my body, making me very weak. I was very close to having a blood transfusion. I was not happy about having that because of the potential diseases I could pick up if the blood were tainted. Breathing was also difficult. I had to blow into what looked like a huffer machine to get a recording to a certain level, but I was so weak that the recording was barely above zero. I was not doing very well. I was also advised that there was a 15 per cent chance that I could get an inflammation of the heart and the lungs, and if that happened, I would need to stay in Auckland for a few extra days instead of the usual 7–10 days after an operation like this. I was not happy about that either, because all I wanted to do was to get home.

After 10 days, I was released from the hospital. My first problem was to avoid the media, who had strategically positioned themselves to see me leave from the front door. Fortunately, the hospital staff had organised my departure through the Chapel and out through the back entrance into an awaiting car. Karen was the decoy, going in another car that was waiting at the front of the hospital. The staff had protected me very well.

Paul Holmes was keen to get an interview but I was in no condition to talk to anyone and I did not want people to see me looking as bad as I was looking or feeling. I advised Paul that he would get the first interview when I was ready and he respected that and I honoured that commitment in due course.

I was 'smuggled' onto an Air New Zealand flight to Christchurch and sat in business class to be away from the other passengers. This was a very nice gesture from our national airline. I was still feeling lousy on the plane. It was a testing experience because I did not want to cough or sneeze or eat. All I wanted was to get home to my own bed. When the plane landed in Christchurch, Karen's sister Susan was permitted to drive a car onto the tarmac to avoid the media waiting in the terminal to get a glimpse of me. No one saw me and the plan worked to perfection.

Two days after arriving home, I was rushed into isolation at Princess Margaret Hospital, suffering from an inflammation of the heart and lungs. I had been in bed at home and in some discomfort with a pain down the left side of my body and feeling very miserable. Karen had gone out for a couple of hours and left me alone, but when she returned she knew that I was in trouble. She needed a wee break and it gave her a chance to see how much I had deteriorated. Action needed to be taken.

She called Ian Crozier, who had no hesitation in saying that I had to go to hospital. As I was helped from my bed I could hear a family friend and former nurse say: 'Richard looks as though he is in his last few days of cancer.' As I was helped along the hallway of our two-storeyed house, I passed Nicholas's room and could hear him crying. Then I heard him say: 'Daddy is going to die.' I was in no condition to say anything to comfort him.

I had seven days in hospital to recover from the inflammation. It was a very quiet time, with only a few visitors and family coming to see me. It was a boring time really because there was nothing to do. During that period, I was given a book that recalled each of the 86 test matches that I had played. To take my mind off the boredom and some of the pain that I was experiencing, I read the book from cover to cover and replayed all those test matches. I generally don't enjoy reading, except the sports section and the television page of the newspaper, and I will never be seen with a novel under my arm. However, something about this book, *The Sir Richard Hadlee Story*, caught my interest. It was, in fact, very positive because it helped me to focus on getting fit and healthy again, and to be active instead of being miserable and angry.

When I eventually got home, I was still very weak. It took me two hours to undress, get into and out of the bath and dress again. I had no energy whatsoever and the level of oxygen in my blood was very low. Even two weeks later, just sweeping the garage floor was still a monumental task — it took so much out of me. In all, it took about nine weeks to recover to the point where I felt I had the confidence to do things without too much restriction.

During my ordeal, I received over 700 cards and letters from well-wishers. It was a humbling experience to know that so many people cared. I really appreciated their support, and those cards and letters gave me greater strength to recover as soon as possible. I made every effort to personally respond to all the mail that had a return address.

The BNZ were wonderful employers during this time. Obviously, I was unable to work for a certain period, but Lindsay Pine, the Managing Director, made sure that my family had no financial worries by paying the balance of my year's salary in a lump sum cheque. That was a remarkable gesture and totally unexpected. I wanted to be able to return to work as soon as possible and to thank them for their generosity and support. In 2008 I had completed 18 years as the BNZ Ambassador and during that time I was totally committed to them.

One result of this experience was that I began to focus on what life is really about and how precious it is. We are not on this earth as of right, rather we are privileged to be given life and be here. Life is to be enjoyed and made the most of, and not wasted or abused, as we only have one go at it. In my life I see terminally ill kids in hospitals and aged people who are in pain, perhaps waiting for the inevitable. I also see people who abuse or waste life by taking huge risks with drugs and alcohol, and this unfairness frustrates me greatly.

Some people only get one chance in this world. I believe I am having my second chance. Life is about making decisions and not allowing oneself to stagnate or drift along, without happiness, purpose or direction. Obviously, apart from good health, happiness is paramount, as are achieving things and having a sense of pride. There is a saying that 'Life is not a rehearsal, you only live once' and, unless you are James Bond, that seems about right.

Over the next few years there were no problems with my heart condition except for the odd time when my heartbeat got out of rhythm — from time to time it would miss a beat or two and go a little too fast. Medication very quickly controlled the condition and while I was out of rhythm I also needed to take five small tablets a day to keep my blood thinned to prevent a stroke. It is interesting to know that this drug, called warfarin, is the same used to poison rats, but luckily I don't hallucinate rats and bloodied teeth any more.

I have experienced some setbacks in my life. This heart problem was tough, and so was the depression I experienced in 1983, but I believe I have come back stronger from those challenges. I decided not to have any regrets about decisions made or not made. I am happier now than I have ever been, and know I have grown emotionally. J.C. Penny, an American retailing store magnate, said: 'I am grateful for all my problems. After each one was overcome, I became stronger and more able to meet those that were still to come. I grew in all my difficulties.' That reflects how I feel about the setbacks I've experienced. You cannot change the past because it is gone forever. We do not know what will happen tomorrow, but we can look forward to the future with some optimism. The present is today, live for the day, make the most of the day and make decisions today. We only have one go at living.

A New Life

In 1995, after 22 years of marriage, Karen and I separated. Leaving my marriage and home was one of the most difficult things I have ever done. It was a time of great stress, sadness and heartbreak for everyone involved. After much contemplation, I came to the realisation that I needed to move on and make decisions and changes in my life.

Many times I drove to our holiday home at Hanmer Springs, about 130 kilometres north-west of Christchurch, to spend time by myself. I would walk in the forests, play some golf, and listen to music. During these times I was acutely aware of a heaviness that seemed to consume me. I was conscious that I was not happy in my relationship.

It was a devastating period, and especially difficult for the boys to lose regular, daily interaction with their father at such young ages (they were 10 and 14 at the time). I felt awful, but consoled myself with the thought that I was only a phone call away. Of course, when it was appropriate I would see the boys and share time with them — activities such as ten-pin bowling, go-carting, paintball shooting, or watching them playing their sports, taking them to movies and going out for dinners. But it was a tough time for everyone.

After the separation, I moved back home and lived with Mum and Dad for about 12 weeks before buying a house. Mum and Dad were obviously upset and disappointed that we had separated, but as parents they were very supportive and understanding.

My separation took all my family by surprise, especially as they hadn't seen any overt signs of concern. But I am not greatly surprised that they were unaware of what was happening in my life, as it has never been in my nature to discuss personal issues. I spent a lot of time by myself, dwelling on what had happened and mulling over what I was going to do. I was fortunate that I was busy with my Bank of New Zealand work around the country: work helped me get through the days, but nights were a quiet and reflective time.

The family rallied around and made life a little easier, but I was at the crossroads. At 44 years of age, there was still plenty to do and I needed to look forward, to find some fresh challenges and grow as a person. I am sure that the heart problems I had suffered four years previously had a major impact on the decision making in my life. I felt a need to be proactive.

The experience of living with Mum and Dad again was enlightening. I was back in the spare room, in a single bed with an annoying sag in it that caused some slight back stiffness. I had a few sleepless nights as I tried to get comfortable. Living at home meant that I now had an opportunity to get closer to Mum and Dad, whereas in the past, because I had been away so much, I had not had anywhere near enough contact with them. I had been neglectful in that area and unaware of the effect it had had on them.

In many ways, they both enjoyed having me around their house. My cricketing lifestyle had taken me to all parts of the world and the work I was doing in New Zealand meant that I was still often away from Christchurch – sometimes as much as six months a year. But I was now having daily contact with them and it was an opportunity to catch up on all the family news that in the past I had only been getting spasmodically, if at all. I realised that I had missed out on far too much and that here was a chance, though admittedly in unfortunate circumstances, to redress the balance with more family contact.

Summer was coming, and with it the cricket season. I would soon be away on the road again with the international series sponsored by the BNZ. It was during this time that I asked a friend, Dianne Taylor, to join me in New Zealand. We had been introduced some years previously by mutual friends, and from time to time our paths had crossed. I had always enjoyed her company. She challenged me and the conversation always seemed to flow. We had many things in common and she had also been through a personal experience similar to that confronting me. Although she is a New Zealander, she had been teaching in Queensland for the past 16 years and during that time had taken out Australian citizenship. Now, with dual nationalities, whenever New Zealand plays the Aussies in any sport, she is always on the winning side. Clever strategy that.

It was important that Di was introduced to Mum and Dad as soon as possible. I felt that it was always going to be a difficult experience for her, but I was both relieved and very pleasantly surprised to see how well Mum and Dad took to her, and she to them, and the genuine warmth and affection they shared. Indeed, as time went on, Mum and Dad found that Di very much considered them her 'adopted' parents, as hers were living on the Gold Coast in Queensland and she saw less of them than she would like.

Dad was in his element, meeting Di. She is a great listener and communication is one of her strengths. She also has a very dry sense of humour and calls a spade a spade. Dad must have seen the word 'target' printed on her forehead and it wasn't too long before he was educating her with stories of his many travels and experiences in cricket. Like all the family, I had heard these stories many times and could see the funny side as Di sat through some of the stories for the fourth or fifth time! She soon wised up, letting him know when he tried to sneak in repeats. Dad was pretty cunning, though, and could manage to bring 'the 1949 cricket team, of which I was captain' into any topic or conversation, and then he'd be off on a roll. Even the 1937 team (Dad's first tour of England and when he met Mum on the boat) got a mention from time to time.

I could be described as being somewhat of a loner or an insular person — boring to some people. That is probably the case, as I enjoy following my own pursuits and have seldom felt the need to seek out others for company, although I have always enjoyed the camaraderie of a drink or a meal with team-mates at the end of the day. I had never been used to sharing my innermost thoughts or emotions. Such thoughts were private, and from as far back as I can remember I had chosen to keep those sorts of things to myself. It had always been difficult for me to express myself to Mum and Dad, or my brothers, with regard to personal and private issues or feelings. I avoided such situations and tended to gloss over possible delicate issues.

I was fortunate to be able to learn many things from Di. With many years' experience in education and counselling in Australia, she was to have a major effect on the emotional side of my personality. She would have described me as being 'emotionally challenged' and taught me the importance of letting go and expressing myself and sharing my thoughts with someone who I knew would listen and trust me.

Our relationship has grown by the day — we are the best of friends, soul mates, and we have no secrets between us. It is a blessing to know that we trust each other implicitly, and, where possible, we always travel together, as we enjoy each other's company. When I am away for the odd trip by myself we will ring each other daily to keep in touch.

Over the last 15 years I have learned to discuss the things that touch me emotionally. There are even many times when I am reaching for tissues during movies or sad news on television, which is something I have never done before. Not surprisingly, many people have noticed changes in me. According to friends and family, I have become much more relaxed, approachable and easygoing — which makes me wonder what they had thought of me previously!

After living together for nearly four years, Di and I decided to marry while we were in England for the Cricket World Cup in 1999. It was important for us to formalise our relationship, so early in May we married in a private ceremony in Annan, a small fishing village in Scotland near Gretna Green. It was a simple occasion, and all we needed were a couple of witnesses to attend the formalities. It had been decided that an American couple who were going to be married before us would witness our wedding and we would witness theirs, but something happened to their travel plans and, at the last minute, they failed to turn up. We had a potential problem, but fortunately the celebrant had also asked a couple of young lads to join us. I gave them a tenner each for their efforts. It was quite funny really, but I suspect that Di didn't find it entirely romantic.

But being together on our own made it a very special time and we generally managed to keep the event from the media, although there was some mention in the English press. The following week an article and photo, taken during the week in London, appeared in New Zealand on the front page of the *Sunday Star-Times*. At least now we didn't have to notify people.

On the morning of the wedding we were in phone contact with both Di's parents in Queensland and mine in Christchurch, and it was great to know of their support, although they were all somewhat saddened by not being with us. Our parents understood that this was something we needed to do together and that we did not want a big fuss.

My two sons, Nicholas and Matthew, are now adults. It took them time to accept Di as my new partner, wife, and as their stepmother but as the years have gone on there has been a warming in their attitude towards her and they enjoy a chat and a laugh – I am delighted to know that that relationship has settled.

This year, Di and I celebrate our tenth wedding anniversary. Time has flown by, as it does, but our lives together have been full and we have fitted much into a very hectic lifestyle. Perhaps somewhere in our busy calendar, we can fit in a second honeymoon!

I value the opportunity that cricket has given me of meeting many wonderful people. Of all the people I have met, Nelson Mandela, one of the greatest people in the modern world, impressed me most. Anyone who knows anything about South Africa and Mandela will know that, as leader of the ANC, he was incarcerated for 25 years on Robben Island, just off the coast of Cape Town in South Africa. What is impressive is that when he was finally released, he chose to forgive those who had placed him in that environment — that is an attitude, a generosity of spirit, almost unheard of. Mandela had a dream that all South Africans would be free and equal. When apartheid was finally abandoned he went on to become the President and lead his country as the figurehead of the new South Africa. In world history he would rate as one of the greatest and most inspirational persons to have lived.

On 11 January 1995, New Zealand was playing South Africa at the Wanderers in Johannesburg. The President arrived at the ground and was introduced to the crowd, which gave him a standing ovation and rapturous applause. It sent a palpable tingle through my spine to witness that, to see that this man had earned the respect of an entire nation, and what was also clear in that moment was that it meant the future was more important than the past. South Africa, through the example of this man, was not denying its past but was affirming that the future would be better. To see black, coloured and white people in unison honouring this man was a sight to behold.

I was fortunate to be in the same room as the President for lunch. I was formally introduced to him and was a little surprised to find that he was aware of who I was. It was a brief conversation but very special, and I could not resist the opportunity to ask him for his autograph. His signature is my most prized autograph.

Life as a Selector

In the late 1990s, the Bank of New Zealand decided not to renew their sponsorship of New Zealand Cricket's international home series. It had been a very successful relationship, through some tempestuous years for the international team. During that time, cricket had been televised on free-to-air channels, and my services as a television commentator were provided by the Bank of New Zealand as part of its sponsorship package. The end of the BNZ's sponsorship meant that I was no longer involved in commentary — a change that came at a good time for me, as I was losing my desire to continue with that aspect of the position. The National Bank took over the sponsorship of the international home series and Sky Television paid for the rights to broadcast cricket.

I enjoyed having some distance from top level cricket, and regularly played President's grade cricket for High School Old Boys in Christchurch. My team-mates were great, and the times we had were special, although from time to time I did wonder if I would ever be involved in the international scene again. Then, in 2000, Chris Doig, the Chief Executive Officer of New Zealand Cricket, approached me to see whether I would be interested in applying for the role of selector, with the intention of being the new the convener of the panel. When I asked how much time would be involved, Chris responded with: 'Oh, not too much.' I later found out that the position would in reality be very time-consuming and I would devote at least a hundred days a year to selection issues.

I indicated that I would be happy to apply for the position provided that I went through the interview process, and that if appointed, it would be on merit. After all, I had had no previous experience in the role. It was agreed.

I was interviewed by Chris, John Reid (NZC Operations Manager) and two NZC Board members, Peter Sharp and Martin Snedden. Prior to the meeting, I produced a Selection Panel Philosophy document with the intention of outlining my initial thoughts and focusing on areas that I felt needed to be addressed, should I be involved. We would have to start from somewhere, and I felt that the current documentation and policy needed to be built on. Over the past 10 years I had been encouraged by the direction of NZC, and felt that the organisation was focused on ensuring cricket had a bright and positive future. While I respected the wonderful history in the game of cricket and what New Zealand cricket teams had achieved over the years, I believed that change was inevitable, healthy and necessary if we were to keep pace with our competitors.

The interview went well and I was duly appointed convener of selectors, with Ross Dykes, Brian McKechnie and coach David Trist appointed to the panel. I was delighted to have Ross involved because he had a wonderful knowledge of the players and protocols, and as a former convener of selectors for Canterbury, Brian was also knowledgeable and experienced. As far as I was concerned, we had a nice blend of experience in several areas and we were all highly motivated to see the Black Caps move forward under our new direction.

Many of the key thoughts included in the document I had prepared for the interview became the cornerstones for developing our panel's operating philosophy. The documentation of that philosophy has since grown into a sizeable document, reflecting input from many others, but the areas I wrote about (in some detail) concerned our policies for the selection of individuals and teams, the selectors' responsibilities and duties, expectations of the national team (and the New Zealand A team and development squads) with regard to playing style and approach to the game, along with a list of issues that, as I saw it, urgently needed addressing.

It was important that we understood the reasons for selecting players: clearly we had to select first and foremost on form, but many other considerations, such as a player's dedication to improvement, his ability to analyse the game, his understanding of the game's history, the balance of the team in terms of the range of skills required, the need to develop younger players while ensuring that there is adequate stability within the team, these and many other considerations must all be given due weight in the process. Similarly, I was keen to clarify the roles and responsibilities of the selectors: we were to select a squad of 20 players for the national team and to assist with the selection of Acadamy squads; we had to keep our knowledge of players up-to-date by attending sufficient games and by liaising with coaches and other interested parties, including the media, who continually observed and evaluated players' performances. I also wrote about the lines of communication among the selectors, with NZC and coaches, and directly with the players regarding selection decisions, so that expectations were clear and misunderstandings would be kept to a minimum.

I stressed that we were responsible for creating and encouraging a competitive, match-winning style of cricket. As selectors it was important to envisage the way we wanted the team to play the game — the team need to approach training and personal development seriously and positively, to play with controlled aggression but always within the spirit of the game, to be mentally tough enough to come back from difficult positions and to close out games when ahead.

There were, of course, some urgent issues: we needed to find a settled and effective opening partnership; we needed to develop a larger pool of players capable of playing at the international level and in particular we needed to develop more fast bowlers; we needed to address some obvious concerns within the current team, such as where to bat Stephen Fleming, the need to develop a successor for Fleming in terms of the captaincy, the need to get Mathew Sinclair and Craig McMillan back on form, and so on; and I was also interested in the possibility of getting Jeff Wilson, with all his experience of sport at the international level and his wide range of talents and positive attitude, into the team.

I believed that it was important for the players to understand two key words in relation to selectors — 'perception' and 'proactive'. What we heard and what we saw allowed us to judge a player's form, ability and value to the team and NZC. If a player was proactive and was seen to be doing more than was asked, the perception was that that player wanted it more than someone else.

The official announcement of my new position as convener of selectors came while I was in England doing a promotional tour which coincided with the New Zealand A team's tour. I watched the A team play Sussex at Hove and Chris Doig was present at that match.

He was sitting in a deck chair next to the sightscreens at one end of the ground. I walked over to Chris and we discussed my new role. I had always felt that the role of a convener was simply to chair meetings, but I saw my role as being more than that. I was accepting full responsibility in the role, coordinating my panel, reporting to NZC and keeping my department running efficiently, while also being the spokesperson for the panel. I also noted that the selection panels from England, Australia and the West Indies all called their 'leader' of the panel, the chairman of selectors, and I wanted to bring New Zealand into line with other countries. I asked Chris if we could change the name — and thus also the nature — of the position. It was my first request to Chris — perhaps not a large request but one that I felt was important — and it was accepted on the spot. I felt this bode well for our future relationship.

When I returned home all the selectors met, for the first time, at the High Performance Centre at Lincoln University, just south of Christchurch. We sat down and reinforced the philosophy outlined in the document that I had produced, building on it by adding many other thoughts. It soon became apparent that we needed to clearly identify our goals, and we produced a comprehensive list of objectives.

Our objectives were:

- To select the best players and team to represent New Zealand.
- To improve our international ratings in both test and one-day cricket.
- To be respected as a cricket nation.
- To be competitive every time the team took the field and win as many matches as possible.
- To create opportunities for players to fulfil their potential.
- To build for the future through the development of a succession plan.
- To create greater playing depth so that there is competition for places.
- To develop a pool of fast bowlers so that players can be rested or rotated to prevent burnout and/or injuries.
- To develop a pool of spin bowlers who are up to international standard.
- To play bright, attacking and, where possible, entertaining cricket.
- To compete in world tournaments with the view to winning them.
- To show a consistent individual and team selection policy.
- To provide support and encouragement for selected players.
- To watch domestic cricket as often as necessary to best gauge form, skill, fitness, potential and mental qualities of all possible international players. Ideally, each selector should see every provincial team at least twice in each form of the game.

I felt it was important to keep a direct line of communication open with all the provincial coaches. After all, they were our eyes, ears and legs. They would watch every ball bowled and their input on players would be invaluable. I appointed Brian and Ross to liaise with three coaches each and I would contact the coaches at any given time. It was important that the coaches had a good understanding of our philosophy and the players we were interested in. We welcomed and encouraged the coaches to contact the selectors at any time to discuss issues. We now had an open policy for all involved.

As selectors we were not looking for any credit or kudos, or in fact any headline at all. But I was now in a high profile position, and I needed to accept that every decision, every move, every word said would be analysed and commented on by the media and public. Perhaps I was naive to think that the decisions we would make would automatically be accepted. I felt that the game was there for the players and we wanted them to enjoy it, do well, succeed and grab the headlines. As time went on, however, if there was a prize for getting headlines, then it seemed as though I would get it. That disappointed me, because the game was not about any one person, especially a selector, but I was, I suppose, a very big target.

At times we were hammered in the media, especially in the *New Zealand Herald* by their reporter Richard Boock, but we soldiered on. Early on, I was sensitive to criticism — although I believe I often had every reason to be, as many of the criticisms made by Boock were little more than personal attacks. No one else 'bagged' us as Boock and the *New Zealand Herald* did. However, the panel remained very strong, almost defiant, and we were determined to fulfil our objectives to the best of our abilities. As time went on, a new word entered my vocabulary: 'skimmer'. It was a pearl of wisdom from Di, who said: 'Let things go over your head, Richard, instead of up your nose.' Good advice.

Criticism went with the job and we accepted that there would be a million or more armchair critics. But, at the end of the day, it was our responsibility to make the decisions and put the players on the field. We never had the benefit of hindsight. In fact, it often felt as though we were being asked to predict the future — without a crystal ball — when we picked a player or settled the final composition of the team. Selection is almost an impossible task because we could not perform for the players but had to trust their capabilities. Once we had done our job, it was up to the coach, captain and support staff to get the best out of the players.

As I had learnt when I had heart surgery, you can't control everything. You choose where you place your faith and then it is out of your hands.

The big picture for us always remained team and individual success. We based our selectorial decisions on the facts, advice and information that we had. We had more privileged information than the media or anyone else about the players, and such information often influenced our final decisions. Of course, such information could often not be divulged as the players deserved to have some things remain confidential, and in such situations the media could never be fully informed.

It did not take long to realise that if a player or the team we had picked failed, then it was almost a cause for national mourning. It was our fault for picking the wrong player and the wrong team, and if only we had done this or that, the results would have been different. We were always in a no-win situation and at times that situation was not easy to deal with, especially when I read the papers or listened to *Talk Sport* radio the following day. Fortunately for my sanity, I came to realise that this was sport, this was our national siege mentality and this was part of the job. Later I chose not to listen to *Talk Sport* on a regular basis, but instead turned my attention to the Breeze radio station to listen to music — it was certainly more entertaining and relaxing.

Listening to some of my former playing colleagues on radio or television commentary was always both interesting and frustrating. While I appreciated that it was their job to call a game as they saw it and to be loyal and honest to their listeners and viewers, at times I felt they needed to take a step back and show more understanding of what the players were going through and doing, and what the team was trying to achieve. I often thought that they could have looked at their own careers and their failures and disappointments and how many opportunities they had been given, to be more understanding and appreciative of the situation, especially when they were calling for a player to be dropped. Often they would quote statistics, too many statistics, to back up their arguments. While statistics can tell a story, from a selector's point of view, if we picked players on statistics alone, a computer may as well be used to pick the team, and the best players with the best average and strike rates would always be selected. Statistics do not tell us how good a player's technique is, the conditions played in, the quality of the opposition, the match situation and how the player will fit into the team balance when certain tactics are to be employed. There is more to consider than mere numbers.

There were, of course, many enjoyable success stories and much positive feedback about our role as selectors, but, as I've said, a great deal of criticism also came our way. I believe that I have grown through the experience of this often bitter criticism, and I can now say that I am better prepared to handle such situations: if people disagree with me, then it does not matter; it is their problem, not mine.

There was always a lighter side to selection that kept me entertained. From time to time, I listened to *Talk Sport* radio, especially during talkback, when callers had a chance to express their opinions on a subject. It made for interesting listening — some callers had some very sound and constructive comment, while others were away with the 'pixies'. I recall listening to an old guy called Peter, a regular caller, who said that the selectors should all be replaced: 'They have a wicketkeeper (Ross Dykes) and two all-rounders (Richard Hadlee and Brian McKechnie). They have no one who knows anything about batting. They're all out of touch with the game.'

Graham Hill, the radio host, quietly suggested that Richard Hadlee could bat. He asked this bloke who he thought should be selectors. Peter responded by saying: 'They should have people like Bevan Congdon, Vic Pollard and Gavin Larsen as selectors. They know a bit about cricket.' The reality was that Bevan had been a selector previously and was now in his mid- to late-sixties and was doing other things in his life; Vic, who was nearing sixty, was deputy headmaster of a high school and would struggle to find time for the job and may not have been interested anyway; and Gavin was a commentator and employed by the National Bank (sponsors of the international series and the Black Caps) as their cricket ambassador, and there may have been a conflict of interest if he was to be a selector.

Graham teased more information from this bloke and finally asked him if he watched much cricket. The old fella responded by admitting that he didn't watch it because he didn't have a television and added that he didn't actually know all that much about cricket. No doubt, some listeners thought he was an expert anyway! You had to laugh.

During my eight-year term I received hundreds of letters. Some were from people offering advice on what we were or were not doing as selectors. Others came from young people overseas, wanting to come to New Zealand to settle, play cricket and hopefully play for New Zealand. There was nothing I could do about that. I vividly recall one such incident which occurred in August 2000 when I was manager of the Academy tour to India alongside my brother Dayle, who was the coach. Dayle had received a letter from a young Indian cricket enthusiast who wanted a trial with the ambition of coming to play and live in New Zealand. This young lad was about 19 years old, and travelled 24 hours by train from the war-torn Kashmir region in the north to Madras in the south to meet us. We did the youngster the courtesy and allowed him to practise with the team.

He advised us that he was a leg spin bowler who could bat, which was an enticing prospect for us as we were short of spin bowlers in New Zealand at the time. The first ball he bowled landed on the top of the net, the next ball found the right hand corner of the net, and the next the left hand corner — inconsistency appeared to be something of a problem. During the 20-minute bowl, he did not impress and even less so when he batted, not getting into line at all against the faster bowlers. He was obviously very nervous, and that may have had something to do with it, but, on the evidence, Dayle and I decided that we could do nothing for him. We both felt terrible because here was a young lad who had taken the initiative and seen an opportunity to start a new life and we had crushed his dreams within an hour.

Dayle offered to pay his train fare back home, but he refused, saying that he was too embarrassed, that he had let himself down and must leave. At that stage he had nowhere to go and he was faced with another big trip home. It was tough for us all. However, we presented him with a New Zealand Academy tour cap and a shirt, for which he was very grateful. Goodness knows what ever happened to him.

Life as a selector can be testing at the best of times. Sometimes there needs to be a moment when you can have a good laugh at yourself. In 2002, I was at Rangiora, 20 miles north of Christchurch, to watch Canterbury and Northern Districts play a State Championship match — there were several players I wanted to watch.

It was a typical hot, dry and windy nor'wester day and I was sitting in my vehicle, a 4WD Mitsubishi Pajero, watching the game with the radio and the air-conditioning on, and the driver's door slightly open. I was unaware that the inside light was also on. About an hour and a half later, I tried to start the car and the battery was dead. I made arrangements for a local bloke to bring his car alongside mine and restart my car with his jump leads.

Peter Sharp, a radio commentator, had noticed what was going on and decided to tell the nation what was happening: 'Ladies and gentlemen I have to report that the chairman of selectors, Sir Richard Hadlee, has a flat car battery. He has been sitting in his "penthouse on wheels" listening to the cricket with the air conditioning on, the front door open and the inside light on, and he is getting help from a local supporter to get his vehicle restarted.' Peter then continued with the cricket commentary. About half an hour later, when I knew Peter was back on the air, I started my vehicle and drove it very slowly in front of the tent where Peter was commentating and then stopped in front of him, so that he could not see the cricket. The commentary continued very smoothly: 'Ladies and gentlemen, I am pleased to announce that chairman of selectors, Sir Richard Hadlee, now has his "penthouse on wheels", mobile again.' I then repositioned my vehicle so that Peter could continue with the cricket commentary, but I just wanted to let Peter know that his words were being heard by at least one listener!

Facing the Issues

As a player I was very passionate about the game, and my love for cricket never diminished as a selector. I took the view that the players we put on the field of play were our boys and we wanted them to succeed individually and collectively. I lived every ball that was bowled and every ball that was faced. I shared each player's emotions, whether they succeeded or failed. I felt the disappointment when the team was beaten and I was fulfilled when they won. I invariably had a tear in my eye whenever a new player took his first international wicket or scored his maiden test 50 or century. Not only had we, as a team, enjoyed that success, but perhaps we had also launched a promising career. All in all, it was both draining and rewarding.

I genuinely enjoyed my role as a selector and I was privileged to have worked with many outstanding individuals during my stint as chairman and selection manager. We always worked hard, and we made some good choices and some tough decisions. I felt that although the team suffered from inconsistency, progress had definitely been made with the players and we were getting some good results in both test and one-day cricket.

We have some very talented cricketers in New Zealand and a strong base to work from. The High Performance Centre and Academy have produced quality players and the future looks positive, provided the players are prepared to listen, work hard and maximise their potential.

They need to be mentally tougher in match situations and when the game is there to be won, they need to lift the intensity. The Australians are so good at that.

As selectors we faced many different issues and we had to deal with them as they arose. We were challenged on many occasions.

The captaincy

The new selection panel inherited Stephen Fleming as captain of both the one-day and test sides. Stephen had been appointed as the New Zealand captain in 1995/96 after changes at New Zealand Cricket saw the demise of Glenn Turner as coach, Gren Alabaster as manager and Lee Germon as captain. There were also some player casualties. Rumours were rife about the dysfunctional nature of the New Zealand cricket team at that time: there were player revolts and widespread disharmony among the ranks. Fleming was posed with a choice of styles as captain: to continue with the more autocratic style that had failed under the previous regime or develop an environment in which all the players were accountable, self-sufficient and involved in decision-making — even though he, as captain, would make the final decisions. Stephen opted for a leadership style that involved the players. He gave them responsibility by asking them to take on tasks such as scouting and analysing opponents, tactics and venues, and bringing their findings to a team meeting to be discussed and debated.

There was a brief period when he was struggling, his results were only average and he appeared to lack confidence and be doubting himself as a player. There were some suggestions within the panel that he be relieved of the one-day captaincy, clearly an added pressure on any player, but this became unnecessary when, after accepting the invitation to open the innings with Nathan Astle, he responded to the challenge and lifted his performances — in both forms of the game — to another level.

His captaincy skills also continued to develop and Stephen was highly respected and admired by his peers around the world. Stephen was a prime strategist and very much the team leader both on and off the field. He was a student of the game and was well educated in the history of New Zealand and world cricket. He was passionate about the game and wanted team success. The selectors believed that Stephen had matured into an outstanding captain who was the obvious front-man of the team.

If we selectors had a criticism, it was that at times Stephen tended to overshadow and almost downgrade the profile and role of the coach. When he took over the captaincy under Steve Rixon he was young and relied heavily on the coach. Midway through the tenure of David Trist, Stephen had assumed greater responsibility, and in Trist's last year, the coach was happy to see Stephen assume the major focus as leader. Denis Aberhart inherited this situation, and he appeared happy to go along with the status quo to avoid rocking the boat. Stephen did not rate Denis as a coach, probably because Denis had never been an international player. Stephen, who was quite confident of his abilities as a captain at that stage of his career, gave me the impression that he was able to manipulate situations to his own advantage, especially with regards to selections and where he wanted to bat.

I suspect the relationship between John Bracewell and Stephen was mixed. They were both strong personalities with clear ideas about how to move the team forward. Initially, they developed a wonderful and successful relationship, but that may have soured towards the end of Stephen's career. Perhaps Stephen felt he was being undermined by Bracewell and the selectors. There was a huge shift from the selectors in terms of wanting more from the players in both personal and team performances. Results were not good enough and too inconsistent. Perhaps Stephen felt interference when losing some of his right-hand men. After all these were friends he'd come to rely on before they were dropped.

The selectors maintained a distance from the team environment. It was important for us to ensure that Stephen did not let personalities and friendships cloud his judgment when it came to which players to select in any given situation. We asked Stephen for his thoughts as often as possible but we felt that he had a tendency to favour some players ahead of others and could be reluctant to discuss or accept other points of view. Indeed, at times he was almost dismissive of other points of view.

Discovering Shane Bond

One thing that really kept us motivated was seeing a new player do well. The emergence of Shane Bond was one of the greatest success stories a selector could ever desire. We had selected the New Zealand A team to play in the Buchi Babu tournament in India in 2001, a tournament that included some up-and-coming Indian stars. Scott Styris had withdrawn from the team due to injury and we were looking for a replacement player. The selectors were having a meeting at the High Performance Centre at Lincoln and Dayle, my brother, said: 'Your replacement is in the nets now — it's Shane Bond.' We had been thinking that we needed a bowler who could bowl fast instead of selecting another multi-skilled player or another medium-pace bowler. So Bond was definitely what we were looking for.

Following the meeting I asked Shane whether he would be interested in going to India for three or four weeks. He said he was keen but would need to get some leave from his job with the Police. This was clarified very quickly and he was soon on the plane to India.

When we announced Bond as the replacement for Styris, Basil Netten, the Central Districts convener of selectors, was outraged, claiming that it was Canterbury bias and that Brent Hefford should have been selected. This was a strange comment when Hefford, a capable medium-pace bowler, hailed from Basil's own province. Was this Central Districts bias? At the end of the day we wanted someone who was different from the many other medium-pace bowlers we already had. Bond was in a rare category — he was a one-off. I spoke with Craig McMillan, who said, 'Bondy hits the bat harder and faster than any other bowler in the country.' Those words were taken to the selection panel meeting for discussion.

Shane impressed Ross Dykes, who was manager of the team on the

Indian tour. He bowled fast, he unsettled the Indian batsmen and by taking seven wickets in one innings he won us the match that allowed us to qualify for the finals and eventually win the tournament.

When we selected the Black Caps team to tour Australia in 2001/02, we picked the pace attack around those who had served us well in recent times, but also included some experienced bowlers returning from injury — Chris Cairns, Dion Nash, Shayne O'Connor, Daryl Tuffey and Chris Martin. Although I was very keen to find a place for him, the reality was that we needed as much experience as possible to take on the Aussies and there was no room for Shane. But we did advise him that he was on standby and to keep working, because knowing our history with injuries, there was a chance he would join the tour at some stage.

As soon as Dion Nash and then Shayne O'Connor broke down in the first test at the Gabba in Brisbane, Bondy was on the plane. He impressed in the two tests he played and then became the 'Player of the VB One-day Series' when he destroyed both the Australian and South African batting. He impressed the Australian and South African players, and the Channel Nine commentators, and all of a sudden his career was launched. He provided Fleming with an attacking option which in time proved to be a very potent and successful weapon. It was an exciting time.

Dropping players

One of the most difficult jobs we had to do was to advise a player that we had dropped him. I usually took it upon myself to do this job and although NZC had developed an exit protocol for a player who had been dropped, it was never easy. I had been dropped myself, so I knew the feelings and frustrations a player would experience. We were instructed by NZC that we could only give a player a brief explanation as to why we had dropped him. NZC felt that we were not qualified and that it was not our role. They considered it best if the coach and the technical advisor talked with the player regarding the reasons he had been dropped as they could also let him know what he had to do to get back into the side. The selectors accepted this, but reluctantly, as we were, of course, very well aware of the reasons for why we had or hadn't selected a player. In most cases the players accepted a brief explanation from me as to why they were dropped.

The protocol was for us to contact a player, where possible, two days before the team was to be announced. This would allow the player time to accept the decision before being contacted by the media for comment. If I could not speak to the player directly, we were instructed by NZC to leave a message on the player's mobile phone advising him of our decision and that if he wanted to discuss the matter further, he could contact me for further clarification. This would avoid me having to repeatedly try to make contact with a player who couldn't be reached.

The only difficulty I had when presenting a player with the bad news was when we decided to drop Adam Parore from the one-day team to play England in 2002. Adam had left the team in Australia to fly home early for private reasons. While Adam was flying home, Denis was advising all the players who were still in Australia of the one-day team we had selected. I did not know when Adam would be home but when I rang his mobile he could not be contacted. So I left a message on his phone, saying: 'We have left you out of the team and selected Chris Nevin. Ring me if you have any queries.' It was all very polite, and from NZC's point of view, the procedure was correct.

I never heard back from Adam but I read on the front page of the *Sunday News* that Adam had been advised of his omission from the team by a voicemail message left by the chairman of selectors, Sir Richard Hadlee. He said that I had left a message saying: 'Don't come Monday.' This statement caused a real stir and a national debate on radio. The selectors had been publicly embarrassed and we were criticised for using those words when advising players of their non-selection. The truth of the matter was, of course, that this was not our method at all when advising a player he had been dropped and I felt unhappy with all the negative publicity when we had done nothing wrong.

Adam then declared that he was unavailable to play for Auckland in the remaining five State Championship matches because he was exhausted.

This placed the selectors in a very tough position when it came to picking the test team to play England as it would be difficult to consider Adam for the test series against England if he was not playing cricket. I made a statement to that effect — the only statement we made on the matter. We accepted that he was tired and probably needed a break.

Adam then declared himself available to play for Auckland, but, in a surprise move, Auckland did not want him to play. We were advised that the Auckland team did not want him because his selection was likely to upset team morale. We wanted Adam for the test series, but Auckland had made life difficult for both him and us as he was faced with having no cricket at all. One of the requirements of selection was that if a player had had a layoff because of injury or was not playing for a specific period, he had to prove his form and fitness at first-class level for his province before being selected for the national team.

Then we heard a surprise announcement from Adam that he would play in a club match to try and satisfy our requirements, even though it was at another level. We all felt that this was the best we could get to satisfy our criteria — to prove his form, fitness and desire to play again. I contacted Martin Snedden to let him know that the selectors felt that we needed Adam to set the record straight in the media as to the 'Don't come Monday' message.

Sneds agreed and the three of us had a meeting in Christchurch at which everything was very amicable. It was agreed that Adam would appear on Murray Deaker's television show, 'Deaker on Sport', and clarify things. He was to confirm his commitment to the English test series, confirm that he had no issue with his dropping, confirm that there was no issue with the communication of his dropping, confirm that he had no issues with me, and express an opinion that the media went too far and went down the wrong track relating to Hadlee versus Parore. To be fair to Adam, he did a very good job with Murray Deaker, except that he did not mention the 'Don't come Monday' message. However, he said that he had no issues with the selectors and that if he was a selector, he would have left himself out of the team.

Within days, Adam announced that he would be retiring from all cricket at the end of the test series if he was selected. He had been thinking about retirement and a change of direction for some time as he was not enjoying the game. His dropping from the one-day team had only hastened his decision. In the end, we selected him for the tests and he played very well, helping New Zealand square the series.

I had the utmost respect for Adam's ability as a player and although I was aware that at times he was not popular with his team-mates, I liked him as an individual. He was one of our finest ever wicketkeepers and had a world-class reputation. His batting in both forms of the game was very valuable and he played some fine innings for New Zealand.

Chris Cairns and the captaincy

Just before the player's strike ended in early November 2002, Chris Cairns phoned me to say that he wanted a meeting. As it turned out, Ross Dykes and Brian McKechnie were in Christchurch, so we met at the Heritage Hotel. It was an informal discussion over a beer at which Chris advised us of his plans, how he felt about his fitness and the roles he wanted to play during the Indian series at home in 2002/03 and the World Cup. He expressed a real desire to lead the one-day team and take over from Stephen Fleming if appropriate, and at the time, given our current thoughts about the leadership in the team, that interested us a little. Chris, however, also made it very clear that he would happily play under Fleming if we decided that the status quo should remain. At that time Fleming was struggling for form, his position in the team was not clear cut and the performances of the one-day team had been less than dazzling, with about a 36 per cent success rate in the past few seasons. We knew that Chris would lead from the front and he might energise the one-day team — he had done it so well when Fleming was unavailable for a one-day match at the SCG against Australia a year previously. We had won that match from being in real trouble at one point. The thought obviously had merit, but on balance we opted for the status quo. We did, however, appreciate the idea of a player like Chris getting things off his chest and confronting the issues — full marks for initiative.

As it turned out, Fleming had the best few months of his career as a player and captain when he led the team to defeat the Indians at home, then secured some very good wins at the World Cup and won the tri-series in Sri Lanka. He scored over 1500 runs in both forms of the game — an outstanding performance that pleased us all.

Technical and tactical problems

As selectors we were faced with trying to solve three major problems with the Black Caps as a team and as individuals: 'at the death' bowling, the ability to score runs freely and effectively from the final few overs, and opening-batting partnerships.

In one-day cricket we were aware that of the eight test playing nations (excluding Bangladesh and Zimbabwe) our bowling strike rate in the last four overs of the innings was the worst. Bowling 'at the death' requires pinpoint accuracy to deny the batting side any opportunity to thump the ball to the boundary. It is a vital stage of the innings and can determine the winning or losing of a match. Too often we were conceding around 90–100 runs from the final 10 overs, which did not help our cause.

Nor was our batting in the last few overs particularly effective, with only Sri Lanka and England performing worse. Somehow the coaching staff had to address those two issues, as we felt we had selected the best players to try and do an all-round job.

The other major problem was with our opening batsmen in both forms of the game, but more so in the one-day game. We were aware that from January 2000 to January 2004 the New Zealand team had played 112 one-day international matches and the first wicket had fallen before the team had passed 10 in 55 of those matches, that is, that half the time we were losing a wicket while still in single figures — this was not only an area of great concern for us but it was also an appalling record. New Zealand had lost 35 of the 55 matches in which the opening partnership had failed to deliver — a telling statistic. Even the Zimbabwe and Bangladesh opening batsmen had performed better.

Part of the blame was placed on the selectors: it was felt that we had tried too many different opening combinations — in those 112 matches we had tried 23 different opening combinations — and consequently not given any particular pair the time to learn to bat together. It was true that we had tried many different players in that pressure position — including Nathan Astle, Matthew Bell, Craig Cumming, Stephen Fleming, Matt Horne, Richard Jones, Craig McMillan, Brendon McCullum, Chris Nevin, Adam Parore, Mark Richardson, Mathew Sinclair, Craig Spearman, Daniel Vettori and Lou Vincent — but some selections were made because of injuries and unavailability and others because of constant failure and the need for change. Nonetheless, we were acutely aware of the problem and were always looking for players capable of taking on the challenge.

We were also well aware of the need to establish a successful test opening batting combination. During a period of 12 years, from 1995 to 2007, 21 players had opened the innings in test matches. Bryan Young was a middle-order batsman who reinvented himself as an opener with some success. He was gritty and determined, batted within himself in an effort to occupy the crease, and achieved a highest score of 267 not out against Sri Lanka. Blair Hartland was tried, failed and tried again only to average 16.83. Blair Pocock averaged 22.93, which included six half-centuries. Mark Greatbatch had most of his test successes in the top order and was quite successful as an opener. Darrin Murray played eight tests and averaged 20.20. Roger Twose floated up and down the order, while Craig Spearman scored just one century in 19 tests. Justin Vaughan averaged 13.25 during his tour of Pakistan in 1996. Matt Horne scored a superb 133 against Australia in his first test innings and was one of our more successful opening batsmen, but he was injured, then lost form and never regained it. Matthew Bell averaged 22 in 13 tests. Gary Stead scored 17 and 78 on debut against India in 1998 but was hardly used again, as he was more of stop-gap opener in the first place. Adam Parore was tried as an opener during the 2000 tour of South Africa but he was normally used in the middle order. But we did find one very good opener. Mark Richardson was by far the most successful opening batsman in recent times, amassing 2776 runs in four years at an average of 44.77. He surprisingly retired in 2004. Mathew Sinclair opened for the first time against Zimbabwe in 2000 and again in 2004/05 but with only moderate success. He preferred batting at number three, where he enjoyed his best results, including two double-centuries and 150. Lou Vincent made a stunning debut century against Australia at Perth in 2001 and another century against India in 2003 but loss of form and technical issues saw him back in domestic cricket to rebuild his flagging career. Stephen Fleming accepted the challenge to open the innings on some occasions as there were few other options — on the tour of Sri Lanka in 2003 he scored 69 not out. But as the best batsman in the team he was always better suited to batting at number three and using him as an opener was therefore only tried when no one else could be found. Michael Papps scored 59 in his first test innings against South Africa but injury meant that he was unavailable for selection and his shortcomings in his technique against quality new-ball bowlers seems likely to hinder his progress. Craig Cumming and James Marshall were introduced against the 2005 Australians. Cumming started well, with a debut 74, and James Marshall grew in stature during that series and against the Sri Lankans but faded. Hamish Marshall was tried against the West Indies and the South Africans in 2006 but struggled. Jamie How had his technique exposed against the West Indies. Peter Fulton also had his technique exposed, especially to the short-pitched ball, but after sorting that out he looks like being our best option at number three. Jamie How remains a future prospect and when Matthew Bell was recalled to play against Bangladesh in 2008, he notched up a century, but struggled against England, was dropped and missed the tour of England.

Without any clear and established opening pair, we had a tendency to pick our best six top-order batsmen and fit them into the order so they could all play. That invariably meant one or two players had to bat up the order, perhaps out of their normal positions, where facing the new ball became a greater mental and technical challenge.

During the 2006 test series against Sri Lanka we reverted to picking specialist opening batsmen — Craig Cumming and Jamie How. That meant two top-order batsmen were left out of the team (Peter Fulton and Hamish Marshall) as there were too many middle-order batsmen contesting four positions. It was evident in domestic cricket that there was a reluctance for some Black Cap players to seize the opportunity and open for their provinces instead of hiding in the middle order and then taking pot luck with selection. There were clearly vacancies at the top of the order for those who wanted the job.

When is the right time to inject a new player?

I considered that part of my role as chairman was to be positive and proactive — to stimulate a thought or two that was outside the square and to bring about debate. That way we would come to a better conclusion, with no stone unturned. NZC's overall philosophy was 'Pushing the Boundaries' and '. . . to be daring so that we ensure we are ahead of the field'. It is fair to say that we did just that.

We did our homework by knowing what a player had achieved and what we thought he was capable of achieving. We watched a lot of cricket at first-class and international level. We talked to many people in the game. We took some big punts on players, especially Ian Butler, James Franklin, Brendon McCullum and Hamish Marshall.

We always learned some valuable lessons whenever we introduced a player into international cricket, even if it turned out to be 'too early'. If that player performed, then we were proved right, we had introduced them at the right time. If we had to drop a player, we would then find out if he had the mental toughness and the ability to correct his problems to prove a point. And if we then gave a player another chance, we would quickly learn whether or not he had the goods to succeed. In our own minds, either way, we could not be wrong.

Great players will overcome their lows far quicker than lesser players, who sometimes never overcome them at all. But any player, no matter how good, can have a bad period, and we had to be mindful of that as selectors and not discard players on the strength of a single or only a few performances. For that reason, it was always important that we persevered with a young player to give him ample opportunity to perform. Balancing that, of course, was the need to recognise when a player was continuing to fail at the highest, and most testing, level. All too often the media were telling us who to select and who to drop, with no thought given to the incumbent player and what we were trying to achieve through our overall objectives. We did not pick players on a whim — we had specific reasons for doing it. Certain players were targeted. In some cases their opportunities came earlier than expected due to circumstances such as injuries and loss of form of key players.

I had no problem injecting youth into the team. If a young player was performing, why not advance his career? Why hold him back when there was a chance he may provide something special and make the most of his opportunity? Surely that player deserved a chance or a lucky break based on performance. It was not uncommon for Indian and Pakistani players to be selected to play for their countries at the tender age of 16 or 17. Even Daniel Vettori was picked by a previous New Zealand selection panel at 17. Former player and commentator Martin Crowe and columnist Ken Rutherford expressed concern that young players were being exposed too soon to international cricket — this view was largely based on their own experiences when they had initially struggled to come to terms with the demands of international cricket. It was interesting to note that in other New Zealand sporting codes 19- and 20-year-olds were given an opportunity without too much fuss.

My early career was less than distinguished but the experience was valuable because I knew I had a lot more work to do to get to the next level. Crowe and Rutherford both had a point and it was a fair observation but we needed to have a succession plan and introduce young players when we could. Gone are the long tours that would have had 10 or 12 county games during an English tour, which would allow a young player to learn and to develop his game. Today the tours are much shorter, with one or two build-up matches followed by a three-match test series and then the one-dayers. If a young player was selected, he had to develop, learn and perform when it mattered in a full international match. We could not afford to carry three or four young players on a tour unless we felt they were good enough to play at the highest level. At times we took a big punt on a player or two for that reason.

It was also important to ensure that we recognised some of the journeymen in first-class cricket and rewarded them for their performances over a long period of time. We had to look to the future and try to create more depth, which inevitably would lead to more competition for places. I detest the words 'comfort zones' and 'complacency' in sport. Players always needed to be aware that other players were looking for opportunities to take their place, and that form is important. As time went on some of the senior players were looking over their shoulders as some of the new and younger players were out-performing them. That must have been an incentive to perform, I believe, and must be good for the game in this country.

There is no doubt that the biggest problem we faced as selectors was the number of injuries players suffered. In the first few months we selected more than two rugby teams to play for New Zealand, either at test or one-day level — 33 players in all. Of those players, 18 players were unavailable for a match, a series or a tour.

Player contracts and how the players were rated

The selectors were asked to analyse what a player had achieved during a 12-month period and what his potential value to NZC would be over the next 12 months. These ratings were used to determine the income potential and the futures of the players over the following year. We were given a simple formula to work with — rate the top 25 test players in order and the top 25 one-day players, give them points, add them together and we would come up with the top 20 players in the country. Points allocated to a test player were multiplied by 1.25 because a test player had fewer matches and opportunities to play than a one-day player. It was obvious to us that this system had its shortcomings: the specialist test or one-day player would be disadvantaged because he would not get enough points, whereas an average player who played in both forms of the game could almost guarantee a top 20 position and be rated reasonably high, ensuring a better pay packet.

While I was in Australia I spoke to Trevor Hohns, the chairman of the Australian selection panel, and he advised me of the system that they were working with. It was a good idea because it rewarded success and if players were conscious of their rating and were motivated by money, they would need to perform better to move up the list.

We were confident that the recommendations made to NZC and the decisions we made were as accurate as possible, but, of course, they were always very subjective. If players had performed well during the contract period they were rewarded accordingly, while others who disappointed were dropped down the list and earned less money — in some cases players were not offered a NZC contract as they had slipped out of the top 20 all together.

From 2002 to 2004 we had been asked to place the top 20 players into one of five categories differentiated by the amount of money they would be paid. For the 2003/04 season we recommended that each position in the pecking order should have a different fee payment structure. The idea was accepted by NZC and the CPA.

We felt the contract system could have both positive and negative effects. A player might question why he was rated below another player when he might consider that he had performed better than that person. There was no doubt that every player would know where all the other players were rated. They would, naturally enough, talk among themselves.

Then again, the ranking system and the fact that better rewards came with higher rankings might motivate a player to get ahead of someone else in the pecking order by outplaying his mate.

Each year the media tried to speculate where a player was rated and how much money he would earn. Some were very close but no one got the final pick right. I was of the opinion that the official ratings should be made public — why hide it, when tennis and golf ratings are well known? It would have created a lot of debate and interest but NZC and the CPA agreed that it should all remain confidential.

Leading Teams concept

NZC engaged the services of an Australian company to help the players and team grow as leaders with the aim of generally helping in personal development and hopefully improving individual and team performances. It was envisaged that players would learn to have the confidence and ability to challenge team-mates through peer assessments, which would spur team members to higher levels of achievement, and John Bracewell was a great supporter of this concept.

The approach was called 'Team First' and involved the players taking ownership and responsibility for their own and the team's performances and being bold enough to question anything and everything and confront team-mates if they were not acting in the best interests of the team. Players were taught to be fearless in their comments, to review players honestly, confront issues and not hide behind them, and, importantly, not to take offence. This proved to be a tough ask for all players and management.

Players voted, in front of their mates, on establishing a Team Leadership Group that would interact with management and the players — six players were elected onto the committee. If a player exhibited non-compliance with the team's objectives — which included behavioural, cultural, training and playing issues — the Team Leadership Group would act decisively and give that player a clear message to improve. They would also offer the player any support that was needed to get that player back on track.

Some players were shocked not to be voted onto the Leadership Group, or to not even get a vote from their mates. The process was no doubt at times hurtful for players and management but it offered insights into all members of the group. Did players feel better getting issues off their chests? Did players go into their shells? Did players respond and take action to correct their faults? All very good questions.

The concept was sound, but I felt that in practice it created more issues than solutions, and failed in its main goal of helping individual and team performances. There was no real evidence to suggest we were a better team and got better and more consistent results. What I did see was that some players benefited and grew from the experience whereas others were not happy with the concept and did not want to have anything to do with it — they often became reluctant participants only because they had to, which in itself was destructive and undermined the overall goal.

Some of the senior players and management who were peer-assessed did not enjoy the 'hot seat' experience. Younger members of the team had the opportunity to say what they really thought of a player or a support staff member but often this was without having too much knowledge about that person or their role in the team — some highly personal issues were raised and that did not sit comfortably with some players or management. Ignorance can be fraught with danger. There appeared to be too many put-downs and many felt they had been put through the wringer and were left with a shattered perception of themselves and others. There were suggestions that some senior players retired prematurely because they did not enjoy, or even see a need for, the Leading Teams concept — and that may be so.

The concept was replicated throughout the provinces, again with a negative overall effect. Hundreds of thousands of dollars would have been spent but with very few players improving as a result. The main area of concern for me was that too much time was devoted to meetings, discussion groups and peer assessments when more time should have been used to develop skills, which is our biggest weakness. It isn't rocket science: if we want to be more competitive and beat the better teams more consistently, there is an urgent need to improve our skill level.

Selectors challenging the players

For the team and players to be successful and fulfil NZC's edict that we had to be the number one team in world cricket (this was later changed to being number one or two) in both forms of the game, things had to change. Inconsistency of player and team performance plagued us badly, and results were frustrating. Yes, we would win some games, but then lose some badly. It was difficult to get on a roll where we could win five tests or 10 one-day games in a row.

Personally, I felt the common denominator was that some players were in cruise control and did just enough to be selected for the next match. They were not being challenged because they knew their positions were safe and they did not need to look over their shoulders at a younger player keen to take their place. Batsmen would average 30 to 35, bowlers would strike and get their wickets at 30 to 35, and we would not win many tests with those statistics, especially when opposition batsmen were averaging 40 to 50 and opposition bowlers were getting their wickets at less than 25. We were always behind before we started a game.

The selectors felt we had to get the players to lift their games, get better results, show more intent in training and start winning more games in both forms of the game. We challenged them and put pressure on them to perform, and if they had a run of poor to mediocre performances then we dropped them, which they did not like, especially some of the senior players. Sometimes it seemed as though they felt they had the right to automatic selection. Their attitude seemed to be one of outrage that the selectors would put pressure on them to perform and question their play and commitment, a resentment that we were playing around with their job. In my view, you have to earn the right to play for your country and there is no automatic right to stay there. Everyone should be judged on form at the time and their ability to make a contribution that is worthy of future selection.

Our approach may have 'forced' some players into early retirement but at the end of the day it was their decision to leave the international arena and not ours — you are a long time retired. Our depth of talent was severely tested as Cairns, Astle, McMillan, Vincent and Tuffey pursued other interests in the game.

Injury and unavailability

Injuries were a constant problem for the Black Caps and that meant that we had no choice but to select some new faces. That was especially true for the tour of Africa in 2000. Most of the replacements came from the New Zealand A or the Academy teams simply because they were the next tier of players. Communicating with the Medical Panel was almost a full-time job in itself. The phone would be ringing at all hours of the day and night as yet another player broke down. We then had to make quick decisions about a replacement player to get him to Africa in time to be of some assistance to the team. Every time this situation happened, the team balance was upset and addressing that was another challenge.

During the tour, Geoff Allott, Chris Cairns, Stephen Fleming, Matt Horne, Dion Nash, Scott Styris, Daniel Vettori, Brooke Walker and Paul Wiseman all suffered injuries and were unable to play at times. Kerry Walmsley, Andrew Penn, Chris Martin and Hamish Marshall were sent over as replacement players but they were all injured too. We had no choice but to select some new players who would have the opportunity to gain valuable international experience which would hopefully benefit New Zealand cricket in the future.

And who would have thought the 2007 tour to the republic would be 2000 revisited? It was another tour from hell. Shane Bond pulled a stomach muscle, Craig Cumming fractured a cheek-bone, Jacob Oram pulled a hamstring, Stephen Fleming fractured a thumb and two players suffered sickness. Replacements were called for and sent. The most difficult team to select was the 2003 team for the short tour of Pakistan. The tour was going to last only 10–12 days and involved five one-day internationals, but several players — Lou Vincent, Scott Styris, Craig McMillan and Ian Butler — had announced their unavailability. NZC had given all players on the tour of India an opportunity to consider their positions for Pakistan. Everyone understood that the situation involved some uncertainty relating to terrorist attacks and accepted the right of players to opt out if they wished — there was no point in a player being in an environment where he was not happy.

Understandably, it would be difficult for them to concentrate and perform — memories of the bomb blast that killed 14 people in Karachi a year before would no doubt have a lasting impact on those players there at the time. They were only metres away from the incident. Some players took the view that there is more to life than playing cricket in hostile parts of the world. They had a valid point. However, the players effectively forfeited their positions in the team and allowed other players an opportunity.

As selectors we were comfortable with the situation — we needed to find four more players, not impossible. The team returned home from the Indian tour for a few days before departing for Pakistan. We then found out that Matt Horne and André Adams were also unavailable for the tour. Paul Hitchcock had bowled only a handful of overs in India and was recovering from a side strain and had yet to prove his fitness. Nathan Astle was still recovering from a knee injury and Shane Bond was on a strict rehabilitation programme to have him fit for the home series, therefore both were unavailable. There was a possibility that Daniel Vettori would be unavailable to travel due to the failing health of his grandfather, and when Jacob Oram and Kyle Mills returned home from India with a virus, we were faced with sending a very inexperienced team. Kyle Mills was eventually unfit to travel after spending some time in Middlemore Hospital with a lung infection.

Things started to get more complicated from that point on. Stephen

Fleming withdrew from the tour because of an abdominal strain and we had to drop Chris Nevin due to lack of form and a struggling and unconvincing technique — as it turned out, he too suffered a viral infection and was too sick to travel.

We therefore needed to find eight players. It was decided that Craig Cumming, Richard Jones, Tama Canning and Matthew Walker would be the players to replace the four who were originally unavailable. We recalled Mathew Sinclair, Kerry Walsmley, Michael Mason and Hamish Marshall. Only Sinclair had previously played a one-day international. Chris Cairns was given the captaincy and Daniel Vettori the vice captaincy. What a challenge!

The tour was undertaken to fulfil NZC's obligation to tour Pakistan and it would tell us whether some new players were able to rise to the next level. Against such quality opposition, they would learn about themselves, and if the players were able to address the two glaring deficiencies in our game — opening the batting and bowling 'at the death' — the tour would be deemed a success. Quite frankly, I was excited about the prospects, because if the new players did perform, we would have more depth and more competition for places. It was important that all the players had at least two or three games each — there was no point in going to Pakistan to make up the numbers.

In reality, the inexperience of the team meant that we were almost conceding the results of the matches in favour of individual performances, something that captain Chris Cairns had to deal with — he was on a hiding to nothing playing against formidable opposition in their own back yard. To win a match would be pleasing, two would be fantastic and to win the series would be one of the greatest achievements ever by a New Zealand team offshore. The likelihood of winning a match was very remote, and as the tour progressed results were disappointing, although not unexpected, as we lost the five-match series 5-nil.

However, the success of Hamish Marshall batting at number four was the undoubted highlight of the tour. He compiled 243 runs at an average of 81, with a strike rate in the eighties — he also scored his maiden century at the highest level, along with two half-centuries, which was a magnificent achievement. In addition, Richard Jones, Matthew Walker and Tama Canning put in some useful performances, so the tour had its minor triumphs.

When is it time to move on?

We cannot allow emotion to guide our selection choices, but sometimes the decisions that have to be made so the team can move forward and perhaps get better results can be tough. We decided to drop Chris Harris from the one-day team in 2003/04. He had been a wonderful servant of New Zealand cricket. In 238 appearances he had scored 4250 runs at an average of 29.51, with a strike rate of 66.43, and had also captured 199 wickets at an average of 37, conceding only 4.29 runs per over. Those statistics were very impressive. His first-class and one-day record for Canterbury was even more outstanding — he averaged over 60 with the bat in first-class cricket and nearly 45 in the one-day game. On top of this, he was also a world-class fieldsman.

We thought the public and media reaction would be severe on us but generally the decision was accepted. There was the odd banner at grounds saying 'Bring back Harry' but most people realised that he was coming to the end of his international career. Harry had expressed a desire to play in the 2007 World Cup in the West Indies but the reality for us was that the style of play, the team dynamics and the balance of the team had changed. The team now had wicket-taking bowlers who were performing quite well in the middle of the innings. We were not prepared to simply have defensive bowlers just getting through their 10 overs while the batsmen got set for the final 10-over slog — the best way to stop a batting team from dominating is to get wickets. Even before we dropped him, Harry was being used only sparingly, bowling no more than three to six overs in a game. That was not enough for us.

Harry also typically had high anxiety levels when he came out to bat and would struggle to get bat on ball, with his pads being hit too frequently. He needed time to get set and the run rate would often slow considerably. This, in turn, made it difficult for other batsmen when they came out to bat, as they had to take more risks while Harry was still getting settled. At the end of the game, Harry may have been 40 or 50 not out, with a reasonable strike rate, but a lot of damage had been done to the innings.

Harry was asked by John Bracewell, the new Black Caps coach, to hit the ball when he came out to bat and show that he could keep the score moving and win matches from his batting position. Braces wanted each player to do a specific job well, instead of being, as it were, a bits-and-pieces player who could bat a bit and bowl a bit, without mastering either skill. Harry needed to prove that he didn't fall into that category.

Interestingly enough, Harry was still recalled for the odd match when pitch conditions suited — on his comeback match against South Africa at Eden Park in 2004 he won the Man of the Match award with a run-a-ball 55. He had demonstrated that he had taken the message on board and had improved in the area of his game that concerned us — get bat on ball and hit it. But in the end Harry's time ran out and he did not go to the 2007 World Cup, eventually signing for the Indian rebel league, ICL, to ensure some financial security.

Mark Richardson — was he a one-day player?

One of the most contentious issues we faced as selectors was the non-selection of Mark Richardson for the one-day team. Public demand and media hype created strong pressure to select Mark to solve our opening batting woes. But we stuck to our guns in the knowledge that it would be highly risky to play him, let alone think that he would do the specific job required.

He had four matches against the world champions in Australia in 2001/02, where he scored 42 runs at an average of 10.50 with a strike rate of only 43.29 runs per hundred balls faced. Those four matches confirmed what we already knew. 'Rig' — his nickname being short for 'rigor mortis', a comment on his lack of flexibility and mobility — was slow when running between the wickets, had difficulty scoring runs quickly and was indecisive with his calling. Moreover, his lack of mobility in the field could be costly — after all, the difference between losing and winning a one-day match can be as little as just the one run. In his first one-day international match he ran out Brendon McCullum with a poor call, which tended to confirm the view that he could be a poor judge of a run.

During the 2003 pre-season matches at the High Performance centre, Mark played for the Academy team against several of the provincial teams. He ended up with a batting strike rate of 31 runs per hundred balls, which was too slow, he had a poor average and ran his partner, Jesse Ryder, out three times in four innings. He also dived over the ball on several occasions in the field. He was eventually dropped from the Academy team. With the national selectors present, including the new coach, John Bracewell, it was a time for Mark to impress, but he was unable to do so. He was later omitted from the Auckland Aces State Shield one-day team for 'tactical reasons'. In other words, he was no longer required for any type of one-day cricket by any team in New Zealand. Surely our justification for not selecting him was more than valid.

The truth of the matter is that Mark knew that he was not a one-day player and admitted as much to me. He was keen to play if selected, but we all knew that his real value to NZC was to prepare for test matches, where his record was outstanding. We were not prepared to compromise that position by confusing his batting roles in both forms of the game, but preferred for Mark to keep a very specific focus on his test match role. There were many critics of his non-selection, from both cricket lovers and the media. Even Richard Boock from the *New Zealand Herald* felt that we had to swallow our pride and pick him, especially as the top order batting was continually failing. Most critics based their arguments around Mark scoring runs and batting for long periods of time so that other players could play around him. The theory was sound, but there were no guarantees that he would score runs, nor could we know just how many balls he would face to score those runs. If he scored 80, he may have taken 150 balls, half the innings. He would therefore deny other batsmen the opportunity to face the bowling, and this scenario would put added pressure on other players to take risks, increasing the likelihood that they would lose their wickets. Stephen Fleming was adamant that Mark would be an all-round liability and all the selectors agreed.

Sports writer Mark Geenty wrote an article that appeared in the *Dominion Post* in December 2004 about Richardson, who had just announced his retirement from all cricket. In it Richardson was quoted as saying: 'I am 33 but I have the agility of a 55 year old. Physically my body is really starting to struggle and fielding-wise, my agility's nowhere near what is required to contribute. In test matches, I was sick of fielding under the helmet and getting hit and I could not justify fielding in any other place.' The reality was that the selectors knew about his lack of mobility and agility three years previously.

Jacob Oram — a batsman who bowls, a bowler who bats or a genuine all-rounder?

I first noticed Jacob Oram on the Academy tour of India in 2000. He was the captain of the team and I was the manager. There were early signs that he was a very capable batsman who could take an attack apart by bludgeoning the ball to all parts of the boundary — in one innings he scored an amazing 168.

At that time he was only a part-time bowler but he had the raw basics to be an all-rounder who could make the Black Caps team within a year or two. He bowled some useful overs at medium pace and I noticed that because he stood at around two metres he was able to get the ball to bounce and make life difficult for the batsman. From that point on he was encouraged to do more bowling, to get fitter in general terms and to get bowling fit specifically. He needed an extra yard of pace and to be more efficient with his technique. While he was going through this change his batting suffered a little at first-class level. Central Districts Cricket were very concerned that we had changed his role from being a batsman who could bowl a few overs to a bowler who batted. We copped some early flak over this from several people in the CD area but we advised Central Districts Cricket that there was definitely a role for him to play in the New Zealand team, but if he wanted it, he needed to be a better bowler.

Somehow, I think Jake would have been very happy with what we suggested and he emerged as an integral part of the team and an all-rounder of note. He went on to score test hundreds and filled the third or fourth seamer role to good effect. In one-day matches he bludgeoned the ball and bowled very effectively, sometimes with the new ball and sometimes at first or second change, and did a fine all-round job.

Craig McMillan — an enigma

Craig McMillan became a very frustrating player to watch and manage. He was capable of dominating attacks, but also had the ability to invent new ways of getting out. He was in and out of the team because of his inconsistent performances and his poor shot selection and decision-making at crucial moments. He might have considered himself to be hard done by at times, but enough was enough. His bullish approach and run-ins with the media and public were seen as arrogance, but he had ability. He was often motivated by negative newspaper reports and then performed well, but would relax, until further misses got the media going again.

I became very frustrated with player performances. I am realistic enough to know that players will have their misses and low points during a career. I am also realistic enough to know that players need to turn their performances around and get back on track reasonably quickly, especially the more experienced and senior players. That's the reality of cricket at the international level.

I have always believed that with experience and opportunities players should progress their careers and show improvement, advancement and be more consistent. Unfortunately for Craig his career was regressing and not progressing — there were concerns over his general fitness, weight, work ethic, eyesight and diabetes problems, all of which may have affected his decision-making and performances.

There are times when players needed a bit of a tune up and, rightly or wrongly, I made the odd public statement about how some players should start performing or they would be dropped. Without mentioning names, I suggested that the middle-order batting needed some better results — the papers naturally assumed that I was talking about Craig McMillan and Nathan Astle (which was correct). The next test match was against Zimbabwe at the Basin Reserve, Wellington in 2001. Both players were under pressure and scored very good hundreds. The newspaper cartoonists enjoyed the moment and a cartoon duly appeared with me pulling up the

socks of both Craig and Nathan. Good humour that! I could not resist the temptation of getting a copy of the cartoon and asking both players to autograph it for me. They both had smiles on their faces and enjoyed the banter, and no doubt also got the subtle message from the chairman of selectors!

In 2007 Craig embroiled himself in controversy. He had been left out of the team for a year, missed a NZC contract and tried unsuccessfully to find other work. To his credit, he realised that cricket was all he knew and he changed his attitude and worked hard on his game, with the result that he received a NZC contract and was recalled to the one-day team with immediate success. In my view he had at least three or four years of international cricket left in him, including test cricket. But he then announced his retirement from all international cricket. It was all very suspicious, especially with the advent of a rebel Indian Twenty20 league called the ICL (Indian Cricket League).

Craig had signed his NZC 2007/08 contract and NZC had every right to hold him, like any other contracted player, to his contract, otherwise contracts were not worth the paper they were written on. By signing his contract he had agreed to be available to play for New Zealand whenever selected to do so. Contracts are there to protect both parties, not just one.

NZC decided to release Craig from his contract on compassionate grounds — health and family reasons. He had diabetes and he felt that in a steady home environment he could control his health issues better. He also wanted to spend more time with his family and not undertake the intensive tours any more. NZC made it very clear that they would be disappointed if he were to join the rebel league following his release from his contract. Everyone knew, though, that he was about to sign for the ICL (if he had not already done so).

Next thing we knew, he was in Hong Kong playing in an international sixes tournament. Weeks later it was announced that he had signed for the ICL for a period of time. To me, Craig's credibility had been damaged.

Soul mates — with my wife, Dianne.

At a coaching clinic I coached a very young Shane Bond who later went on to become one of the world's best fast bowlers.

The two RHs: me and Robin Hood in Nottingham, England.

As an ICC Cricket Ambassador, I presented Craig McMillan with the Man-of-the-Match award — a watch — and the words 'It's about time!'

The family celebrates Dad's eightieth birthday. From left to right: me, Dayle, Barry, Mum, Dad, Martin and Christopher.

Dad's Memorial Service was held in the hall at his beloved school, Christchurch Boys' High School, in 2006 — an emotional time for all.

One of many speeches, 'The Great Debate', New Zealand (me, Ken Rutherford and John Morrison) vs Australia (Ricky Ponting, Doug Walters, and Greg Chappell) — we won.

Riding for charity to help Heart Kids in the Taupo Challenge. I am Patron of the Kidz Zipper Club.

'Blue September' — supporting Prostate Cancer Awareness Month, 2008.

Sunset at the Taj Mahal in India. Sitting on the 'Diana' seat with Di — it was a breathtaking experience to be there.

The day I officially became Sir Richard Hadlee.

In 2008 I was awarded an Honorary Doctorate from Nottingham University. I am now known as Sir Richard Hadlee, Kt Bach, MBE, Hon.DLitt.

With my sons, Nicholas, 27 (left), and Matthew, 24 (right), celebrating Matt's birthday in 2009.

Kyle Mills — accused of chucking by Ian Smith

There were times when the selectors had to deal with some strong opinions from ex-players who chose a career in the commentary box. Ian Smith had been very critical of some bowlers in the game who in his opinion 'chucked' the ball when they delivered it. He challenged us, as selectors, not to pick Kyle Mills for the Black Caps because his action was suspect. Certainly, Smithy is entitled to his opinion but I had to explain to him that it was not our role to prejudge a player and that it would be irresponsible and unprofessional for us not to select him just because other people felt he was a 'chucker'. It was our job to select him as a player first, if we considered that he was good enough. When he was finally selected for the Black Caps he would then be scrutinised by the umpires and the match referees and if there was a problem, due process would be enforced. To my knowledge there was never a problem and Kyle was selected and has done a good job for the team.

Chris Martin — when is it time to recall a player?

The decision to recall pace bowler Chris Martin to the test team in 2004 for the second test against South Africa at Eden Park was made of *Boy's Own* fairytale stuff. It felt something like a stroke of genius, as Chris went on to capture 11 wickets in the match to be named Man of the Match. It was the first time he had taken 10 or more wickets in a first-class match — truly, a remarkable performance.

Coach John Bracewell was keen to play Chris in the test because he was likely to bowl well to the South African left-handed batsmen. As selectors we agreed that he had earned a recall based on some solid performances for Canterbury during the domestic season. Chris had also taken the initiative to go to Australia in the pre-season and play some club cricket to build up for the home domestic season. His decision to spend time building himself up physically paid dividends and he was rewarded for his efforts. A year earlier Scott Styris and Daryl Tuffey had done the same thing by going to Australia and their performances for the Black Caps had been enhanced dramatically. As selectors we can only admire those players who are keen to better themselves and improve their chance of performing. I was always impressed with Chris and his work ethic. After spending time at the Academy and on tours that I managed at Academy and A-team level, I knew that he went about his business and physical preparation in a responsible manner — he appeared to do all the right things and was always fit to play.

On the morning of the first day of the test I congratulated Chris on his recall to the Black Caps, saying that it was well deserved. I said: 'Go out there and get a bag of five wickets.' He replied: 'I'll be trying.' But I don't think even Chris himself could believe what he had achieved by the day's end.

The disastrous 2004 tour of England

There were high expectations of the 2004 tour of England. The objective was to beat England decisively in the test series and regain our position as the number-three-rated team in test cricket. Some of the media and former players rated this team as the best New Zealand had produced. Chris Cairns also said that this was the best team he had ever played in. There was no doubt that this team was a very good one, but the best ever? I had reservations. To be a great team or the best ever, you need to be judged over a period of time and produce match and series wins in different parts of the world. The reality was that we had won one test in the last 12 months and England were coming off a high after beating the West Indies in the West Indies 3-0.

The pre-test build up did not go well for the team — there were injury problems, losses to Essex and Leicester did not help and were perhaps an omen for what was to happen in the test series.

We lost the first test at Lord's by seven wickets in an epic encounter that could have gone either way during the last session of the match. We were thrashed at Headingley in the next test by nine wickets and lost the third test at Trent Bridge by four wickets to be whitewashed 3-0. The last time England had done that was in 1978, a series that I had played in. The players were hurting in 1978 and again in 2004. The results during this tour were extremely disappointing and also embarrassing after all the build up and expectation.

There is no doubt that England deserved to win the series. They showed great determination and skill and they produced the mental toughness to win crucial sessions. In each match the Black Caps had an opportunity to put the opposition away and play them out of the game to perhaps win the match or at least make it more difficult for England to win. But the opportunities weren't taken.

We had the players to perform in English conditions but we batted poorly in the second innings of each match and our bowlers failed to produce the form they were capable of. I could not believe how inconsistent our bowlers were — their line and length varied too much and the number of no balls conceded was excessive.

The injury toll during the tour was one of the worst I had seen — of the 14 players selected, eight suffered injuries. Fleming had a groin injury, Oram a side strain, McMillan and Papps had broken fingers, Bond did not play a test because of recurring back injury and returned home, Vettori pulled a hamstring, and during the third test Martin suffered a hamstring injury and Mills injured a muscle in his side. That left only two fit bowlers, Cairns and Franklin, to bowl England out twice in the third test. They both bowled superbly and put in a huge effort — taking 14 of the 16 wickets that fell — but there was not enough support from other players to put England under more pressure.

The selectors were criticised for having only 14 players on tour. John Bracewell wanted 14 and we all agreed with his rationale. Braces, with his knowledge of the English conditions at that time of the year, felt that all the batsmen on tour would need to play in as many of the build-up games as possible, we needed only one spinner because pitches at that time of the year would be more seamer-friendly and we could rest or rotate the faster bowlers so that everyone would get enough cricket before the tests started.

What the critics failed to realise was that although we'd only taken 14 players, NZC had ensured that several standby players were playing cricket in England who would be available if we needed them — Mathew Sinclair, James Franklin and Michael Mason (who was on holiday but had his boots with him). What we did not bank on was the excessive injury toll and losing our only spinner, Vettori, which meant we went into the last test without a spinner. That proved costly, as was demonstrated by Ashley Giles, the England spinner, who took four wickets in our second innings.

The critics also said that Ian Butler should have been on tour at the outset to give us some added pace in our attack, especially as there were some doubts over Bond's fitness. The fact was that prior to the tour Ian was not fit and was going to have surgery on an ankle injury. During the tour we learned that the surgeon had decided not to operate and that a cortisone injection might solve the problem. Once we knew he was fit, he joined the team for the one-day series but he was underdone in his general bowling and proved to be very expensive.

The Black Caps picked themselves up for the one-day series, though, and salvaged something from the tour when they first eliminated England and then went on to defeat the West Indies in the Natwest tri-series final at Lord's.

On-tour selectors

NZC has generally had a policy of not sending a national selector on tour. I suppose the argument is based around the fact that the coach is a selector and represents the selection panel — and, naturally, the cost of having another person on tour is a factor that has to be considered. But other nations see some value in having selectors on tour: England and Australia send a national selector on tour and generally rotate their selectors during a tour.

I found it frustrating to be sitting at home watching games on television while the on-tour selection panel was overseas trying to work out how the team for each game should be selected: how each player should be used and in exactly what role. At times I would get a phone call or an email to discuss what was happening, but this was rare. The same old message kept coming through from the coach or manager that as they were the ones on tour they were best able to assess the conditions, the fitness of players and other matters pertinent to team selection. That may be so, but having an independent selector on tour would be aimed at augmenting, not replacing, the selection process undertaken by the on-tour selection panel, which consists of the coach, captain and vice-captain or another senior player. An independent selector would offer another perspective and could also assess many things that the coaching staff and players may not have the time for, and such an input may be beneficial.

To me, it also made a lot of sense to have a national selector on tour as an observer to determine whether the process of selection was correct and to help ensure that the players were given a fair go in the role for which they were selected. Having a selector on tour would also offer objective views and balance to any agendas, conscious or otherwise, by the on-tour-selection panel. Looking at some recent tours, I think that if a national selector had been on tour, there would have been times when the playing XI would have been different, and we may have achieved different and more positive results.

In addition, there is also the possibility that if those on the national selection panel are experienced enough they could also be used in other roles on tour — perhaps to assist the coach in a specialist role (batting or bowling), or to help the players with skill work, captaincy and general playing experiences, or simply to help with the general odds and ends that help the team to function.

The tsunami disaster

On Boxing Day 2004 the world went into mourning as we witnessed on television compelling yet disturbing images of human suffering, loss of life and massive destruction. A tsunami had struck parts of Indonesia,

Thailand, Sri Lanka and India, killing local inhabitants and tourists and destroying millions of homes — over 300,000 people lost their lives.

We were hearing stories of how people on coastline beaches had noticed that the sea had disappeared hundreds of metres back into the ocean as it was sucked backwards by the advancing wave, and then, within minutes, the first big wave hit the beaches, followed by a second wave, which did most of the damage. Some of the water, moving at pace, went up to five kilometres inland, tearing up everything in its path — buildings, trees, motor vehicles, animals and humans. Some fishing boats ended up two kilometres inland. The damage and loss of life were horrendous.

The Sri Lankan tour of New Zealand, which was currently under way, was understandably postponed to allow the Sri Lankan players to return home to be with relatives and friends, and to grieve for those who had lost their lives and help wherever they could. There was no way the players could stay in New Zealand to concentrate on cricket, knowing that their nation had lost 20,000 people and millions more were homeless. Sanath Jayasuriya's mother was injured, other players lost relatives and friends, and the Galle Cricket Ground had been totally destroyed and washed way. We had heard that champion spin bowler Muttiah Muralitharan had just visited Galle to do a cricket promotion where he was signing and giving away cricket bats. He left the ground to return home and 20 minutes later the waves struck. By all accounts he was very lucky.

The severity of this tragic event touched millions of people and there were some unbelievable fundraising activities and aid provided by governments, sports teams, sports individuals, the general public and companies. The cricket world came together and within 15 days the ICC, Cricket Australia and FICA (Federation of the International Cricket Players' Association) had arranged a cricket match to be played in Melbourne at the MCG to try and raise money for World Vision, who were helping rebuild millions of lives. The wave of destruction had now become a wave of compassion.

On 3 January 2005, I was watching Canterbury play a State Shield one-day match against Wellington at Timaru when the phone rang. It was a representative from Cricket Australia advising me that there was going to be a cricket match played on 10 January with the Rest of the World playing an Asian XI in a 50-over match and would I be available to help select the World team along with former Australian captain Steve Waugh? Naturally, I was very keen to assist in any way I could. I phoned Steve immediately and we discussed the choices. England and South Africa were engaged in a test series in South Africa at the time and consequently we couldn't pick any of those players. But very quickly we agreed on 12 players — Ricky Ponting (Captain), Matthew Hayden, Adam Gilchrist, Shane Warne and Glenn McGrath from Australia; Stephen Fleming, Daniel Vettori and Chris Cairns from New Zealand; Brian Lara, Chris Gayle and Dwayne Bravo from the West Indies; and Darren Gough from England.

We had a very strong team with four opening batsmen, and three fieldsmen who could field at first slip. Ricky Ponting was going to have a headache trying to work out the batting order and fielding positions! The Asian team would be selected from India, Pakistan, Sri Lanka and Bangladesh, so players from eight test playing nations were available, all waiving their match fees to help the cause.

People in New Zealand were exceptionally positive about the game and the fact that three New Zealand players had been selected created a lot of interest. There was a thought, too, from some people that Stephen Fleming should have been named as captain of the team in light of his status and respect around the world. But it was also reasonable for Ponting to captain the team as he was leading the current Australian team, the best and most successful team in the world, and again because the match was being played in Australia. I have always liked his demeanor on the field where he is always in the face of the opposition and he plays the game positively and hard — he is a very busy cricketer who tries to wear down the opposition with his presence, both when he bats and when he is in the field.

The original idea was for all 12 players to participate during the day but the ICC then decided that the match would carry official one-day status and all player performances would count in their career statistics, so, as the Laws of Cricket stated, only 11 players could actually play. Dwayne

151

Bravo drew the unlucky straw and was made twelfth man, although he did play his part by fielding during the match.

The Asian selectors put together a very competitive team — Sourav Ganguly (captain), Virender Sehwag, Sachin Tendulkar (who did not bat due to an injury but fielded during the match), Rahul Dravid, Anil Kumble and Zaheer Khan from India; Sanath Jayasuriya, Kumar Sangakkara, Chaminda Vaas and Muttiah Muralitharan from Sri Lanka; Yousuf Youhana and Abdul Razzaq from Pakistan and Alok Kapali from Bangladesh, who was twelfth man.

Although both a serious and competitive match, the players enjoyed the encounter which was played in great spirit. All players were driven by personal pride to succeed in front of an official 70,103 spectators at the ground and millions more who watched the match on television. The match was televised to 120 countries around the world.

The World team had a convincing 114-run win but the result was secondary to the fundraising effort. It was, however, pleasing to see all three New Zealanders perform with and against the best players in the world. Chris Cairns featured strongly with the bat, scoring 69 in 47 balls, including two sixes, and he picked up one wicket, with Stephen Fleming taking the catch at slip. Fleming batted down the order and scored 30 in 28 balls, playing some lovely chip shots, and Daniel Vettori was 27 not out in only 17 balls, also capturing 3/58 from his 10 overs. But the star of the show was Ricky Ponting, who scored a superb 115 from 102 balls — he raised $265,000 from his personal performance.

The match raised an estimated $16,000,000 a truly remarkable performance. Qantas flew the players from all over the world at no charge, the Mobile 3 Company (official sponsors of Australian cricket) provided $1000 for every run scored ($576,000) and Toyota sponsored $50,000 for every six that was hit during the match up to $500,000. The Packer family (Channel 9 TV and PBL Marketing) provided another $3,000,000. E-bay ran an auction on the internet and the players' signed shirts from the match fetched some unbelievable money. Shane Warne's shirt generated over $150,000 and other shirts were sold for between $3000 and $30,000.

The match coin used for the toss exceeded $500,000. There were many very generous people who dug deep to assist those who were less fortunate. This was an emotional time for everyone.

The return match to be played in Calcutta, India in April was cancelled. It was going to be too hot at that time of the year.

The FICA matches and the selection of Jeff Wilson

When the Sri Lankan tour was postponed in New Zealand it left a gaping hole in New Zealand's international calendar. Four one-day matches and two test matches were lost in the month of January and February. Through the magnificent efforts of Martin Snedden from NZC, Heath Mills from the New Zealand Players' Association and FICA, a three-match one-day series between the Black Caps and the Rest of World was quickly arranged.

The selectors decided to pick the same team that had defeated Sri Lanka in the Boxing Day one-dayer at Auckland, with only the injured Ian Butler not being included in the 12. We saw a huge opportunity to select the golden one, Jeff Wilson. 'Goldie' had played for New Zealand in 1993 as a 19-year-old and hit 44 not out from 28 balls to help New Zealand win a match against the Australians at Hamilton. Jeff later left cricket to pursue a professional rugby career where he became a very successful All Black rugby winger, scoring 44 tries in 60 test matches.

There is no doubt that Jeff Wilson was one of the most talented and multi-skilled sportspersons that New Zealand had ever produced. He had the Midas touch in every sport he played — cricket, rugby, basketball, tennis, golf. When he retired from rugby he decided to return to cricket but injuries over a three-year period restricted his appearances and performances, but there were some positive signs that he still had plenty to offer. At least he was fit in 2005. He was staying on the park and there were some encouraging early performances. Glenn Turner, his Otago coach, said that he was still a very talented cricketer and would offer more than some of the other multi-skilled players currently in domestic cricket, including some who had played for the Black Caps. The question was whether he could still offer anything after a 12-year absence from international cricket.

We discussed him and decided that it was a perfect time to select him, and I rang Jeff to advise him of his selection. Apparently, when his phone rang, he knew it was me — he must have had my number in his mobile phone list as it came up on the screen. He later said that it was just as well he was sitting down because he was very surprised, yet delighted, to be given an opportunity to see whether he could make a successful return to the top level. He almost sounded apologetic, but he was very gracious and thankful.

Jeff's selection caused mixed reactions. Some said it was a 'staggering recall'; some cynics thought, incorrectly: 'That it was a publicity stunt to get more bums on seats to help raise additional funds for the tsunami victims.' Dipak Patel was a little confused and couldn't work out what role Jeff was going to play in the team. Dipak also felt that there were too many all-rounders in the team and that there were no specialist batsmen in the top six of the order. I am not so sure that Stephen Fleming, Nathan Astle, Mathew Sinclair and Hamish Marshall would agree with that! Chris Cairns and Jacob Oram are also useful batsmen. Danny Morrison and Dion Nash, however, both thought that it was a very positive move and they summed up the feelings of most people when they said that they were looking forward to seeing what Jeff could do.

When I phoned Stephen Fleming to advise him what we had done the first thing he said, perhaps with tongue in cheek, was: 'Are we playing an exhibition game of touch rugby at half-time or something?' I sensed then that he was not entirely happy about Jeff's selection. A couple of days later, when Wellington played Northern Districts at the Basin Reserve, he tapped me on the shoulder at lunchtime and asked if we could have a chat. He asked me to talk him through the rationale of Jeff's selection because he had difficulty working out how he could use him in a match and what role he would play. I said that there was a concern about what would happen if Chris Cairns was injured or retired tomorrow or there was an injury to Jacob Oram. What choices would there be? Adams and Canning were, at best, only marginal reserve selections as multi-skilled players, and it would be useful to see if Jeff could contribute at the same level as Cairns and Oram. Because these were unofficial games there was an opportunity to assess what Jeff could offer in the dressing room based on his international cricket and rugby experience and what he could provide on the field as player. Jeff had the X-factor in the past and could win games; he could bowl at a brisk pace and maybe he could be a useful 'death' bowler, which was still an area of concern in the Black Caps team. Maybe he could hit some useful runs down the order. He could field well and had a positive attitude to everything that he did, and here was an opportunity to find something out with three games of cricket in five days.

I thought I had a convincing argument. There had to be far more positives than negatives to his selection. I also indicated that had we been going to play either Sri Lanka or Australia tomorrow, Jeff may not have been a possible option and we may have played a more cautious hand in our selection philosophy. I asked Fleming to embrace the situation and give it a chance — if Jeff struggled, then we lost nothing, and if he succeeded, we had another positive option to consider for the future. Fleming did not appear to be too convinced, but at least he said that he had got it off his chest. Next day Fleming appeared more relaxed about the situation after having had some further discussions with John Bracewell.

The Black Caps won all three matches in convincing style and Jeff played his part. He was our quickest bowler, at 139 kph, he took 5 wickets, did not look out of place and showed us that he still had something to offer. The Australians soon arrived and we lost 5-0. Jeff struggled, as did all the team except Hamish Marshall and Daniel Vettori. Ankle injuries to both feet did not help Jeff's performance, so much so, in fact, that he did not complete the whole series. The sad thing was that those injuries spelled the end of his international cricket career. Who knows what he could have done?

The 2005 Australians in New Zealand

The Australians came, they conquered, and then departed, leaving the Black Caps and all associated with New Zealand cricket in disbelief at what they had achieved — they had won the Twenty20 match convincingly, and had won the one-day series 5-0 and the test series 2-0. They were perhaps the greatest team to grace the field, certainly in the modern era, if not of all time, with at least five players making their greatest team of all time — Hayden, Ponting, Gilchrist, McGrath and Warne. Throw in Martyn, Langer, Lee, Gillespie and their rising star Michael Clarke, and they had a team that could beat anyone, in any type of conditions, anywhere around the world. Their batting was brilliant, their fielding superb and their bowling magnificent. They had all parts of the game covered and they had the attitude and belief that they were good enough to win every match, from any situation they were in. Their greatest strength was having the ability to get out of difficult situations: without fail one or two players would lift their performances by scoring a hundred or producing a bowling spell that would win them the match.

They had a physical and mental presence that intimidated us — they upped the ante and were ruthless against any new players, almost saying that this is a hostile environment and only the strong will survive; if you are weak, you will be exposed, exploited and given a reality check. It was fascinating to see how they worked on and then destroyed their opponents.

As selectors we were severely criticised by Ian Smith, who must have had a bad week. The knives were out and on *Radio Sport* he attacked the selectors, saying that NZC could save themselves a lot of money by sacking the selectors because they do not do anything and that we were not giving some form domestic players a go. Even the 'Man in the Stand', an anonymous person who conveniently hides behind that name when he does his weekly stint on *Radio Sport*, said the selectors 'are brain-dead'.

During the one-day series we selected 18 players to do the job but we were not good enough to undermine and defeat this great Australian team. Even some of the players that Ian Smith was promoting were eventually given an opportunity, and were found wanting as they too struggled against the best players in the world. At no stage were we able to put our best playing 11 on the field, with several players unavailable through injury — Bond, Butler, Oram, Styris and Adams missed the series, and Papps, who had been recalled, was hit on the head by a bouncer from Brett Lee and missed the last two matches. Astle also missed a game through injury, and Wilson, Mills, Cairns and Hamilton all carried injuries into the matches. We were severely weakened and the gap between them and us was huge in both forms of the game.

Even during the three-match test series changes were made, with McMillan axed and Paul Wiseman and James Marshall given an opportunity. Somehow, I think we gave players a chance to impress and as selectors we made decisions!

TV One introduced a sports programme called the 'Sports Hour: All Fired Up', which was introduced by Andrew Saville. Former All Black Richard Turner was on a discussion panel and put things in perspective. He said: 'The All Blacks are rated the number one test team in the world and if they were playing the number seven test team (Argentina), they would expect to win every game. The fact is that Australia is the number one cricket team in the world and they were playing the Black Caps, rated at number seven, and they would expect to beat New Zealand every time they played them.'

We had to accept that we were just not good enough, lacking skill, technique and confidence, but convincing the public was a futile exercise.

Being a World XI selector for the Super Test and One-day series against Australia 2005

In February 2005 I received a phone call from the CEO of the ICC, Malcolm Speed, asking me whether I would like to be part of the six-man selection panel to pick the test and one-day teams to play the world champions, Australia, in the Super Series to be held in Australia during

October 2005. To be part of a panel headed by Sunil Gavaskar (India), the chairman of selectors, and which included former players Clive Lloyd (West Indies), Aravinda de Silva (Sri Lanka), Michael Atherton (England) and Jonty Rhodes (South Africa), was a great honour for me.

Our brief was quite simple — come up with a test and one-day team that could beat the Aussies. We were asked to select an initial group of 30 players in both forms of the game by April, reduce it to 20 players in June and have the final group of 13 players selected by August. This was going to be a daunting task because 30 of the world's leading players from outside Australia does not divide into the final 13 test and 14 one-day players — some quality players would miss out.

When I first got the news of this appointment I wrote down on a piece of paper the 30 names that in my view we would need to select initially. My list in fact extended to about 35 players, so I was keen to be involved with the first meeting, when there would doubtless be some robust debate and some important decisions made. We had our first conference phone call on 18 April 2005 at 8.00 pm New Zealand time. In some ways, it was a little chaotic as we were all in different parts of the world and trying to keep the phone links going was an almost impossible task. Our chairman, Sunil Gavaskar, disappeared three times and we were talking among ourselves until he was reconnected. I was lost for 20 minutes and Jonty Rhodes was at the airport waiting to catch a flight and could only spare 30 minutes. After an hour and a half Mike Atherton had another meeting to go to, so continuity was a problem. However, the end result was pleasing and the 39 players that made up the test and one-day playing squads were sound. Not one of the selectors had a personal agenda — we were not interested in continually pushing our own countrymen but coming up with the best of the best. We all had good knowledge of our own players — and in some cases that information meant our own players missed out.

On 29 June we had our second conference phone call. Sunil, Mike and Aravinda were at the ICC office in London, whereas Jonty, Clive and I were on our phones. The two-hour meeting was very orderly and the cull to 20 test and 20 one-day players was made without undue fuss.

After final deliberations the following two teams were agreed on. ODI team: Shaun Pollock (captain), Sachin Tendulkar (vice captain — later replaced by Rahul Dravid following injury), Virender Sehwag, Kevin Pietersen, Herschelle Gibbs (replaced by Chris Gayle), Brian Lara, Jacques Kallis, Andrew Flintoff, Kumar Sangakkara, Shahid Afridi, Shoaib Akhtar, Makhaya Ntini, Muttiah Muralitharan and Daniel Vettori. Test team: Graeme Smith (captain), Rahul Dravid (vice captain), Sachin Tendulkar (later replaced by Inzamam-ul-Haq), Virender Sehwag, Brian Lara, Jacques Kallis, Andrew Flintoff, Shaun Pollock, Mark Boucher, Steve Harmison, Shoaib Akhtar, Muttiah Muralitharan and Daniel Vettori.

We had the world's top rated players in the batting and bowling performances throughout that year. Some decisions were unanimous and other decisions went to a vote. The general comment was that the players selected deserved their selection, although one or two players may have been unlucky not to make the team. We all thought that the teams should create a great challenge for Australia, who had just lost the Ashes to England in England and were looking a little vulnerable at the time.

From a New Zealand point of view, the omission of Cairns and Fleming caused some minor ripples but the reality was that there were better-performed players in other parts of the world and neither could justify selection based on their recent performances against Australia — that was the time to stand up and perform and put one's name in front of the selectors. Brendon McCullum nearly made the final selection but lost out to Boucher for the test spot and Sangakkara in the one-dayers. He got my vote for both forms of the game, but I was outvoted 5-1.

The one-day matches at the Telstra Dome, an indoor venue in Melbourne, proved to be a huge disappointment with Australia winning 3-nil and by big margins — 93, 55 and 156 runs. Australia went on to win the six-day test in four days, with an emphatic 210 run win at the SCG. The world team had batted 50 overs or less in all five innings — this was a remarkable failure given the batting talent on show. The world champions had humbled and embarrassed the champion players of the world, and the selectors were hammered for picking some players who underperformed and who should not have been there in the first place. Hindsight is a wonderful thing for those who love to criticise! I thought the balance and the composition of the two teams was very good but it is difficult to foresee such quality players failing: Brian Lara made scores of 0, 5 and 0 in his three one-day innings, Kallis (the ICC Player of the Year) scored 21 runs in three innings, Pietersen made 18 runs in two innings and Dravid didn't do much better.

However, I was pleased to see a couple of players perform and enhance their reputations. The real highlights in the one-day series were the two spinners, Muralitharan and Vettori, who cemented their reputations. Dan did well with 2/38, 0/55 and 1/34 from his 10 overs in each match to climb into the top 10 of the one-day bowling ratings.

In the test match, the batsmen failed again — twice in the match being bowled out for under 200, in fact, 190 and 144. Inzamam, who did not make the original test team, had criticised the selectors for not picking him and had been backed up by Javed Miandad and the Pakistan Cricket Board. When Tendulkar was injured, Inzamam played, only to score one and nought. Were the selectors therefore right not to have selected him in the first place? As selectors we have no way of knowing how a player will perform in the future. It will always be a judgment call based on current form, team balance, doing a specific job and adding value. At the end of the day, as a selector, I felt very frustrated, disappointed and let down by the players.

The commitment of the players was severely questioned — many people said that a player is more likely to be committed to his country, where a do-or-die effort is required, than a world concept when team harmony can be disjointed. John Wright, the coach, questioned the team commitment when he said the intensity level from the players was far less than what would have been required if they were playing for their countries. Some players were content to just hit the ball out of the park at practice when their shot selections in matches needed to be more than that.

The players were also criticised for picking up huge financial gains for their lack of effort — the Australians won most of the money and no one can deny them their spoils, about US$120,000 each, but the world players who played in all the games profited by nearly US$50,000 each for seven days' work. The *Daily News* in Sri Lanka, where I was watching the games, at the time quoted some angry spectators: 'They are all a bunch of greedy players who came here [Australia] for the money and prestige and not to perform as a team and they will be laughing all the way to the bank when they get home.'

The real losers were probably the sponsors, Johnnie Walker, and the ICC. The sponsors would not have been happy with an event that failed to live up to expectations and the ICC will have to determine whether this concept has future merit. The initial thoughts were that it would not happen again, at least not in its current format.

Dropping Chris Cairns

In September 2005 the new selection panel of John Bracewell, Glenn Turner, Dion Nash and I knew we had to review the playing career of Chris Cairns. In 2004 Chris had decided to retire from test cricket but had indicated that he was available for one-day international cricket and would like to play in the 2007 World Cup in the West Indies. We were keen for Chris to keep playing but we were concerned at the amount and quality of cricket he would play to prepare himself for one-day international cricket. In our view, a few games of club cricket and one-day cricket for Canterbury were not going to be enough.

In order to give him an opportunity to play some competitive cricket the new panel wanted Chris to go to Sri Lanka with the New Zealand A team, but we were advised that he was unavailable. I guess we could have forced him to go under his contract agreement with NZC, but what was the point if he was not interested? Chris Harris and Daryl Tuffey, who were both returning to cricket following enforced injury layoffs, were very keen to go to Sri Lanka to test their fitness and skill levels, and as I was the manager of the tour I could assess them. Chris Cairns, however, did not see this as an opportunity to prove to us that he was committed.

We selected Chris for the tour of Zimbabwe in 2005 knowing that he was under pressure to perform and prove his fitness, and to find out where he was with his skills. On both counts he failed. He developed further injury concerns and his bowling and batting skills were not at the level we required. For those reasons he was dropped from the tour of South Africa that followed.

In the media he reacted defiantly, saying that he wanted to regain his place in the team and that he would play more cricket to prove his worth: 'I am not finished yet, and I certainly do not feel all washed-up. I probably underestimated the effect of not playing first-class or test cricket but this has forced the point now. It is effectively asking me: how much do I really want this? Well, my answer is that I want it a lot, to the extent that I will now play first-class cricket for Canterbury as well as the one-dayers in a bid to force my way back into the squad.'

John Bracewell, who made the press statement as well as taking it upon himself to tell Chris of his demise, said: 'It was one of the hardest decisions of my career so far but a necessary one in terms of challenging the all-rounder to address the problem before it was too late. Chris was omitted because of his lack of cricket fitness and he needed to confront his workload to force his way back in contention.'

The reaction from some of the players I spoke to was that they had seen his dropping coming. Chris was no longer the player he once was, and if he was not prepared to put in the effort then why should he be treated as the exception? It also sent a clear message to all the players that there were standards of fitness and skill that needed to be achieved.

The Black Caps one-day tour of South Africa was disappointing, with a 4-0 series loss and one match abandoned because of rain. Media reports suggested there was a rift between Stephen Fleming and John Bracewell over the axing of Cairns, and hypothesised that had Cairns been on tour the team might have won. This type of speculation and mischievous reporting, from Jonathan Millmow of the *Dominion Post*, was way out of line. The players on tour had the responsibility for winning and losing the games and had the top order batting performed, the results may have been different. The failure of Astle, Marshall and others cannot be attributed to Cairns's absence from the tour. There was also a suggestion in a newspaper article from Martin Crowe that Cairns's dropping was the doing of new selector Glenn Turner, who had had a clash with Cairns in the mid-90s when Glenn was coach. This was all rubbish. The new selection panel was unanimous that Chris be left at home to sort out his fitness and commitment to the game.

To his credit, Chris went away and worked on his fitness, played in some pre-season games for Canterbury and showed a desire and commitment to return to the national team. We recalled him for the three-match Chappell-Hadlee series and for the four-match series against Sri Lanka, where he had moderate success with the bat. His bowling, however, still concerned us, as he was conceding more than six runs an over. In January I received a phone call from John Bracewell saying that Chris wanted to retire from international cricket and requested to bow out after the Twenty20 match against the West Indies at Eden Park in February. We supported the request to allow him to leave the scene with his dignity intact, especially given the significant contribution he had made to the game, but at the back of our minds it confirmed that he would have difficulty retaining his fitness, enthusiasm and form going through to the World Cup in 2007. It was a wise decision for him to make.

The rest and rotation policy

There was an enormous amount of debate in the media and among the public about our resting and rotating players during the Sri Lankan series prior to the 2007 World Cup. The All Blacks had done it successfully and fielded different combinations that were good enough to win. We did not deliberately follow the All Blacks' philosophy, but it made sense to ensure that when we selected the best 15 players to go the World Cup, everyone would be fit and available. Based on our history and our high player attrition rate, to be without key players would weaken our chances of success when it really mattered. As it turned out, Oram, Styris and Mills were all injured and unavailable for that series. It was, therefore, important to manage players to get them through the year.

We also decided to rest Nathan Astle, Stephen Fleming and Shane Bond, so there were vacancies and it gave us an ideal opportunity to try some fringe players in different roles to see if they could take the opportunity and be successful at the highest level. To be able to win matches without senior players would allow the team to grow emotionally and for individuals to enhance their skills. Ross Taylor, Mark Gillespie and Jeetan Patel proved the point.

In the absence of Stephen Fleming, Dan Vettori captained some games to give him some experience. If we did not have Fleming at the World Cup for any reason, at least Dan had some experience leading the team instead of going into an important match as a novice. The team won two of the three matches he captained against Sri Lanka.

The plan was sound, but we were not prepared for the backlash, especially when we started to lose matches and some of the rested players looked horribly out of form. We were prepared to sacrifice some results, although every time we took the field there was a desire to win matches. The priority was the World Cup, followed by the Champion's Trophy, the tri-series in Australia and the home series against Sri Lanka. We did what we felt was right at the time, but in hindsight some players who were rested, especially the batsmen, could have kept playing at domestic level to maintain or regain form.

We reached the semi-finals of the World Cup for the fifth time but went no further, so, like the All Blacks, who were knocked out of the rugby World Cup at the quarter-final stages, our policy was questioned.

Changing the captaincy

After New Zealand was eliminated from the World Cup, Stephen Fleming announced his resignation from the one-day captaincy. I was somewhat stunned and surprised while sitting in an Indian television studio making comments on the World Cup, to hear Stephen's press statement. He indicated that it was time for a new one-day captain to take over and that he could not take the team any further under his leadership. He also felt that he could concentrate better on his batting without the pressures of captaincy and get his playing record to the point where he felt it deserved to be. Very quickly, Dan Vettori was appointed the new Black Caps one-day captain.

The selectors were now faced with the decision of who would be the test captain. We were unclear about Stephen's future. Rumour had it that he was going to sign for the rebel ICL which would mean his New Zealand international career would be over — he would be banned. There was silence from Stephen for about a month. We needed to know what he was going to do and whether he would be committed to New Zealand cricket in the future, but we had no confirmation. We were running out of time, with future captaincy decisions needing to be made. Then he announced his retirement from one-day international cricket, while also saying that he was still keen to be the test captain. With his decision to retire from one-day cricket, we could only assume his playing days were coming to an end — we could look at having two captains, one for limited over cricket and the other for test matches, but would that work?

With still no clear indication from Stephen, we decided it was time to move on. Senior players were retiring and we were entering a new era. It was time for Dan Vettori to take over in full. We had heard that Stephen would likely retire from test cricket after the 2008 tour of England and there seemed little point in waiting until then to make the change. We welcomed Stephen continuing to play test cricket, provided his form and commitment to preparation were there still. He was now placed in a position of being just a player, but we also felt he still had a lot to offer as a player and batsman and he could also help Dan through his transitional period as captain.

We knew that Stephen was very disappointed to lose the captaincy — after all, he had been captain for 10 years or more. There was a sense of anger in him when I came into contact with him either face to face or on the phone. I am sure if he reflected on how he went about things, he would realise that he placed himself in a delicate and vulnerable position — if he couldn't take the one-day team any further, how could he take the test team further? He almost forced us into making a decision about the captaincy. He was frustrated and annoyed, but to his credit he contributed to the team while he was still playing test cricket.

I noted with interest that Ian Chappell, the former Australian captain, and one that I admired, felt that there should be a change of captaincy every four or five years. Even the players within the team were pleasantly surprised at how Dan had accepted the challenge and how well he had settled into the role. His style was different but he earned respect very quickly. The team needed the change of captaincy, especially with retirements and new players gradually being introduced to the set-up — it was a new era. According to one player, it was a breath of fresh air. Dan would show his emotion on the field of play and even at practices — he was very competitive and wanted to win. He wore his heart on his sleeve — and hopefully, in time, we will see Dan grow in the role and become a very successful leader.

Lou Vincent and depression

I had known Lou from his early days at the NZC Academy and in 2000 I was manager of the Academy team that toured India. There was no doubt that he was a talented player but there were definite signs and issues with his temperament and anxiety levels. Over the years, we learned that if Lou was in form we should pick him, but when he was struggling with form and consistency, it got to him and could have a negative effect on the team. It was, therefore, not surprising to read in the papers in February 2008 that he was suffering from depression.

Having been through a bout of depression myself in 1983, I could relate to what he was experiencing and I understood the effect it was having on him.

He said: 'I didn't like myself. I was beaten by it. I let it get to me and it just took over. For as long as I can remember, I was riddled with self-doubt. I had no self-belief. I have hated the guy I've seen in the mirror.'

As selectors, we knew he was fragile. When it appeared that he was going through some low periods we needed to remove him from the limelight. When he was in that state of mind, there was no way he could focus and produce the results we needed from him. Playing international sport is no place to be when suffering from depression — to be exposed to the opposition, the public and the media would not help anyone's mental state in this situation but only make things worse.

We also needed to protect Lou's privacy with this issue. It would have been irresponsible for us, as selectors, to go public with this very personal information just to explain why he was in and out of the team. Once Lou broke the story, for which he should be complimented, it certainly helped explain why he wasn't always picked for the side.

There was a suggestion from some members of the media that he was treated unfairly by the selectors and John Bracewell, and some media stopped only millimetres short of accusing us of causing Lou's depression. But that was never the case and we always had his best interests at heart. With professional support, Lou had to overcome his anxiety levels and other issues and go through a process to reach a state where he felt good about himself again before he could again be considered as an international sportsman.

The Indian Leagues

The emergence of the two Indian leagues in 2008 decimated our player depth. Players who joined the rebel league called ICL were banned from international cricket. Some players who signed had already retired — Chris Cairns and Nathan Astle — so that was not a problem. Others did not see themselves being selected again for the Black Caps, so they chose to become a 'rebel' — Chris Harris, Hamish Marshall, André Adams and Daryl Tuffey. Others pursued the overseas dollar and ended their international careers prematurely — Craig McMillan and Lou Vincent.

Shane Bond made a career decision that forced him to choose between international cricket and 'rebel' cricket — he chose the latter. Shane's situation was different to the other players. Originally Shane had sought, and was granted, approval in writing from NZC to sign for the ICL and still be available to play international cricket. He had the best of both worlds. Unfortunately for Shane, the goal posts changed and the powers that be — notably the Board of Control for Cricket in India (BCCI) — forced the hand of NZC, who changed their mind on allowing him to play international cricket if he continued with his ICL contract. Shane, a man of high integrity, had signed an ICL contract in good faith and wanted to secure his financial future, which was fair enough and understandable for a man of his age. This was a sad time for New Zealand cricket.

Adam Parore came out of retirement to earn some quick bucks, which was no problem to us as he wasn't remotely in our consideration. But the net result was that NZC lost a lot of experienced players in a short period of time.

The Indian Premier League (IPL), a league sanctioned by the ICC, was set up as direct opposition to the ICL. This created different problems. Senior players saw an opportunity to make mega-dollars for a few weeks' work. Stephen Fleming announced his retirement from all international cricket to be available for all IPL matches to increase his value. Scott Styris retired from test cricket to concentrate on one-day cricket and be available to play IPL and increase his value, although he would have been disappointed with the money he got compared with other New Zealand players. Daniel Vettori, Brendon McCullum and Jacob Oram profited hugely when they were auctioned off by team franchises, but they were to receive their payments on a match basis — play to be paid — so their loyalty to NZC was compromised when international tours and matches clashed with IPL games. On the 2008 tour of England those players understandably wanted to arrive well after the rest of team so that they could earn $30,000 to $40,000 per match in India.

Perhaps the biggest problem that may develop is when a young player bursts onto the scene and does well. The talent scouts from the rebel league could entice a player to sign, thereby ending his international career and playing future. Some youngsters with an eye on the dollar may be misguided and misjudge, and perhaps regret the decision made.

No matter what happens with either league, the player drain will severely challenge our game, and it seems likely that new players will need to be introduced more often. Clearly, having inexperienced cricketers playing will affect our performances and ratings. Challenging times lie ahead for NZC.

The 2008 Tour of England and the IPL

I strongly opposed the late arrival of Daniel Vettori, Jacob Oram, Brendon McCullum, Kyle Mills and Ross Taylor on the tour of England. I believed it was fundamentally wrong that we arrived in England missing five of our players for the practice games and lead-in to the test series. England is the tour of tours and we were embarrassing ourselves by not having our captain, vice-captain and some senior players in England to prepare for the series. Has any team ever done this?

The IPL had always stated that international commitments would come first. In order to protect world cricket and the future tours programme, players must be available at all times to play for their country. For me, a tour starts when the team assembles. The players were contracted to NZC. Contracts are there to protect both parties and must be enforced so that everyone knows where they stand and what their expectations are. The players had known for many months what the tour dates were — to disrupt the tour and its preparation was unprofessional.

I am more than happy, in a vastly changing cricket world, to see players secure their futures by accepting IPL contracts. I can understand the players not being happy if they are denied the opportunity of earning some big and 'relatively easy' dollars, but, in that case, they also needed to understand that NZC had given them the opportunity to be involved with IPL. The players needed to be reasonable and show some loyalty to the hand that had fed them over the years; they needed to accept that a tour of England was a commitment. Playing for New Zealand had given them the international exposure that their market value was based on, and that had to count for something.

Although the ECB were apparently happy with late arrivals, I wonder if those counties who were hosting matches and had sold hospitality packages thinking they would have a full strength team at their venue were so accepting. Would NZC be happy with this situation if it happened to us?

NZC's mandate was to have the Black Caps ranked in the top two positions of world cricket. It seemed to me that arriving in England with 10 players (and five other younger players) meant running the risk of being under-prepared and setting ourselves up for failure and potentially seriously compromising our ranking. With five senior players arriving only 10 days before the first test, there was a danger that the last practice match before the first test could be rain-affected or rained out (the English weather, especially in the start of the season, can be, at best, marginal) and those players would get little or no playing time and would be underdone. Look at what happened to Steve Harmison and Matthew Hoggard when they arrived in New Zealand in 2008 after playing only one first-class match — they were under-prepared and bowled poorly in the first test at Hamilton. Surely we should have learned from that. Bowling 20 overs a day and backing up the next day with another 10 to 15 overs, and ensuring that that performance is polished and effective, is hard work.

From experience, I knew I needed three or four first-class matches and to bowl 100–130 overs to find my rhythm and confidence and to know that I was in a perfect condition to have a better chance of performing. Likewise, batsmen who had been playing Twenty20 cricket would not have had much batting time and played the sorts of long innings required in tests. The mental, physical and technical demands of the different forms of the game can be a major adjustment and some players have difficulty with this.

On the 2008 tour we were also faced with having some players in the team who might not yet have been worthy of wearing the Black Cap and silver fern. Are we happy to make representing New Zealand easy for players? I can understand giving young players some experience of touring and playing in other countries but that, to me, is not the issue — when we select a team it is supposed to be the best team we can pick.

There is also the question of what happens to players who are acting as cover for players in India. If they do well, we may want to select them. Or should we just send them home irrespective of their results. That would seem unfair. It seems to me that allowing late arrivals creates more issues and problems for us to solve.

For the England tour, the team had indicated they were happy to have late arrivals, but I would seriously question the validity of that stance — there were the 'haves' and 'have nots'. Would any of the younger players in the team have seriously challenged the captain and vice-captain? I believe that this sort of thing must surely affect team morale. NZC had spent a lot of money on 'Leading Teams' and the 'Team First' concept. Did anyone really think that 'Team First' was working in this situation when there were so many players serving their own interests? To me, the concept had been seriously compromised and possibly destroyed.

There were also conflicting messages given by some players. In South Africa, where we were well beaten by the Proteas, players felt they were under-prepared, as they hadn't had enough games leading in to the test series. Yet Dan and the others playing IPL cricket said they only needed a few days' preparation in England. Who were they kidding?

As a selector I was not comfortable selecting a team that was not competitive, where several players were under-prepared, where morale was possibly affected, and players were unavailable (for personal gain) at the expense of their team-mates who were putting in the hard yards for others who were placing themselves in a position to under-perform. Our credibility could also have been compromised, especially if team and individual performances were sub-standard. We lost the test series 2-0. This, after having England on the ropes at Old Trafford in Manchester, only to let them off the hook with a poor second innings batting display. It was a game we should have won.

Here had been an opportunity for NZC to stand tall and lead world cricket and set an example for other countries to follow. Players should be available for all international cricket and not be dictated to by India and the IPL — we must protect the world game and what is in the best interests of our own game.

On Strike

In 2002 the standoff between the New Zealand Cricket Players' Association (CPA) and New Zealand Cricket came to a head and the players withdrew their services from the game for six weeks. Player associations can have a powerful impact on the game. After all, if the players do not make themselves available to play, there is no game.

I had belonged to the England Cricket Players' Association during my 10 years of professional county cricket with Nottinghamshire. The Association was very generous in its support of players who suffered injury or permanent disability and also advocated for players' needs. Every month subscriptions to the association were deducted from my pay. I accepted that the players' association was there if and when a player needed to use it — every player had a right to be represented. I guess it was like an insurance policy — if we were all in it together, we had the power to enforce change and ensure the quality of our working environment. I never needed the association to represent me, largely because I had developed a wonderful relationship with my employer, Nottinghamshire County Cricket Club. We negotiated our deals in a friendly and open manner, and with a little bit of give and take everyone was happy, and we all got on with the job.

It was understandable that the players in New Zealand were keen to get the best possible deal for themselves and for their colleagues. What the players had to remember, though, was that the money they could make in

New Zealand was relative to the income that NZC produced. NZC had an overall responsibility to cricket at all levels, including youth development, junior cricket, women's cricket, A team and Academy tours, coaching and umpiring, and not just to the international and the first-class players. There was little point in our players wanting parity with players in other parts of the world. The earnings of the Australian, English and Indian players, for example, were probably two, if not three or four times the amounts in New Zealand, but those countries produced probably 10 to 20 times the revenue that NZC could ever hope to make.

Under the circumstances, NZC had looked after the players well. There were base contracts and depending on how good the player was — and perhaps how good his negotiating skills were — he was offered a deal backed up with test and one-day appearance fees, some win bonuses, prize money and a few add-ons. It was felt that a top-class player in New Zealand could earn a base contract fee of around $60,000, plus appearance fees and bonuses, along with having all expenses covered, which would allow him to earn perhaps over $200,000 a year. One would have to say that is a very acceptable salary package. Chris Doig, Martin Snedden's predecessor, said publicly that 11 players were paid in excess of $200,000 under his leadership.

A young player new to the first-class scene may be offered a salary of $15,000 to $20,000, plus match fees. It was a far cry from the $100 I got for playing my first test, although in 1981 I was contracted for $10,000 and towards the end of my career, from 1987 to 1990, I was contracted to NZC for varying amounts of up to $36,000. That was a very good deal in those days.

During the standoff in 2002, from the players' point of view there was more to it than their own salaries. It was not all about the elite international players and their needs, but also about the needs of the first-class players, who in some cases had taken time off work to play domestic cricket and consequently suffered a loss of income. Employers were under no obligation to reimburse employees for their time off.

One of the major problems facing New Zealand cricket at that time was the number of experienced senior domestic cricketers retiring from the game in their late twenties and early thirties in order to secure their own futures in other areas. The result was that the standard of cricket had fallen dramatically. It was therefore considered vitally important to keep those players in the game as long as possible, in order to improve the competition and allow the younger, less experienced players to learn from those who had been around the scene. In my time, it wasn't unusual for players to stay in the game — Bevan Congdon, for example, played until he was 40 — but there was more pressure on today's players to secure a future, especially as more cricket was being played, which meant more time away from work.

The New Zealand Cricket Players' Association was led by Rob Nichol — who was also involved with the Rugby Players' Association — and Heath Mills, brother of Black Cap Kyle Mills. In the eyes of the public, they became the villains, the people who were about to disrupt, and perhaps destroy, our game. As the dispute went on, a public radio poll indicated that 80 per cent of the public supported the approach taken by Martin Snedden, the CEO of NZC. NZC had put their final offer on the table and it was rejected by the association. There was a breakdown in the negotiations, so the players withdrew their services and went on strike.

Although it wasn't the only issue, the standoff was primarily about money, and how much NZC was going to earn over the next few years, with the players wanting more of the pie and more say in the running of the game. The players also wanted their association to be funded by NZC, which I thought quite strange. Why would NZC want to fund an organisation or a union when that same union could work against them if they did not get what they wanted and go on strike? Surely it would be counterproductive. Nichol's argument was that the New Zealand Rugby Football Union and the Australian Cricket Board paid for their association bodies. Snedden disagreed with that principle. He felt it was unethical, if not unconstitutional, to provide the players' association with exclusive partnership rights in terms of its operation.

The players eventually took strike action for six weeks. They said they did this as a last resort to settle the matter, but Snedden took a firm hand, indicating that NZC had done all it could and that the offer on the table was fair and reasonable. NZC had made some movement and offered an additional $440,000 to the players' pool. That in itself was a generous concession.

Snedden made a very clever move. He went public on most of the issues, much to the disappointment of the CPA, and he made it very clear that 'cricket will be played this summer'. He flexed his muscle and sent a very clear message to all the players that they should accept the deal and get back to work. On behalf of NZC he had made a reasonable offer to the players and by doing so he also indicated that NZC would be forced to reassess its finances and how the monies within NZC would be redistributed. There would be budget slashing within most departments of NZC to cover the additional funding made to the players, something that did not sit well with the public.

If the CPA did not accept NZC's final deal, then NZC would take the first step and cancel the Max cricket tournament in November. The players continued to refuse and the tournament was duly cancelled. NZC had spoken. Snedden said: 'The players' association had been adopting a strategy which could still have us at the negotiating table when the Indians arrived — and therefore over a barrel. It could have well got to the stage where there was about two days left before the tour started, and still no resolution in sight.'

People got frustrated with both Nichol's manner and his comments. Public relations were not his strong point as he repeated himself time and time again, often talking in riddles. He would constantly say: 'We are comfortable with where we are at . . . we are prepared to negotiate.' Nichol claimed that the players, reputed to be 120 strong, had signed up and were 100 per cent behind him. I wasn't aware that we had 120 first-class players in the country — perhaps 90 would have been more accurate and even then some of those would have been pushing the boundaries to think they were of first-class ability.

The CPA covered their bases by contracting as many of the first-class and second-class players around the country as they could — and it may be hearsay, but it was my understanding that some high school First XI players were also contracted. The CPA had the players they wanted to bring an abrupt halt to the game.

Many people felt that Nichol was not the best person to lead the negotiations and that a former player who had both the players' and cricket's best interests at heart would have been better to deal with Snedden. Snedden, I felt, bent over backwards to help the players and he understood what their needs were. Just how they were going to get what they wanted was a different story. There appeared to be a clash of two strong personalities.

But the dispute left us as selectors in a very difficult situation. We had not had the opportunity to have an end of tour debrief with Stephen Fleming after the recent West Indies tour, something that was essential to our planning for the upcoming Indian series at home. Normal practice was to have a meeting within days of the team returning home from a tour. Worse yet was the simple fact that there were no players available to select a test and a one-day team from for the upcoming season, nor were we allowed to make contact with them. We had no way of knowing what they were doing as far as their preparation was concerned.

All the pre-season matches against the Academy team had been cancelled. Those matches would have been an opportunity for the players to play on grass, to get the feel of the bat on ball and bowling on turf pitches. It would have been an ideal build-up for everyone. It was proper cricket and it would have allowed us to make some pre-season judgments as to where we felt the players were in their preparation.

We decided to take the initiative and Ross Dykes, Brian McKechnie, Denis Aberhart and I assembled in Rangiora to view the match between Canterbury and Otago — fielding what was, in effect, their provincial C teams. Each province had tried to be proactive and recruit whatever players they could, even if they were ordinary-grade cricketers. Some of the players were induced not to sign up to the CPA and were offered $1000 to be available to play first-class cricket for their provinces. Ben

Yock was the first player to break ranks from the CPA and commit himself to Canterbury cricket. Was there a chink in the CPA's armour? Were they starting to fall apart?

As it turned out, the match at Rangiora was a good game of cricket and as a starting point we were putting some names down on paper. We had not heard of many of the players until then and in some cases we did not know how to spell their names. Unfamiliar names such as Paul Rugg from Weedons and Brendon Donkers from Rangiora stood out. It was all very surreal. We were faced with the real possibility of selecting 11 debutants, which should only happen once in a nation's history.

As the strike went on, the papers grabbed the headlines — 'Selectors may have to pick second-string sides', 'Credibility on the line for union man', 'Petulant cricketers let the side down'. Then ex-players waded in on both sides of the dispute. Former Black Cap Adam Parore said that the players should be given more money. Martin Crowe publicly stated that Chris Cairns and Stephen Fleming should replace Rob Nichol and Heath Mills, and that Nichol and Mills did not have credibility and should step aside as they had failed. Crowe also felt that Fleming, the Black Cap's captain, should be more involved. Later on, when the dispute was settled, Fleming told me that in his opinion it was nothing to do with him and was in fact a dispute between the CPA and NZC.

Dion Nash, a former Black Cap and now a 'staunch militant' of the CPA, went public with a personal attack and crusade against NZC. He said that: 'NZC had picked up three or four players and paid them very well — but the rest of us could go to hell.' He criticised Chris Doig and NZC regarding how he was treated as a player, although Doig's version of events involving Dion was very different. But the attack backfired and only had the effect of severely denting the credibility of the CPA. It was highly emotional stuff.

Emotions, in fact, were running high right throughout the sport; players, administrators, the media and the public were all affected. One of the saddest aspects for me was seeing my father, a highly respected former player, captain and administrator, who had given his life to cricket for no financial reward, his face filled with emotion, tears in his eyes and his voice quivering, saying: 'The players have abused and betrayed our game — all for personal greed. They have held our game to ransom.'

I had heard that any player who would not sign for the CPA or who would break away from the association would find life difficult — they would be intimidated by the militants of the CPA and other players. It appeared that some ugly tactics were being employed. I had also heard that some fast bowlers would bounce non-contracted players in the nets and in club games — even bowl bean balls. Hopefully, this did not happen — as far as we were concerned any player involved with that sort of behaviour would not play for New Zealand again.

Part of our selection criteria included — 'To honour and respect the true values, history and traditions of the game. To respect past players and reflect on their achievements and glory.' All of a sudden, those thoughts had become meaningless.

The dispute, in its entirety, continued from May until November 2002. At that point, Chris Cairns, a senior player, eventually put his reputation on the line, broke silence and in a joint statement with the CPA and NZC announced that an agreement had been reached, much to the relief of all concerned — and especially the selectors. We rubbed out all the names we had pencilled in and started to get back to normality.

The players went back to work, player payments and fringe benefits increased, and NZC were left to juggle the books so that the 94,000 people playing cricket in New Zealand would somehow be looked after. In a final gesture of goodwill, NZC agreed to fund the CPA.

In my view, there is no doubt the players went back to work because they knew how serious NZC was and that their jobs were on the line. They were all off contract — no play, no pay, no Indian series and no World Cup. The players were effectively unemployed and in danger of having to find another job, which for some may have been difficult. All of a sudden, it dawned on some of the international players that they could earn between $100,000 and $200,000 a year playing cricket, compared to the $30,000 to $40,000 they might get in the workforce. And if they continued to refuse to play, then other players would be found to take their jobs. Reason had to prevail.

The players now had to regain the faith of the public and the media, and restore credibility to the game. The only way they could do that was to perform both individually and collectively. The public view was that if the players wanted more money, then we should get better performances.

The player strike had started in October 2002, not long before the beginning of the domestic and international season, and we were very concerned about the players' fitness and their general and specific preparation and mental state for the upcoming matches. The players were apparently working behind the scenes but the coaches, selectors and administrators had no feedback or way of monitoring the players' progress.

The selectors felt that the players needed to know where we thought they were at and what we expected over the next few months. In early November, with NZC's and the selection panel's approval, I sent a memo to all the contracted players and some other fringe players, expressing our views about recent substandard performances, especially in the ICC Champions Trophy in Sri Lanka; of where players needed to be in terms of world rankings; of the need for better and more consistent batting; and of our perception that some senior players were resting on their laurels and needed to train harder. I reminded them that they had a responsibility to NZC, the public, the sponsors, the team and to themselves to achieve better results and that, as selectors, we would be looking for performance, commitment and desire.

By the time the season had ended, the Black Caps had produced some very positive and rewarding results. The team performed very well at home against India, winning the two-match test series 2-0 and the one-day series 5-2. It was a convincing victory, although the Indians would claim that the pitches, especially for the tests, were almost unplayable and greatly in favour of the ball over the bat, that is, very useful for our seaming bowlers and negating their strength in spin. Although we failed to make the semi-finals of the World Cup, the team competed well, winning five of our eight matches, including our first ever win over South Africa in South Africa. Wins over the West Indies, Bangladesh, Canada and Zimbabwe were impressive. We won the Bank Alfalah Tri-Series Cup in Sri Lanka, beating Pakistan in the final. We had won our second ever one-day final overseas.

Over the preceding three years, our one-day performances had been very disappointing — we had won only 36 per cent of our matches. But as the 2002/03 season progressed, things improved — at one stage the team produced 11 wins in 14 matches. By the end of the season, we had won 15 of 26 completed matches, a 58 per cent win rate.

At the end of the Sri Lankan tour in 2003, we had several players rated in the top 20 test and one-day rankings; indeed it was the first time we had so many players in the top 20. Progress was being made.

In 2006 NZC and the CPA had discussions to renew the agreement. While I am sure there were changes made, and no doubt in the future there will be some 'testing issues', there appears to be give and take, and the relationship is now very cordial.

Should I Walk?

The appointment of Martin Snedden as CEO of NZC took me by surprise. Why would a former player now involved in a very successful law practice want to become a cricket administrator and move from Auckland to Christchurch to start a new life? The answer was quite simple — Sneds, who was a NZC Board member, still had a love for the game and felt that he had something to offer, and on 31 July 2001 he officially took office.

Sneds appeared to fit comfortably into the role and he gained the support of the public and the media for his transparent approach to all issues. He was a decision-maker and his public profile grew in stature to the extent that people were saying that if there was a Sir Murray Halberg Award for 'Best Sports Administrator of the Year', Martin Snedden would be the winner — high praise indeed. In my view, his greatest quality was the depth of understanding he brought to situations and the empathy he had with other people — he showed passion for the role and compassion for the people he had an influence on.

Sneds had many issues to confront during his tenure and they began immediately. On his first day in the office he found himself involved in a dispute with John Turkington, the CEO of Northern Districts Cricket, when Hamilton was overlooked as a venue for the England test series. Then, following the terrorist attack of 11 September 2001 on the twin towers in New York, Sneds decided to bring the team back home from Singapore where they were *en route* to Pakistan, as it was apparent Afghanistan was going to be a target and US forces could launch an attack from Pakistan. In 2002 he brought the Black Caps home from their tour of Pakistan following a bomb blast, and the women's tour of India was cancelled for security reasons. The advent of the Players' Association and the players' strike in 2002 brought cricket in New Zealand to a standstill and Martin and NZC were forced to take tough measures. Death threats and security issues became a major problem prior to the 2003 World Cup. New Zealand had to play a match in Kenya, where Westerners were going to be targeted — a terrorist attack rocked Mombasa. Fines imposed on NZC by the ICC for not going to Kenya during the 2003 World Cup was going to severely dent the income of NZC and disrupt all future programmes and the stability of the organisation — later, fortunately, common sense prevailed and no fines were imposed. In 2004/05 the Sri Lankan tour of New Zealand was postponed due to the tsunami disaster in Sri Lanka and other parts of Asia — there was no international cricket in New Zealand during January and early February, but at short notice Martin was able to get a World XI, captained by Shane Warne, to play three one-day matches to resurrect the summer. When Black Caps player Daryl Tuffey was videoed in a compromising situation, NZC fined him $1000 for bringing the game and NZC into disrepute — but the public questioned whether NZC had the right to be judge and jury on a moral issue. The tour of Zimbabwe in 2005 caused outrage at government and public level. President Robert Mugabe's atrocities in his own country fuelled an anti-tour feeling, but NZC were caught between a rock and a hard place — if the team did not tour, massive fines would be imposed by the ICC, and if the team toured Zimbabwe, NZC and the players incurred the wrath of the government and the public.

Sneds had been involved in several major crises within a relatively short period of time, with all incidents handled in a disciplined and a sensitively explained manner. One of the key qualities Sneds brought to the position was the common practice for lawyers of documenting everything. This meant there was an official record of everything that had happened and that events could be not be disputed or challenged. Communication was a key component of his style of leadership. NZC could have taken up shares in the forest and paper industry with the amount of paper he used!

I learned very quickly that Sneds had two sides to his personality within the role. He did not have the time to mince words and his method was to be direct and to the point, which meant that everyone knew where they stood. Such emails were typically addressed 'Richard . . . from Martin'. On the other hand there were also friendlier emails saying, 'Hi Paddles . . . Regards Sneds' — perhaps those ones indicated that I was doing a reasonable job!

Obviously, Sneds wanted to make an impact within NZC. All departments within NZC underwent a massive review and he wanted to find ways to improve the organisation and make it better. All CEOs in any business would see this as stamping their mark on the job.

After the disappointing results in the World Cup there was a clear indication from Martin and NZC that they were not happy with the team's overall performances. Under the current management structure, the personnel involved had done a job but if the Black Caps were going to move forward and get better results, especially in the one-day game, changes needed to be made. Sneds' view was that if we were third in test cricket and sixth in one-day cricket, how would we get to being number one? If we kept doing things the same way, how would we progress?

I knew there were changes in the wind. The manager, coach and all the selectors had to reapply for their positions. That was a NZC Board instruction. This was normal practice after a term in office, with everyone having a performance review, except that, strangely enough, the selectors had never had one. At the end of the 2004/05 season, Jeff Crowe had made it very clear that he was finishing in his role as manager of the Black Caps. The question was whether Denis Aberhart and the selectors would survive.

It appeared that NZC was very concerned over where the responsibility and total accountability for the Black Caps' performances should be placed.

Was it the players, the coach, the selectors, or me as chairman of selectors who would be blamed for the failures and be held accountable for the results? Personally, I felt that if one individual was to be held accountable for the losses against Australia and India in the World Cup that I would willingly accept the full blame for that as I had had the final say in selections, even though the decisions were unanimous. But apportioning blame for failure is, of course, more complicated than that. Many people play a part: the selectors (including the coach) pick a team and hand the players over to the coach and the captain. The coach prepares the players and the team, and the captain is responsible for decisions on the field. The players, in turn, are accountable and responsible for their own performances.

NZC considered four options regarding the selection process. They could continue with the existing Black Caps selection panel; they could appoint the Black Caps coach as sole selector; they could appoint the Black Caps coach as chairman of a three- or four-man selection panel; or they could appoint the Black Caps coach as sole selector but put in place a selection advisory panel to assist him.

We, as the current selection panel, were asked to submit our thoughts and rationale as to the future structure of the selection panel. On behalf of the selection panel, and in consultation with them, I responded that we felt it was in the best interests of NZC and the players for the status quo to remain, and after considering our arguments NZC did in fact retain the independent selection panel concept. There was much to be said for the status quo: we covered all domestic cricket, were independent and not too close to the players, we were a source of alternative ideas for the coach and captain, had good lines of communication with coaches and other interested parties, and happily took criticism for selection choices, deflecting such attacks from the coach, who would not need that added pressure. The other options, in our view, all placed considerably more pressure on, and demanded much more time from, the coach, to the detriment of actually coaching the team.

NZC's strategic document 2003–07 had the theme of 'Pushing the Boundaries'. Part of the plan was 'to be daring, to ensure that we are always ahead of the field'. Over our first three years, the current selection panel had pushed the boundaries and been daring with some bold selections. We had introduced some new blood, recalled some experienced players and given some of the journeymen in domestic cricket an opportunity to play for New Zealand. We had had some successes, although several players were still trying to find their way at the highest level.

During the last three years we had won three, drawn four and lost two test series. In one-day cricket, we had won the ICC Champions Trophy (our first ever one-day title), the Bank Alfalah Tri-Series Cup in Sri Lanka (our second one-day title) and won three ODI series. We had lost five ODI series and performed poorly in other tri-series tournaments in Sharjah and in Sri Lanka. Obviously, there were some significant test and one-day wins. Our test ranking had climbed to third, which is the highest it had ever been, and we had held that position for nearly a year. We were ranked fifth in ODI cricket (up three places) but we were hopeful that our ranking would improve in the future.

The results in Sri Lanka in 2003 should not have been underestimated. Without some of our experienced players (Astle and McMillan), we drew the two-match test series and won the one-day series. Sri Lanka had won nine of their previous test matches at home and had never missed the finals of a one-day tri-series tournament at home. Daniel Vettori was named Player of the One-day Series (won a car) and Brendon McCullum and Lou Vincent won best batsmen awards (motorbikes). In difficult conditions, we performed creditably with a relatively new-look team.

The advent of the Players' Association and the associated contractual rankings had made the task of selection more onerous, as the panel now had a significant influence in the earning power of our top players. Not only did that place more responsibility on the panel, but it has also highlighted the need for the selectors to maintain a delicate distance between themselves and the players.

NZC now had our thoughts to consider before making a final decision as to our futures as selectors. As we had never had a performance review from NZC, we had no idea of how they thought we had performed in our role. That disappointed me because I had asked for feedback time and time again. We were left to assess our own performance, and all things considered I would rate it as high as 8/10.

The first thing that NZC wanted to address was to find a successor to Jeff Crowe. Lindsay Crocker, the former CEO of Auckland Cricket, was appointed as the General Manager of the Black Caps, which in fact gave him more power than Jeff had had. He would be accountable for everything that involved the Black Caps.

The next job was to address the coaching position and there was a lot of speculation that former New Zealand player and coach of the Gloucestershire county team, John Bracewell, would be appointed and that Denis would be replaced. Before the announcement of both Crocker and the new coach, who did indeed prove to be Bracewell, Denis Aberhart advised me that he had withdrawn his application for the coach's position, and that very soon became official. According to Denis, it was taking NZC too long to make a decision and there was too much uncertainty as to whether he would be reappointed or not. He felt that he needed to be proactive and secure his own future. Denis had a background in education and was later appointed as Head of Department at St Andrews College to assist overseas students with English.

There was speculation that I was next in line to be given the chop. If the papers were right, John Bracewell was going to be appointed as the convener/chairman of selectors. In an interview on *Talk Sport* radio Braces tried to avoid the question, but being pressed he said that he preferred to be in charge of his own destiny but that he would be happy with whatever decision was made by NZC. That first comment suggested to me that part of his package and appointment was that he would be the chief selector. If that were the case, my role was redundant. I felt I was perceptive enough to know that the writing was on the wall and that I would not be reappointed in my role. Was it time for me to walk? Maybe it would be the right time for me to go and let the possible new structure and newly appointed personnel get on with the job without feeling they could be undermined by those who were involved under the old system.

I was very pensive and reflective of the situation that I was in. I questioned myself as to why there needed to be change — for years, England had appointed David Graveney as their chairman of selectors and Australia had done the same with Trevor Hohns. West Indies had just appointed Sir Vivian Richards as their new chairman of selectors and India had appointed Syed Kirmani in the same role, yet NZC appeared to be about to change to having the coach as chairman of selectors. Cricket Australia had also decided not to reappoint their coach, John Buchanan, as a selector — allowing him more time to concentrate on player and team performances, with the selection panel from outside the team having complete control. Different scenarios for different teams!

On 6 July 2003, I emailed Martin and indicated that if it was NZC's decision to appoint the coach as the convener/chairman of selectors, it would be in everyone's best interests if I withdrew from seeking reappointment in that role and I wished Sneds and NZC all the very best for the future. I had decided that it would be best to walk away and allow the new structure and people in strategic positions to push on with the new philosophy.

Over the weekend of 18–20 July the NZC Board discussed the selection panel issue. The first thing they would decide on would be the structure of the panel and then later decide the personnel who would be involved. I had always expressed an interest to continue in my current role, but if that role was to change, I would need to reconsider my position. Our contracts expired on 1 June 2003. Originally, I was contracted for a two-year term but that was extended another 12 months to coincide with the World Cup.

There were grave doubts expressed in the media as to whether I would be reappointed. There was a suggestion that my ego would be too big to allow someone like Braces to take over my position and that I would not be big enough to accept the change. If there was going to be change, I had two choices — accept it or walk away. It was also taking NZC a good long time to reach its decisions. This created uncertainty for me, so much so that I was starting to look for other opportunities. I knew that I had done a good job: progress with the team and some individual players had been made, there was competition for places, there was more depth and choices, the team was competitive, and if I were to get the chop, I would have been very disappointed and disillusioned with NZC.

I also suspected that there was an underlying financial reason for the change. It appeared that NZC was not going to get the full payout from the World Cup because of their refusal to play in Kenya — NZC were going to be severely penalised for the decision not to play, perhaps by as much as US$2 million. If that was the case, and with the CPA's demands for better player payments, there would clearly need to be huge cost cutting within all departments of NZC. The selection department, like all other areas, would also come under the microscope. Perhaps there was consideration being given to having Braces as a sole selector with an advisory panel, or involving the provincial coaches, to reduce costs. There would be a possible saving of around $120,000 to $130,000 within the selectors' department budget from fees, administration, travel, accommodation, telephones, daily meal allowances and other incidental costs.

After Sneds had read my email he asked me to come and see him and have a 'chat'. He was very up-front and forthcoming, saying that he would recommend to the Board that Braces be the new convener of the selection panel because he wanted Braces to be accountable and responsible for the overall results, and to do that he needed to have the final say on team selections. Sneds could see how disappointed I was to hear the news and the change of direction. He said that it was not a matter of money or cost-cutting with the department — he wanted the best system and people in place to take the Black Caps forward.

Sneds informed me that the recommendation he would make to the Board was in no way a reflection of the way I had done the job. He went on to say that he still wanted me to stay on as a selector because I had experience, knowledge of the players and systems, and skills in the role and there needed to be a team selected for the forthcoming tours of India and Pakistan, and it would be important for me to be part of that process until Braces took over in December. I was somewhat pleased and relieved to hear that.

Sneds explained that the only key difference in my role was that Braces would make a final decision on the players he wanted and that he had the right to veto all decisions: 'You would still be involved with the management of the selection panel — the administration, co-ordination in organising meetings and telephone conference calls, reporting, budgeting, logistics of organising the other selectors to be on the grounds viewing matches and the players. The coach would not have the time to do the administration and all the other facets that involve the selectors.' All those things that I had done on a daily basis for three years would continue and would continue to involve about a hundred days a year as issues cropped up that needed to be actioned.

I thought very seriously about the offer being made — it was very generous, I thought. I eventually accepted the new deal and thought that it was important to understand and support the new concept, to at least give it a go, to see whether the team would move forward and get better results. At least I was still involved with cricket and NZC, and there was still an important role to play. I felt that the fact that there was no large change to the selection system was a vote of confidence in the job I had done, and I also felt that there was still some unfinished business. I was very keen to see whether the players and the team that we had selected over the previous three years could go on and fulfil their potential.

In effect nothing was going to change, except that Braces would get the final say, even if he was outvoted by Ross, Brian and me — the 'heat' would now be focused on Braces because, effectively, the selections would be perceived as his and not mine, even though I was still part of the process. It was an interesting thing that our selection process, which involved wide discussion, meant some decisions would be unanimous and others would be made by majority vote, and only once do I recall having to make a casting vote in three years under the old system, yet the teams were perceived by the media and the public, as being mine and mine alone.

Sneds and I had another meeting to confirm my role and to discuss the terms we would use when communicating with the media: the names 'chairman' and 'convener' were discarded and the term 'selection manager' was created for my position. On 28 July a press conference confirmed my new role and the future direction of the selection panel, and in August I was very pleased to see that Ross and Brian had also been reappointed. All the announcements were simple and to the point and the media reaction to the new structure was positive. Everyone involved came through with credit and their dignity intact. I thought that Sneds had handled a very delicate and sensitive situation exceptionally well.

Over the next two years Black Cap results under Braces' leadership were generally good, with the one-day game improving, although the test results were a little disappointing. Braces copped some flak from time to time, but didn't seem to attract the same level of criticism I had. I found myself enjoying my new role as selection manager and the panel was working harmoniously.

When the new contract period came around — from June 2005 to May 2007 — Ross Dykes and Brian McKechnie decided to stand down as selectors; Ross was appointed CEO of Otago Cricket and Brian felt that it was time to move on after having 10 years of selection at first-class and international level. A new panel was appointed, with Glenn Turner and Dion Nash joining Braces and me until after the 2007 World Cup.

I had encouraged Glenn to apply for the role when I knew he was finishing as coach of the Otago team — he had so much to offer our game. I was, however, surprised to see Dion appointed, if only because of the players' strike and his outspoken words against NZC. The media reaction to the new panel was that they would have liked to have been a fly on the wall at our meetings, with four strong-minded egos now on the panel. The reality was that our discussions weren't ego-driven, but we all had opinions that could be expressed and shared and we had some robust and interesting debates.

In August 2006 I was reappointed on a one-year contract, but in December 2007 I advised the new CEO, Justin Vaughan, that I would not be reapplying for my position as selection manager or as a selector when my term finished in July 2008. I had decided that after eight years in the role, it was time for me to move on. Every year since 1972, the Christmas and New Year period had found me either playing or watching the game, whereas for other people it was a holiday time. I needed a break and perhaps a fresh challenge. I was not enjoying the role as much any more — it was time-consuming and I could foresee many delicate issues coming up that would require more meetings, more phone calls, more administration and more frustration when trying to select players and teams. I was tired of the role. I had had enough of phoning players and telling them that they had or had not been selected. It was always stressful for me and disappointing for the players when I had to phone them saying they were dropped from the team. Our decisions were affecting their careers, incomes and futures and I really felt for those players. Selection is about putting emotion aside and making the tough calls. The fact that I was feeling empathy with the players made me realise that it was time for someone else to make those calls.

To be a NZC selector these days is a full-time job. Every other day selectors are thinking about the players, future tours, general issues, talking to fellow selectors or coaches, answering emails, planning for meetings, doing research and working through decisions that need to be made. I believe that selectors need to be rewarded and valued more than we were, in what is a very demanding and challenging role — and there were no pay increases during my term.

For eight years I had been involved in three different structures. For three years I was chairman of selectors and had a casting vote in case of deadlock. The changes made when John Bracewell became coach — specifically, his right of veto — meant that effectively all other selectors served in an advisory role only. The final year — and the first with Justin Vaughan as CEO — saw the rule of consensus implemented: we all had to agree on decisions and if someone opposed a decision, there needed to be a compelling argument to change his mind. This was very time-consuming.

In my view, I believe the selection panel should be independent of the team, meaning that the coach should not be a selector. When the coach is the selector, player trust of the coach is compromised and at times it is difficult for the coach to stand back and be objective. If the independent structure were to be put in place, the coach and the captain would always be consulted, but would be more focused on and have more time for the core business of coaching and playing and getting the results, without all the other distractions. Australia operates under that structure.

I certainly never had any issues with my co-selectors, in fact I had the utmost respect for them all, but trying to lead a group and reach consensus was taking its toll. It was time for me to walk, hopefully with my dignity intact and knowing that I had tried to make a difference. I remain supportive of NZC and its direction and hope the team and the organisation will succeed in its goals to be the number one or two team in the world in the very near future. I will watch with interest.

The World Cups
of 2003 and 2007

New Zealand has a proud record in World Cup cricket. We have reached the semi-finals four times and the quarter-finals twice. There was every reason to have some optimism in 2003. Three years of the selectors' planning had gone into this team. We had experimented and tried different combinations and although we had had mixed results at least we had tried some different things to give us greater options. The coach and the captain, along with the support staff, had done their best to prepare the team, so expectations were high.

The 2003 World Cup staged in South Africa was the most controversial ever. It became a political time bomb when New Zealand decided not to go to Kenya because of security reasons. And when England pulled out of their match in Zimbabwe, the whole tournament lost its credibility and became almost farcical.

The ICC and the World Cup committee were faced with a dilemma. Bow to the pressure of two major countries and reschedule the games or stay with the status quo, and if New Zealand and England did not honour their matches, they would forfeit their points. In the end the status quo remained and Kenya and Zimbabwe picked up four points each, which advantaged them but disadvantaged every other team in the competition. They had gained points for matches that they probably would have lost. This made it harder for other teams to qualify for the Super Six rounds.

This was confirmed when Pakistan, West Indies, England and South Africa, all major teams, were eliminated after the preliminary rounds.

World opinion would say the ICC should have shifted the matches to South Africa to get all the games played on a fair and equal playing field, with no one being disadvantaged.

The decision by New Zealand not to go to Kenya was sound. It was a Board decision, not a players' decision, but somehow I think the players were relieved and grateful that the decision not to go was made. There were severe security issues in that country. A bomb had exploded in Mombasa, causing casualties, only weeks before the World Cup started and there were reports that Al Qaeda cell networks were operating in Kenya and were going to target Westerners. The US Embassy and the Australian Consulate strongly recommended not going to Kenya. When I arrived in South Africa, Dr Ali Bacher, the World Cup Executive Director, said to me: 'Your team should go to Kenya. There is no problem. When you fly to Nairobi, the team will be escorted by MiG fighter jets, and tanks and troops will be positioned on the ground.' That merely confirmed to me that there were severe security issues. Even later on, when it became abundantly clear that the ICC was not going to reschedule the matches, Ali said: 'Your players should fly into Kenya in the morning, play the match and fly out again that night.'

Security was always going to be a major issue during the World Cup. While my wife Di and I were in South Africa, the term CPO was often mentioned. My initial thought was that CPO meant Central Post Office, as it did in New Zealand. However, in South Africa, where security was paramount, CPO meant Close Protection Officer. Di and I had supervision and protection whenever we left the hotel to attend a cricket match, an official function or when we went shopping. It simply was not safe to walk about the streets alone.

But as soon as we forfeited the game against Kenya, our chances of reaching the Super Six rounds were slim. We knew we could beat Bangladesh, Kenya and Canada, but that meant we still needed one win against either Sri Lanka, the West Indies or South Africa to get us through to the next stage — 16 points was the minimum required for some sort of safety, barring huge upsets.

When we lost the match to Sri Lanka, there was immediately pressure on the Black Caps to beat both the West Indies and South Africa, and to ensure that Bangladesh and Canada did not cause an upset by beating us. This scenario would still allow us to get the 16 points needed to qualify for the Super Six rounds. History shows that we made it through, but only by the skin of our teeth, and in the end we were left relying on the results of other teams. It is hard to know which team to thank the most: Sri Lanka for beating South Africa by one run in a rain-affected match or South Africa for misreading the Duckworth-Lewis system by one run, which eliminated them from the tournament. Had South Africa scored one more run, even though we had the 16 points we would have been eliminated and South Africa would have qualified. That is how close it got, through no fault of our own.

In an unusual step NZC decided that as I was going to be in South Africa as an ICC cricket ambassador for three weeks, it made sense to be involved as one of the Black Caps' on-tour selectors. Usually, the on-tour selectors are the captain, coach and a senior player, but on this occasion I was the chairman of selectors and I had the final say. As the tour progressed I was accused by some media of interfering with the on-tour selection process. This was strange criticism, especially when it was my job, along with Ross and Brian, to originally select the players for the tour and then make decisions in consultation with the other on-tour selectors. All decisions we made on tour were unanimous.

My approach at all team selection meetings was to first ask Stephen Fleming for his thoughts, followed by Denis Aberhart's thoughts. I conveyed those thoughts to Ross Dykes and Brian McKechnie, and then added my thoughts (including thoughts, if relevant, from other people I had approached). We then debated all the issues and agreed unanimously on all occasions on the final teams selected. The communication and level of understanding between the on-tour selectors were very positive. We had healthy and amicable debates. Stephen and Denis arrived at meetings with their initial thoughts, and by the time we had discussed and debated all the issues, we found that we had looked at the broader picture and decided on the best possible combinations.

We had never won a one-day international match in South Africa. By the time the tour was over, we had won five of the eight matches we played, including five wins in a row. If the team had lost any one of those first four wins, we would not have qualified for the Super Six rounds. We defeated the host nation South Africa, West Indies, Zimbabwe, Bangladesh and Canada.

Several players had an excellent World Cup. Stephen Fleming batted sublimely on occasions but, in reality, had only one big score, with several other useful contributions. Shane Bond demonstrated that he is one of the world's premier fast bowlers. Jacob Oram and Scott Styris made some very good contributions. Brendon McCullum did a fine job behind the stumps but we still needed more runs from him. Nathan Astle produced three worthy scores, including a century, but also had three ducks. Chris Harris showed his experience on occasions.

There were too many disappointing batting performances from Craig McMillan and Lou Vincent. While Chris Cairns made some useful contributions with the bat, he was dismissed too many times at crucial moments, when he had the experience and opportunity to put the team in a better, and perhaps winning, situation. Daniel Vettori was well below his best, capturing only two wickets. André Adams could not get the ball in the right place, especially when he was bowling 'at the death', the specialist role for which he was selected.

Kyle Mills (hamstring injury), Mathew Sinclair and Daryl Tuffey did not have much of an opportunity to impress due to the situation we were in — after the Sri Lankan loss and points gifted to Kenya, we had to win every match, so we decided to play what we thought was our best team and best combinations.

Some of our selections caused a lot of debate back in New Zealand. But we had our reasons for everything we did. The experiment of batting Nathan Astle at number three proved to be successful. We knew that his home record was very good (average of 56) but his offshore record was disappointing (average 27). Astle was a valuable member of the team — in reality, if he scored big runs, we won. In recent times Astle had been vulnerable to the new ball, and was being dismissed too often within the first few overs. It was decided to protect him (this was discussed in New Zealand and he was happy with the idea) for at least the first five overs — when he came in to bat in the World Cup after the first five overs, he had scores of 46, 54 not out and a century. In contrast, his three ducks all came when he was in before the first five overs were completed. By the time the World Cup was over, Astle had averaged 42.

Craig McMillan was used in different roles. He started the tour batting at number three but without success. Daniel Vettori, who opened the batting against the West Indies, was going to do the job again against South Africa but suffered a slight back injury. McMillan was promoted to open the innings and he had some success — he scored 25 and helped Fleming put together our best opening partnership of the tournament at that time. It was therefore thought that McMillan could do a job for us as an opener again — he scored 75 against Bangladesh, but then failed several times in that role. He was dropped but recalled when Vincent failed in his role in the middle order. The on-tour selectors could have made other changes but we felt that we would back McMillan and his experience to try to turn his disappointing form around, but he failed to deliver.

Daniel Vettori was tried as an opener against the West Indies to unsettle their bowling attack. He had moderate success by scoring 13, but he helped add 40 for the opening partnership and got the team off to a good start. Dan is unorthodox in his style and approach, and there was a calculated chance that he could do a job in that role, as he had done quite successfully for Northern Districts. We tried it again against Australia to unsettle their game plan. This would allow Astle to be protected and we felt that if Dan was dismissed early, it would not be such a huge loss as we were able to include another batsman in the team lower down the order in any case.

We deserved to make the Super Six, but on a technicality we could have been eliminated from the tournament a lot earlier. We beat South Africa and the West Indies, yet had South Africa beaten Sri Lanka, they would have gone through and not us. We also had a better net run rate than Kenya, yet they were the first team to qualify in our group for the Super Six based on the four forfeited points they were given (a win for Kenya).

The bottom line was that we had an opportunity to beat either Australia or India to qualify for the semi-final. Our fate was in our own hands, whereas on other occasions there had been too many scenarios that were beyond our control that counted against us. But our batting failed on both occasions and there were question marks over the mental and technical aspects of some of the players (player decision-making, options taken and whether they were tough enough when under extreme pressure). Some of the experienced and key players did not deliver when it mattered and some of the younger players gave the impression of being overawed when put under pressure to lift their performance and win the match.

To be beaten by the two teams who ultimately contested the World Cup final perhaps puts everything into perspective — they played better than we did when it mattered most. Australia was definitely the best team in the competition, winning all their matches and being undefeated in 17 consecutive one-day internationals, which was a world record.

There was an interesting aside involving Chris Harris that nearly caused me some embarrassment. At all the venues during the 2003 World Cup an up-to-date electronic scoreboard was on the ground. During the day the scoreboard would advertise asking people to text in messages that would then be on view to all those people on the ground. During the Super Six match between New Zealand and Zimbabwe, the Black Caps had performed well, restricting Zimbabwe to 174/7 with seven overs to go. Chris Harris was nearing the end of his bowling spell, having bowled eight overs very well and taking 1/18. While he was performing well in this match, I thought it a good idea to send the scoreboard a text message saying, 'Well bowled Harry. Paddles'. I got my wife Di to type the message into the phone and get it ready to send. I waited until it was the right time to send the message. When Harry had just got a wicket and finished an over, Di sent the message. I was hoping it would flash up on the board in an instant. I thought Harry and the team would enjoy the moment! I was also publicly acknowledging his performance. Well, I waited and waited and nothing appeared on the scoreboard. Harry started his ninth over and Heath Streak hit him for six. I thought then, please do not flash the message up on the screen or Harry and the team would think I was being sarcastic and perhaps offensive. Thankfully, still no message appeared. Harry then started his tenth and final over and the ball disappeared to all parts of the boundary — in all, Harry's last two overs cost 26 runs (21 coming from the last over) and I was anxiously hoping the message would not appear on the board. Thankfully, the message never did appear, otherwise I could have been very embarrassed. I learned later that they did not show personal messages but only more generic messages wishing the teams well. I was very grateful for their policy. When I told Denis and Flem about the incident they laughed but saw the problem it may have created.

Over the next few years, NZC planned for the 2007 World Cup which was to be staged in the West Indies. This would be the first time the cup would be held in the Caribbean.

I was still involved with selection, but I was now the Selection Manager, with Head Coach John Bracewell now having the final say on all selections.

In February 2006, NZC appointed me as World Cup Project Manager (WCPM). It was my role to coordinate our campaign by liaising with all of NZC's Heads of Departments to ensure that targets and deadline dates were met and the Black Caps had all the tools and resources available to be fully prepared.

Before the tournament started there was lots of scepticism as to whether the West Indian islands and different countries were capable of staging a world event. Trying to coordinate this tournament would never be easy. As the tournament progressed, there were problems, one after the other.

It was a logistical nightmare especially for tourists getting from island to island; high ticket prices kept locals away from the grounds — games were initially played in near empty stadiums — tourists were fleeced by profiteers with high travel, accommodation and ticket prices; the decision makers banned the calypso bands at the grounds (this was something that people wanted to see and be part of because this was what West Indian cricket was all about in providing atmosphere at the grounds); some of the new stadiums built in the islands were located outside the city, sometimes in remote areas, therefore making travel and travel times more difficult. There were security issues highlighted by the tragic and untimely death of the Pakistan coach, Bob Woolmer. Suspicion still surrounds how he died — was it of natural causes or murder?

Our build-up for the campaign was very good. We had two NZ A teams playing some tough cricket in Australia against Australian, Pakistan and Indian A teams. This ensured that players in line for final World Cup selection had a chance to impress and show they were in form.

The Black caps performed impressively against Australia in New Zealand to win the Chappell-Hadlee series 3/0.

We selected the team and we had the players we wanted who were in form, fit and ready to go. The management and support staff were experienced and the best available. We had done our scouting in the West Indies and believed we had the knowledge and contingency plans in place to counter any problem that may have arisen. As WCPM, I was very pleased with our overall preparation and there was an air of optimism and confidence that this was going to be our time. However, I was somewhat surprised and disappointed not to be asked to go to the West Indies in my role both as a selector and WCPM — somehow, it did not make sense, especially with the investment already made in our campaign both financially and in manpower.

The tournament started very well for us — we had a great draw in the preliminary rounds and easily dispatched England, Kenya and Canada to comfortably qualify for the Super Eight rounds. Wins over the West Indies, Bangladesh and Ireland meant we had won nine matches on the trot including the games in the Chappell-Hadlee series — we were on a roll. Sri Lanka then beat us, we knocked over South Africa and then lost to

Australia, but we had done enough to qualify for our fifth semi-final.

The loss to Australia came at a bad time. Bond needed a rest and Oram had a heel problem and needed a break. We suffered our worst ever losing margin in a one-day match — a loss by 215 runs. This may have had a detrimental effect on the team; however, in a one off match against Sri Lanka in the looming semi-final, there was still a good chance of winning the match and progressing through to our first ever World Cup final. Again it was not to be. Sri Lanka amassed 290 and at 105/2 we were on target until we lost 5/11 and we lost by 81 runs — it was as though we just gave up, with too many soft dismissals.

Whether it was the occasion, complacency, or the fact that we were just not good enough in tournament play will always be debated. What disappointed me was that we had batsmen and bowlers who were in form and playing well. Styris scored 499 runs at 83.16 with one hundred and four fifties and Fleming, McMillan, Oram and Fulton had all been batting well. Vettori had 16 wickets at 27.93 and Bond had 13 wickets at 16.33, both with excellent economy rates. Oram and Franklin had been doing their jobs well with the ball. We were a very competitive and potentially a dangerous team to play against.

We cannot offer any excuses for our exit from the tournament. We quite frankly blew it — our destiny was in our own hands and players did not perform when it mattered; they cannot blame anyone except themselves.

Reviews will highlight some issues. In reality, we had it all too easy in the early and middle rounds of the tournament. We were winning comfortably and we were not challenged until we struck stronger teams in Sri Lanka (twice) and Australia who beat us easily. Those losses exposed how vulnerable we were against better teams.

Injuries to Vincent, Oram, Taylor, Tuffey and Gillespie (who had a virus that restricted his appearances and performances) were unhelpful. Bowling at the death hurt us badly against Sri Lanka in the semi-final — we were just not accurate enough in our execution and we lacked precision.

It was later felt by those who were on tour that the 'occasion' and distractions with injuries, the toss, performances by our opponents, umpiring decisions and huge downtime between matches that created boredom exposed our inability to handle the big match when it arose. All I can say is why does this have to happen time and time again?

While we finished a creditable third in the tournament, we played to the level of our current world ranking — third. Some players appeared to be happy with that, and felt that they had not failed. For me, with all resources and planning, we had failed. Surely our goal was to go further than we had ever done before and make the final — at least, that would have been success.

In controversial circumstances, Australia went on to win the World Cup against Sri Lanka in a rain interrupted match that turned farcical. The umpires eventually decided to recall the players to the field for three more overs despite a minimum 20 overs having already been bowled which constituted a game. The match ended in total darkness with the Sri Lankan batsmen blocking out.

In my view, the final should have had a provision to be played over two days so that both teams could complete the match in fair and equal conditions. After all, the World Cup final is the glamour event of world cricket that is contested every four years — this event ended in a shambles that did the game of cricket a disservice.

NZC now has to plan for 2011. With a new coach who is not a selector, a new support team, new players in the team and on the horizon, a new selection panel and selection policy with the rule of consensus applying — everyone must agree, it is now back to the drawing board.

The High Performance Centre has a great challenge ahead of it to produce quality and better prepared players; the domestic competition needs to be more competitive and stronger; there needs to be greater competition for places in the Black Caps to keep the players honest with their performances; mental preparation is paramount (there should be no room for self doubters); and there needs to be a series of tougher games against higher rated teams prior to a World Cup to harden and condition the team.

NZC has since made some sweeping changes within the organisation.

Some positions were disestablished, other positions were created and some of the staff were no longer required. Many of the coaching and support staff have now moved on. There is no longer a cricket academy. It is still too early to determine whether these changes will make a difference and whether winning the World Cup is attainable or a bridge too far.

One thing is for sure — whilst we can learn from our mistakes, it all comes back to player performance on the day. As professional players who have the best of everything with business class air travel, five-star accommodation, generous pay packets, skilled support staff, video technology to assist their game, they have to be good enough technically, physically, mentally and skill wise so they can adapt to all situations including pitches, opposition, match situations and pressure and accept responsibility to win games when it matters most.

'Team-mates'. We bowled together. Australian fast-bowling legends Dennis Lillee and Jeff Thomson at Lilac Hill, Perth — ACB Chairman's XI vs New Zealand in the mid-1990s. I bowled first change and took 1/18. We won.

With Keith Miller, the Australian legendary
cricket all-rounder.

With Marianne Faithfull, English singing star of the 1960s.

Three Knights at the Wellbeing Charity Match in England. I am with Sir Victor Blank, the host, and media personality Sir David Frost, our wicketkeeper.

With Freddy Trueman (first bowler to capture 300 test wickets) and Colin Ingleby-Mackenzie (former Hampshire captain and President of the MCC).

With England football legend Sir Stanley Matthews, known as the 'wizard of the dribble' and 'the magician'.

With Phil Bennett, Wales and British Lions fly-half rugby player.

Renewing a friendship with Devon Malcolm. He was my last wicket (number 431) lbw 0 at Edgbaston off my last ball in test cricket, 1990.

Great mate and fierce competitor, India's Kapil Dev, who broke my world record and went on to capture 434 test wickets.

With West Indian batting legend Rohan Kanhai at his home in England.

With one of the world's best golfers, South African Ernie Els, in England.

The Nottinghamshire Cricket Knights: with Sir Garfield Sobers. We make regular trips to Trent Bridge to support the club.

In the Long Room at Lord's having a chat with Pakistan fast bowlers Azhar Mahmood and Shoaib Akhtar (sitting) on the eve of the 1999 World Cup final.

My most memorable test wickets: India's Sanjay Manjrekar (400th) and Arun Lal (world record 374th) chatting at McLean Park, Napier.

With West Indian fast bowler Courtney Walsh (first bowler to capture 500 test wickets) and South African batting legend Barry Richards.

Trans-Tasman rivals at golf in Australia. Former Australian cricketers Doug Walters and Jeff Thomson, All Black great Colin Meads and Commonwealth games athlete and gold medallist, Dick Tayler.

Headlines and Bylines

Who would want to be a sportsperson in New Zealand? Sometimes it seems that the only way the media and public can be happy is for our national sportspeople and teams to win every match, every series and constantly be world champions! As much as we would like to win all the time, the reality is that life is not like that. There are times when we have to say that we are not good enough and acknowledge the opposition by saying that they were better than we were and deserved their success on that occasion. Of course, New Zealand has in fact produced many world champions, gold medallists and world record holders — we have a proud sporting history — but it appears that a very demanding media and public will never be satisfied and they will always want more, no matter what happens.

The public also expect, in fact almost demand, to hear from sportspeople and from those in decision-making positions. Interviews can help the profile of a sport, and can help the public understand the rationale behind the decisions made and how people feel when they succeed or fail. But players, coaches and administrators don't always have the time for every request for an interview, and in the absence of information there are media who are quite content with speculation. As a player and as a selector I found the media played a major role both for good and bad; there were respected reporters and others I felt had questionable ethics and no credibility.

I believe that at times the media distorted the truth. As the saying goes: 'Never let the truth get in the way of a good story.' Reporting the facts is fine, having an opinion is fine, provided that the story is true and the article or the comment is balanced. There will always be sensational headlines to attract a reader to buy a paper or a quote that will attract a listener to the radio or television. After all, it is a reporter's job to dig deep and find an angle that creates interest and reaction. Speculation, however, can be very damaging. It is possible to speculate and be correct, but often such flights of media fancy are proved wrong and as there is a tendency for mud to stick, this invariably damages the person or team who has been attacked. Very rarely would there be a retraction or would a journalist have the decency to say that they were wrong.

After the 2003 World Cup in South Africa, Mark Geenty from NZPA, along with radio commentator Bryan Waddle, requested an interview with me regarding my thoughts on the team's performance. The interview took 20 minutes and went through all the positives and some of the disappointments. Next day the headline read 'Hadlee Criticises Cairns and McMillan'. According to Martin Snedden both Chris Cairns and Craig McMillan were annoyed that I had singled them out. Both players wanted to have a meeting with me and I agreed to meet with them, but, for some reason, the meeting did not happen. I felt that all three of us had suffered from biased reporting here: I certainly hadn't singled out just those two players, and none of the positive aspects of the tour, of which I had noted many in the interview, were mentioned at all.

I had some learning to do about interacting with the media when I first started my position as chairman of selectors. When I had been first appointed, in June 2000, I had been advised by Chris Doig that I had to be available to speak to the media and make comment. But there had been little support and few guidelines from NZC regarding the media for the first six months I was in the role. There were times when I did not want to speak to the media, but I was under instructions to do so. I was left to do what I thought was right, with the best interests of NZC at heart.

Six months into my new role, there were obvious problems and differences with Richard Boock and the *New Zealand Herald*, and it was clear to NZC that my media relation skills needed some fine-tuning. In 2001 I was asked to attend a meeting with Michele Lewis, NZC Media Relations Manager. I believed that I had been somewhat left to flounder in my role as chairman of selectors and, according to Michele, from the NZC perspective I was making comment on all sorts of things that I should not have made. She pointed out that one minute I was talking to the media on all issues, and the next, I wasn't talking at all. It was suggested that I stop reacting and not allow myself to be distracted by the sledging.

Michele felt that I needed to learn to say nothing nicely, learn to buy time, know my agenda and learn to deliver my own message. Most importantly I needed to be aware of my own boundaries and talk about selection issues and not about the Academy and other departments within NZC.

There were five non-negotiables that NZC wanted me to come to terms with — never criticise the players publicly, never criticise the previous panel of selectors and coach, never contradict the captain and the coach publicly, never question team management or tactics publicly, never talk about your salary and do not compare past eras, as this was perceived as being arrogant. It did not leave me with too many things to actually talk about!

At least we addressed the issues and with a much clearer idea of my role in relation to the media I settled more into the role as a selector, and although there were problems from time to time, media relations improved out of sight in most areas.

I had a reasonably honest and open relationship with sports journalists Jonathan Millmow, Geoff Longley, Peter Bidwell, Lynn McConnell, Mark Geenty and Duncan Johnstone. *Talk Sport* hosts Brendan Telfer, Martin Devlin, Graham Hill and Murray Deaker challenged me on many occasions and I had no problem with that. At least they were all courteous and respectful, and they gave me time to answer the question without butting in. They got answers to their questions that may have satisfied their curiosity and then the public debates and the reactions would start. The hosts may not have agreed with me but at least they were happy that I had given them the time to clarify many situations.

But it did not take long to realise that there was a pattern to Richard Boock's attacks. The article that he produced following an interview in 2000 was headlined 'NZC paddles in untried waters' and had no reference whatsoever to the questions that had been asked and the answers that had been given. To this day, I cannot work out why he bothered to interview me. The article was a personal attack on my character and the start of a series of negative comments about my performance as a selector that continued for the next four years.

There was a smugness and flippancy to Boock's articles, as though he was out to get me for some reason. He had the power of the media on his side and it appeared to me that he was using it to his advantage: to get better ratings and circulation for the paper and perhaps to somehow enhance his reputation as a journalist. But all this came at other people's expense. The following quote from that first article illustrates what I mean.

Never mind the King inquiry, one of the biggest gambles in cricket occurred much closer to home this week. The appointment of Sir Richard Hadlee as the New Zealand convener of selectors was notable not only for the great player's return to international cricket, but also for the astonishing lack of experience he brings to the chair. The ultimate decision-making will be left in the hands of a man who — brilliant though he may have been as a player — has yet to coach or select any representative team at any level. In fact, even as a dynamic fast bowler through the 1980s, Hadlee was seldom offered the captaincy of the national side, partly because of fears he would struggle to cope, and partly because of fears the rest of the team would.

Boock had every right to scrutinise my credentials. He would have been failing in his duty as a professional journalist if he had not, but this went beyond examining my background to being a personal attack on my character. He was saying things that were patently inaccurate, or that he had heard from various, unnamed sources, possibly including players that I had played with '*partly because of fears he would struggle to cope, and partly because of fears the rest of the team would*. It was the start of things to come and it made me begin to suspect that there had to be more to this than met the eye.

Following that initial negative article, Boock and other writers in the *New Zealand Herald* sensationalised more and more articles and kept attacking me at every opportunity. Other journalists had their say and I accepted their criticisms, mainly because they had balanced views. I had very few issues with other reporters, but Boock and the *New Zealand Herald* continued to be negative. I got the impression that he was writing his articles with no feeling for how people felt — perhaps it simply did not matter to him.

Within the first six or seven months of my appointment the relationship between us had deteriorated so much that NZC, who were well aware of the problem and very concerned, thought it was a good idea for both of us to meet with John Knowles, the NZC media relations officer, to see if we could somehow improve things. John was a former TVNZ man who had a wonderful knowledge of sports and people in sport. He was aware of many sporting issues and agendas that people had and how the journalistic business operated. The meeting was organised for 1 November 2000.

The meeting between Boock, John Knowles and myself duly took place. I was playing in a corporate cricket match for the Bank of New Zealand but had a few minutes available to try and address the issues. When I saw Boock, we shook hands. It looked as though we may be able to find some common ground, but the meeting quickly turned hostile, with no inch given by Boock or by myself. Boock was very aggressive and I reacted accordingly, even using a few adjectives. We were getting nowhere very fast. I asked why he took the view he had and whether we had any problems. He said: 'I have been bagging you and the selectors for three months . . . It is my job to report, not to support.' At the time, that comment was the only thing that he and I could agree on. Within minutes the meeting ended and we had achieved nothing. Indeed, the war of words had only just started and would continue for years to come.

It had been clear that our meeting had solved nothing and there were soon further personal attacks from the *Herald*. In January 2001, Don Cameron crossed the line when he wrote: 'There is increasingly strong evidence during the early days of the Zimbabwe tour that the lunatics are taking over the running of the New Zealand cricket asylum' and 'They [Zimbabwe] might be used to this condescension, but not from people in long white coats.' Although it did not state it explicitly, the article appeared to single me out and there was a strong inference that I was the 'lunatic' running New Zealand Cricket's 'asylum'. The dictionary meaning of 'lunatic' suggests that Cameron considered me crazy, mad, harebrained or foolish. To me, this was character assassination, pure and simple. The Hadlee name, my professionalism and my role as chairman of selectors was being strongly questioned, and there was a clear suggestion that I was mentally unstable and therefore unfit for the job.

The *New Zealand Herald* decided that I was a fair target, yet again, during the World Cup in 2003. They could not resist it. One of their writers, Chris Rattue, wrote a scathing and ill-informed article criticising me for talking to Bryan Waddle, the radio cricket commentator, about players and their form when I was in South Africa. It had become well known that I sought the opinions of Ian Smith and Bryan Waddle on selection issues. I had actually done this for three years. In fact, I had also consulted many other people to canvass their thoughts. This was not just a whim or a spur of the moment thing.

One of the selectors' philosophies was to seek opinions from those people who were involved in the game. There were many people who had either played or been involved in the game for a long time whose opinions were valued. It was not unusual for me to ask former players Ian Smith, Jeremy Coney, Martin Crowe and others for their opinions. I would sometimes even ask the print media who they would select. This would sometimes give me other ideas to take to the selection meeting to discuss so that we would come up with informed decisions. Maybe there was a thought or two that we had not considered. This approach was really just common sense: we needed as much information as possible.

Bryan Waddle had been to over one hundred tests and seen many more one-day internationals. He had watched many balls bowled and played at, many players, many match situations, and some great New Zealand victories in New Zealand and all over the world. He had worked with many knowledgeable ex-players who had provided commentary alongside him in the box. In short, he has a wealth of knowledge, and has the ability to read the game and make sound assessments of many situations. I also value him as a friend and had sought his comments on numerous occasions, based on the experience he had in the game. Surely he had something special, and perhaps different, to offer for consideration.

The slurs regarding my mental abilities were still to be found in reports made during the 2003 World Cup in South Africa. While we were at Bloemfontein in March to prepare for the match against Zimbabwe, I mentioned to Boock, who wanted an interview, that this was the best one-day team New Zealand had ever had. Boock wrote a nice article, in which he said: 'There is no doubt that this is the best side we have had, certainly in my experience. It's a complete team and Stephen Fleming has options to burn — whereas three years ago he did not even know some of the players. It is a beautifully balanced side, probably better balanced than any other team in the competition.' The team had just won its last four games at the World Cup and had also won 10 of the last 13 matches it had played, so clearly it was difficult to criticise selections or performances. We went on to defeat Zimbabwe, meaning that a win over either Australia or India would give us a semi-final place. Five wins in a row gave us all some confidence and some hope that maybe we would be able to go all the way.

Nine days later, after we had lost to Australia and India and were out of the World Cup, Boock's tune had changed: 'If this was the best New Zealand one-day side then it was also the country's most shambolic World Cup campaign, featuring a selection panel that came straight from the Sybil school of multiple personalities. Only a week after being lauded as the "best ever" by chairman of selectors Sir Richard Hadlee, the New Zealand team was reflecting on one of the country's worst tournament records...' The article continued, saying: 'New Zealand were hamstrung by a series of witless selections... the side might have been better selected from a hat — at least then there would have been a slender chance of getting it right . . . If this was representative of the new initiative to have the panel's chairman operating on tour, then the sooner New Zealand Cricket fit an ankle bracelet to Hadlee and place him on home detention the better . . . While some individuals were still able to shine, there was little sign of collective poise. But, given the destabilising influence of the selections, it was hardly surprising.'

This was severe criticism indeed, with several personal attacks. I felt let down by Boock and felt he had taken one position in the original story and then chosen to come from another angle when it suited. As selectors, one day we would be on a high, and a day or two later we could be on a real low and feel the full force of the media — at times, this was very difficult to accept and also very unfair.

Another recurring tactic used by Boock and the *Herald* was to state that the selection decisions were mine alone and were made more or less on a whim. Headlines such as 'General Hadlee's flawed strategy' were sensational and implied that no one else on the selection panel made decisions. This, I felt, was not only factually incorrect but also demeaning for the other selectors on the panel. Articles talked of 'the heavily bemedalled one . . . so far the number of players Hadlee has selected . . . is approaching 30.' Another article referred to my 'lone ranger style' as convener of the selection panel, which was more baseless nonsense.

I had often wondered about the *New Zealand Herald*'s motives for what were, in my view, continued negative attacks on me. I suspected that they wanted to get back at me because of a legal case I had taken against them during the late 1980s and won. Don Cameron, the *New Zealand Herald* sports journalist, had written an article that had cost them an out-of-court settlement and an apology.

All I wanted from the *New Zealand Herald* and Cameron was an apology and a retraction, but they refused to do so, with the *New Zealand Herald* saying that they supported Cameron's article. That left me with no alternative but to pursue legal action. They had paid for their mistake. Was this now payback time?

Another small goad to the *New Zealand Herald* was that I wrote a newspaper column for a competing newspaper, the *Sunday Star-Times*. The *Herald* clearly disapproved of this, arguing that there was some sort of conflict of interests involved, and their disapproval was confirmed in a letter dated 31 October 2000 from the editor, Stephen Davis. It became an irritation to them and they complained about my articles. I questioned their motives and ethical right to do that. My writings in the *Sunday Star-Times* had been approved by NZC. I had written articles for six or seven years.

To be balanced, I have to give Richard Boock some credit. There were times when his writings were quite witty, and although he had the ability to be critical, he could also acknowledge that he may have made a mistake or two. Maybe he had mellowed. In an article highlighting the success story of Ian Butler's first five-wicket bag in test cricket (when he took six wickets against Pakistan at Wellington) Boock wrote: 'It's easy to see why Sir Richard Hadlee was so excited about the prospect of Ian Butler and Shane Bond spearheading New Zealand's future bowling attack. If New Zealand's greatest fast bowler was beside himself after discovering Shane Bond three years ago, he was almost ready to donate his memorabilia to charity after finding Butler in 2001/02, at which point he predicted happy times ahead for the national team. And, as always, Sir Richard was right.' And earlier, when writing about Hamish Marshall, he wrote what was almost an apology.

I accept that everyone has the right to express an opinion. Life would be very boring if we all thought and did the same things. I enjoy being challenged and if I am proved to be wrong, then so be it. I'll learn from that. But I take great pride in what I do and how I do it, and over the years I have enjoyed a fair amount of success.

There is no doubt at all that over my four-year period as chairman of selectors, there was a series of attacks on me by Richard Boock and the *New Zealand Herald*. The selectors were very concerned at the amount of ill-informed and speculative comment that appeared in the paper on a regular basis. A lot of comment had no substance, with many comments and articles being factually incorrect. Although I was interviewed on a handful of occasions, there was a general failure to ask questions. Boock apologised for the content of the odd article and there was feedback from other people that at times Boock felt embarrassed and that he had gone over the top. But the general theme of Boock's articles was negative and destructive and I felt victimised by his regular barbed and sniping comments. I don't think much of that sort of journalism, it hardly warrants the term in fact, and I think that if Richard Boock was prepared to criticise the selectors, players, captain, NZC and me personally in the public domain as often as he did, then he will have to accept criticism from others and also be challenged.

A Reason to Believe

My taste in music never sat comfortably with some of my team-mates, but I loved listening to songs that had nice harmony and good instrumental backing. The Carpenters and, later, folk singers Peter, Paul and Mary, among others, recorded a song (originally by folk singer Tim Hardin) called 'Reason to Believe'. That little phrase was integral to my success: I had reasons for doing what I did. I was a highly motivated sportsperson and I have to thank my primary and secondary school days for that. In those days, teachers were actively involved as coaches or managers and they took a great interest and pride in their teams' and individual performances. Today, although some teachers are still very involved in coaching and mentoring, there are many who haven't got the time to be involved in sports because of increased workloads in other areas. It would be fair to say that many teachers do not have the interest or the skills in their delegated sport or want to be involved anyway. Today it is increasingly up to sporting bodies, local associations, clubs and parents to get involved in coaching school teams and individual athletes.

During the 1960s the New Zealand education system rewarded ability, effort and success with a School Certificate of achievement. The average student had to work hard to pass exams. Everyone had to work hard to pass their School Certificate or gain their University Entrance. Today, it seems to me that nearly everyone passes. It all seems too easy, and we are becoming a soft nation. It is as though there are no losers, and mediocrity, which is second rate, is rewarded. I have always believed that schools should prepare students for the outside world. When students leave school they enter a very competitive environment and therefore they need to have experienced competition in the classroom and on the sports field. Classroom placings in exams were a true indicator of where I was at and what I needed to do to get to the top in a subject. Very rarely did that happen, but on the sports field it was a different matter, because I knew that I had some skills and a love for sport that gave me a better opportunity and chance of finishing near the top.

In those days school sport was compulsory. Every student had to play some sort of sport whether he was talented or not, whether he could play sport or couldn't, whether he liked to or didn't, or whether he had a physical handicap or not. If the student wanted to be excused from training or a match for some obscure reason, he needed to have a letter from his parents or a doctor. They were tough days.

I was often inspired by a slightly overweight and physically handicapped athlete who competed year in and year out in the school 100-yard dash. He would always finish last, but that did not matter. Parents, teachers and students alike understood what this boy was going through and what he was trying to achieve. With tears in their eyes, everyone would stand and applaud as they spurred him on to finish the race some 10 or more seconds behind the rest. Winning for him was getting past the post and finishing the race. He always had a smile on his face and when he passed the finishing line his arms were upraised as though he had won. He had given his best and achieved one small goal that was appreciated by so many. Even the winners acknowledged his competitive spirit as they congratulated him for finishing. They admired his attitude and knew that he was not embarrassed or ashamed of competing in a league beyond his means. In my view, this person was a real winner and a hero and an inspiration for many students.

Sport taught me a great deal. I learned more about myself and other people by competing in a sport than I ever did in a classroom. I learned how to win and how to lose. The best way to learn was by making mistakes and finding that failure was not a nice option. There were emotions of joy, but also of heartbreak, frustration, disappointment and failure. I enjoyed success, but I accepted defeat graciously and applauded the winners. I found out what I had to do to get better. I had a very simple philosophy — every day that I missed training, it would take me a day longer to improve, and I knew that if I perfected my skill, there was a very good chance that I would be selected in sporting teams.

Sport rewarded my success, it taught me to be competitive and that winning was important. To be part of just fun, fair play and participation — very much the catch phrase today — was not good enough for me. I wanted to know whether the team I played in had won or not, and whether as an individual I had failed or succeeded.

Some years ago Netball New Zealand made a decision not to tell their young netballers the results of their games. I found that extraordinary, although typical of the attitude that the result of the match was not important and everyone was a winner. With that approach there is a great danger that an individual with exceptional ability won't be recognised and won't be inspired to progress; they may even give the game away at an early age through disillusionment and frustration. And in fact the greatest problem and challenge sports face today is retaining 16- to 18-year-olds.

Sport taught me how to be a team player — to encourage the team to perform and acknowledge the team contributions — but it also taught me to recognise individual talent. It helped me develop self-belief and confidence, even though there were times of self-doubt. I also learned how to prepare physically, technically and mentally. All these things made me a better person because I was doing something with my life instead of drifting aimlessly through the days and years with little to show for it. Achieving goals was a significant motivating force in my life.

Motivation runs hot and cold. One minute I was focused and on track but there were other times when I became distracted and lost direction. Motivation is a bit like having a hot bath: when I was in it, I had a warm and fuzzy feeling, I felt good, I was relaxed and everything that I was doing gave me pleasure. I soon realised that the longer I stayed in the bath, the colder it became — motivation would ebb away if I was just doing the same old thing every day — and the more uncomfortable I felt. But I knew that all I needed to do was to turn the hot tap on again — find something that motivated me — and I would feel good again. I needed a hot tap or a mechanism to keep warming me up and keep me focused — and setting and achieving goals was the simple solution. I needed to maximise the skills, the talents and the abilities I had been given to reach my goals. I was motivated to be the best I could be. My most important motivating factor was pride in my own performance and doing the best I could on the day. Pride is about developing, maintaining and enhancing a performance so that fellow team-mates respect what you can do. It is doing the best you can on the day.

I had great pride in representing New Zealand. I wanted to do well and leave the playing arena with my reputation intact, knowing that I had given my best. I knew that if I wanted to be successful, I needed to be fit, have an efficient bowling technique, compete, make the most of opportunities, have belief in my ability, work hard on my skills and get the best out of myself. Anything less would not be good enough. I was motivated by setting and achieving goals and I was determined to prove a point, even if I was criticised and my professionalism was questioned. I was driven by emotion and statistics, and I enjoyed the rewards of success. I believed that if I worked hard enough, the results would come and I would have deserved them.

In New Zealand we appear to have a mentality that only lets us enjoy successful sporting achievements briefly before we pull the sportsperson involved back into line — the 'tall poppy' syndrome. Private lives are exposed to the point where severe damage is done to relationships and one's public credibility is challenged, yet we still admire performances on the field of play. I never understood that, because countries and people need to have role models and heroes to look up to so that they themselves can aspire to greater heights. The media and general public can be very critical and destructive, and I have often wondered if it is an attitude that stems from jealousy.

I also see too many of our sportspeople given praise and then hear them almost make apologies for their success. They tend to downplay their performances. I believe that if someone has excelled, they should accept the compliments by saying: 'Thank you. Yes, I have worked hard for my success and I am going to enjoy the moment.' Unfortunately, that attitude is perceived as arrogance.

In October 2006 I was asked to have lunch with the Kiwi rugby league team prior to a test match against Great Britain and say a few words on what it meant for me to play for my country. I said: 'I value my test playing cap because it was earned; it symbolised the past and it was our future. Every time I played there was a responsibility to play well and do my best. I believed in playing the moment and seizing the opportunity and not worrying about the scoreboard or the time. Execute the skill well and the score will take care of it itself. Complacency and comfort zones are unacceptable at international level — any sportsperson who thinks things are easy will be at their most vulnerable because they are not expecting the unexpected.'

Competition often brought the best out of me, especially when I was confronted with my opponent — I had to beat him, get him out, score runs off his bowling. There were times when I was annoyed, when my professionalism was questioned, especially by the media, so I was determined to prove that the decisions I had made were right. Statistics and records got me focused and the rewards of success were very satisfying. Sometimes emotion drove me, especially if friends and family were watching a match on live television while I was overseas — I did not want to let them down. Various role models within the game lifted me because I could ask questions and learn from their experiences both on and off the field.

I carried a mantra in my cricket coffin (gearbag) with key words as a reminder of what I had to do. I often visualised my future successes by placing myself in the situation when I last did it — what were the factors that enabled me to do that? When I was next playing in the middle I felt comfortable in the environment — I was not overawed or a stranger.

I was driven by setting and achieving goals — small targets (wicket by wicket) that would build up to the ultimate prize, which for me was becoming the first bowler in the history of test cricket to capture 400 test wickets. It took 18 years to achieve that goal and I felt proud to have done so. Along the way, I learned that goal-setting needed three basic ingredients, known as the three 'I's'. There needed to be *inspiration* or a reason for doing something; there needed to be *innovation* and finding other ways of training to prevent boredom but that still allowed me to develop my skills; and there needed to be a way of measuring *improvement*. For me, results on the field of play and in the scorebook were an easy way of measuring that.

By setting and achieving goals, I was able to get the best out of myself. I was not prepared to settle for mediocrity, even though I was realistic enough to know that I would have an off day every now and again. The body is not a machine and sometimes it breaks down and does not work as efficiently as one would like. It is strange really — a sportsperson prepares for a big event and does all that is required to try and produce the desired result but on some days the body is on a different journey and the performance is left wanting. Some people say that you are only as good as your last performance. I would venture to say that you are as good as your next performance.

The key thing I learned from setting and achieving goals was that I could go beyond what I thought I was capable of. There were times when I was guilty of complacency and expected things to happen. While I was in these comfort zones I was vulnerable and would make mistakes and the opposition exposed and exploited those weaknesses. I learned from that. I had to address that situation very quickly or I would have more disappointments and that would always have a negative effect.

Other people inspired me. One person I found very inspirational was the musician John Denver. He wanted to change the world and make a difference. He loved the environment — the mountains, the rivers, the forests — and he wanted to protect Mother Nature and the universe. The words from his song, 'The Eagle and the Hawk', summed up my feelings about striving to better myself and the world around me.

Come dance with the west wind and touch on the mountain tops
Sail over the canyons and up to the stars
And reach for the heavens and hope for the future
And all that we can be, not what we are.

I have the greatest admiration for Australian sportspeople. For a nation of 20 million people, their sporting record is outstanding. They are the world champions in test and one-day cricket and rugby league, they have been world champions in rugby and netball, and they have produced many world champions and gold medallists in a number of different sports.

The Aussies know how to compete and win. In netball they play for 60 minutes, in rugby and in league they play for the full 80 minutes. They know how to win tight matches, pinch the game in the dying seconds, often sparked by a piece of individual brilliance. It is as though they expect to win in almost hopeless situations. In 2003, an understrength Kangaroos rugby league team were 2-nil up in the series and playing Great Britain in the third and final test in England. A win would give them a clean sweep of the series, repeating the feat of the 'Invincibles' in 1986. With three minutes remaining, the Kangaroos were six points down and needed to score twice to win the match. I was thinking at the time that they could still win the match — I have seen too many Australian sports teams in similar situations before — and clearly they were thinking the same thing. Their captain, Darren Lockyer, ignited the team and they scored two tries to win the game and become known as the 'Improbables', etching their names into history forever.

In cricket they would look to dominate the opposition as soon as possible and wear them down. They had a physical presence and they intimidated us. I learned so much by playing against Ian Chappell's Australian cricket team in the early to mid-1970s. New Zealand's test record at that time was poor — test wins were as scarce as hens' teeth. They had all the star players, including Greg Chappell, Keith Stackpole, Ian Redpath, Doug Walters and Rod Marsh — all very hardened, determined and successful cricketers — and we were their poor relations. We were overawed, lacked confidence and played second fiddle to them time and time again. We were just the opposition that allowed them to get cheap wickets and score big runs to help their averages.

When we were in a position to put pressure on, we did not know how to win. We were verbally abused or sledged and felt very uncomfortable playing against them. It was clear what we had to do — take it on the cheek, front up and take the game to them, give a little bit of verbal back and compete, otherwise we would be walked over every time we played them. We won our first ever test against Australia at Lancaster Park, Christchurch in 1974 — that was a great game to remember: Glenn Turner scored a century in each innings and I took seven wickets in the match.

Peter FitzSimons, a former Wallaby rugby lock and humourist, has written some very entertaining articles about his much beloved nation and their sports heroes. He loves the underdog tag. He wrote an article that contained an anecdote about the Australian cricket captain Steve Waugh, who was going through some tough times. Waugh had been dropped from the one-day team and although he was still captaining the test team his indifferent form had many pundits suggesting that he should be dropped, thereby ending his career.

The Aussies were playing England at the SCG and Waugh had struck some good form and had the England fielders chasing leather all day. Finally, it came to the last ball of the day. Waugh was facing on 98 not out, searching for another test hundred to silence the critics.

Former Australian leg-spin bowler Kerry O'Keeffe and former England pace bowler Jonathan Agnew were both in the commentary box. According to FitzSimons the commentary went something like this.

Agnew: 'Well, it is high drama we have here. Kerry, what will he do?'

O'Keeffe: 'He will go for it.'

Agnew: 'But he could come back tomorrow and wait for a trundler to go down the leg side.'

O'Keeffe: 'Stuff tomorrow, Aggers, tomorrow is for silver medallists. We're Australians. Poms come back tomorrow. Australians only want gold and we want it now.' Whereupon Waugh sent the final delivery through the covers for four and guaranteed sporting immortality.

I get the impression that if a Kiwi was in a similar situation, he would take the conservative approach and wait for the next day like the English would. We would be satisfied in giving it another go tomorrow whereas the Aussie would make it happen today. They would take it to the opposition, and if they lost, it was not for the want of trying. If they lost, they would settle the score in another encounter.

Words will often change our lives. Whatever people say can have a lasting effect on us. All too often we hear people say, 'You are not good enough', 'You'll never be able to do that and things are tough out there'. It would be quite pleasing to hear people say, 'You have the ability', 'You can do better than that', 'There is plenty of opportunity out there'. The latter expressions are more positive and helpful than the former, which are destructive and counterproductive.

I once heard some inspirational words from Dame Susan Devoy, New Zealand's squash champion. She won four world titles and she was eight times British Open Champion. She said that she made a lot of sacrifices during her career to be the best she could be. She said that she would be up at 5.00 am training in wind, rain, hail or snow. 'Every time I was doing that, I knew my competitors were still in bed. When I faced them on the squash court, I knew I had a big advantage, mentally and physically, over them because I had prepared better than them.'

How right she was. I just wonder how many of our aspiring young athletes have heard such profound words from the likes of Susan and some of our greatest athletes, Peter Snell (New Zealand Sportsperson of the Twentieth Century) and John Walker. They all had one thing in common — they did the hard yards. It doesn't take much to get a pair shorts, put on a vest and a pair of running shoes and run and run to harden your body — and your mind.

I frequently reminded myself that if I wanted to succeed I needed to be proactive and would use some little sayings to keep me focused on this:

'Winners know a goal is worthy because of the effort that is required to achieve it.'

'Winners do not blame fate for their failures nor luck for their successes.'

'Winners make it happen where losers let it happen.'

'Winners see rainbows where losers see thunderstorms.'

'Winners see choices where losers take chances.'

'It is important to look forward and not backwards. Airplanes do not have rear vision mirrors.'

I believe that my sporting career successes happened because I was professional. The term, 'professionalism' relates to all sports and businesses. Both have common key thoughts. Professionalism is not necessarily about money, although when I was paid to do a job, money was the end result of my efforts. Professionalism is about conforming to the technical and the ethical standards of our work. There are rules, laws and expectations. There is a right way of doing things. If I could get my priorities right and perform, the rewards and the money would automatically follow and take care of themselves. There were many non-negotiable things that I had to do if I wanted to be successful. For me it meant the total package entailed by the word 'professionalism'. It is made up of many different components and it is important that all are working in the same direction and complement each other.

Set high standards: This means for everything, including dress requirements, being on time, looking the part, practising to correct mistakes and doing the fitness work. Taking short cuts will come back to haunt you one day.

Accept responsibility: You must be accountable for your own performances. There will be times when you are on your own and only you can do it — there are no excuses. And if you fail, don't blame the opposition but look to your own performance.

Gain more knowledge: It is essential to be better informed — you must research, read, watch videos and ask questions about the game. The game has a lot of history, tradition and values. Sir Donald Bradman once said: 'We are all custodians of the game.' It is your responsibility to be the game's caretaker while you play it, so look after and respect the game. Never be afraid to learn from history. Great players do the ordinary things very well, and then produce the extraordinary when it is needed.

Accept the challenges: Challenges are never meant to be easy. If it was easy everyone would be doing it. Having an attitude of 'Yes, I can do it' will go a long way towards having success on the field. Accept the big challenges and set yourself apart from the others.

Solve problems: There will be times of non-performance, failure, poor technique, self-doubt, mistakes, injury and frustration. There needs to be a structure in place to cope with these problems. Ask for advice from specialists in other areas. More often than not it is getting back to the basics and doing the simple things well that gives you a base to work from.

Plot and plan your own path to success: Have realistic goals. To remain focused and maintain a sense of progress you need to have specific, achieveable goals — one step at a time. Sir Edmund Hillary conquered Mount Everest by taking many small steps to get to the top — not one giant leap. And if you are not reaching your goals, do not be afraid to reassess them — over-optimistic goals can cause stress that will lead to distress and worry.

Make sacrifices: What are you prepared to give up to reach your goal? Are you prepared to make changes in your lifestyle by giving up smoking, alcohol or spending too much time with your mates? There may be times when family and relationships suffer in pursuit of reaching your goals. You need to be very single-minded and perhaps there will be times when you need to be selfish. But be brave and make the right decisions that will define your career, future and, perhaps, immortality.

Have a real desire to succeed: Be hungry to achieve. You must really want what you are after and remain positive. Motivation is about having the ability to stay focused and keep going.

Be a consistent and a reliable performer: Consistency and reliability are the hallmarks of professionalism. An amateur is generally very inconsistent and erratic. Professionals back up their performances day after day after day. They know what they have to do to prepare and are more likely to implement the game plan and achieve their goals because they have the time and the energy to do it. Playing professional cricket in England for Nottinghamshire between 1978 and 1987 was an important experience for me: it made me a more consistent and reliable performer because I had to establish good habits, disciplines and routines. In simple terms, 'Proper preparation prevents poor performance.'

Make the most of opportunities: Realise when an opportunity presents itself, seize the moment and 'cash in'. My brother Dayle accidentally damaged his toe when it was caught in a lawn mower. He was unable to play the remaining three first-class matches of that season. I was his replacement and that opportunity gave me my first big break to play first-class cricket. If it had not been for that unfortunate injury, who knows when the next opportunity would have arisen?

Have confidence in your ability: Back yourself in any given situation. Confidence breeds success, whereas a lack of confidence leads to excuses and failure. Jack Nicklaus, the famous golfer who won 18 major tournaments, was once asked:

'What do you concentrate on when you are putting the ball?'
'The ball is in the hole.'
'But you missed.'
'Yes, I did. But next time, the ball is in the hole.'

The ball eventually goes in the hole, the task is completed, the job is done.

Maximise your skills, talents and abilities: Get the best out of yourself. We all have these skills, maybe at different levels, but it is important to practise to improve and to get the best out of what we have. The key is repetition. Repeat the skill again and again until it is perfected. And when the skill is perfected, don't stop but keep doing it again and again until you become clinical. Try to be innovative in your training routines and techniques to avoid boredom. I bowled over 83,000 deliveries during my first-class and international career — and the more I bowled, the more I gained confidence in my ability and the better I became. Some people said that at times I was a lucky cricketer. It is strange how the harder I trained, the luckier I became!

Pride in your performance: Dad's advice was: 'Whatever you do, take pride in your performance by doing it to the best of your ability. Be happy with your performance, even if someone does it better.' You can only give 100 per cent — anything less creates mediocrity, and mediocrity is second rate and second rate is not good enough.

Mental toughness: Have the ability to produce the desired result when everything is against you. When you are finding it all too easy and it is difficult to remain focused don't give it away. Cash in and take advantage of an opportunity. This is all about the 'dig deep' theory — to keep going when it is too tough and to stay focused when it is too easy. The Australians, more than any other cricket team, have this ability to keep performing and winning in most conditions and situations. There was a story about Australian cricketer Dean Jones. He was playing in India on one of those days where the heat and humidity were punishing and after having been in the middle, under a pitiless sun, for some time, he began suffering quite severely from dehydration. Deano was on 70-odd when he told his captain, Allan Border, that he needed to rest. Border said: 'That's fine Deano. When you get back to the pavilion, will you send out a real Australian to bat?' Jones stood his ground and went on to complete a double century.

Have a role model to look up to: It helps to have someone who has 'been there, done that', set the standard and is respected, to focus on. Knowing what they have done will help motivate you to lift your performance. Try to emulate, if not better, those performances. Dennis Lillee was very influential in the development of my career in this regard.

Above all — enjoy what you are doing: Some professional cricketers consider playing cricket to be just a job, they turn up and go through the motions, and if they fail there is another day tomorrow and they give the impression of not enjoying it. So why bother? Play your sport for the right reason: because you want to do it more than anything else. That way you will get some fulfilment and satisfaction.

Professionalism is about the eight Ps: Preparing, Practising, Planning, Playing, Performing, Persisting, Patience and Pay packet. Get the first seven in the right order, and the last one will be there.

Where to Now?

In an ideal world I believe that all cricketers should be indoctrinated with the following quote and play the game accordingly. It should be cricket's oath of allegiance. This is an extract from a letter about the game of cricket from Lord Harris to *The Times* (3 February 1931).

'. . . you will do well to love it for it is more free from anything sordid, anything dishonorable, than any game in the world. To play it keenly, honourably, generously, self-sacrificingly is a moral lesson in itself, and the classroom is God's air and sunshine. Foster it, my brothers, so that it may attract all who can find the time to play it: protect it from anything that would sully it, so that it may grow in favour with all men.'

The game, of course, has moved on and professionalism has taken over and attitudes have changed with so much money now at stake.

Sportsmanship

Having been raised in a family that respects values, history and tradition, sportsmanship is a very big part of my life. We were taught to play hard, give our best and play the game in the spirit in which it was meant to be played. Sportsmanship is based around accepting decisions, acknowledging someone else's success and knowing that you have played fair and within the rules of the game. However, I would venture to say that, at one time or another during their career, all cricketers would have tried to make the most of a situation that went in their favour when it could have gone the other way — the plumb lbw appeal that is turned down, the faint edge on the ball that is caught by the keeper but not heard by the umpire and not given. If a player is going to take advantage of those situations, then it is reasonable that he should accept the decisions that go against him. They say that over a career, decisions for and against will even themselves out. That's probably true of most sports.

Sledging or gamesmanship has been in the game of cricket for over 200 years. The only thing that has changed is that television cameras will now expose the culprits, and ICC match referees will deal with the offenders, either with a reprimand, a fine, suspension or, in the worst-case scenario, a ban. All international cricketers know what the expectations are under the Code of Conduct regulations.

I cannot accept dissent, racial abuse, or foul-mouthed verbal bashings of an opponent. The ICC, with the support of the playing nations, is trying hard to rid the game of this aspect and rightly so — after all, the players are role models and influence the superstars of the future, and they need to ensure that cricket is projected positively throughout the world to attract more players, sponsors, television rights and supporters to the game.

However, there is a fine line between dissent and legitimate frustration and disappointment, and each case needs to be viewed and acted upon on its own merits. After all, we are only human and consequently emotions are involved, which will run hot and cold depending on the situation. If a batsman hits a four, or scores a fifty or a hundred, or a bowler captures a wicket, there is the emotion of joy, which is expressed physically for all to see. If the batsman is out for a duck or 99, or the bowler has a dropped catch, or beats the edge of the bat five times in an over, or has a plumb lbw decision turned down, there is disappointment and sometimes frustration. Players are not automatons and can't just turn their emotions off; indeed much of the enjoyment of the game comes from sharing the highs and lows that the players so obviously experience. Umpires and match referees need to have played the game to understand what players go through. Expressing emotion is part of the entertainment of the game.

Banter or saying a few words, or sometimes offering advice to the opposition, should not be confused with out and out sledging. Players try to gain an edge over their opponent to unsettle them and take advantage of a lapse in concentration. I think that is reasonable and acceptable in international sport.

I recall playing against Australia in 1977 at Lancaster Park in Christchurch when Dennis Lillee, the great fast bowler, had just taken the second new ball (which did not happen a lot in New Zealand cricket at that time) and as Dayle, who batted at number nine, walked to the wicket, Dennis pointed at the ball and said, 'This new ball goes twice as fast as the old one, and it hurts a lot more.' That sort of comment, which is not abusive or derogatory, is aimed at unsettling a player's focus and seems fair enough to me. Dayle could have quite correctly pointed out that it would also go twice as fast to the boundary, and that that would hurt too.

On another occasion, Dennis bounced our wicketkeeper Warren Lees and Wally played a tennis serve shot at the ball, with the ball landing at Dennis's feet. Dennis said to Wally, 'Ah, playing tennis are we? Fifteen-love is it?' Rod Marsh, the wicketkeeper, chipped in with, 'It'll be 15-all in a minute, mate.' Good humour, and in my view acceptable.

Bribery, corruption and match fixing

I found the revelations of match fixing, bribery and corruption in the game very disturbing. There had been rumours around during the time I played in the 1970s and 80s, but it never concerned us and there was never any proof of cricket's malpractice. I was never personally approached by bookmakers or agents acting on behalf of bookmakers, or personally experienced any match fixing. Maybe, like many players, there may have been some naivety around in my day.

But the confessions of South Africa's captain, Hansie Cronje, and India's captain, Mohammad Azharuddin, sent shock waves around the world and many other players were no doubt sweating to see if they would be exposed by the ICC's Anti-Corruption and Security Unit. Other players were, in fact, eventually implicated and fined or suspended for bringing the game into disrepute. Cronje and Azharuddin were in positions of trust, they were decision-makers and the decisions they made influenced the course of the match and how the game would be played, if not the final result. Both were harshly dealt with by the ICC and they had to live with the indignity of being labelled cheats and being exposed as having gained financially from dishonesty.

There can be no greater honour than to play for your country whether it be as an amateur or as a professional. I was fortunate to have played for New Zealand as an amateur, which was rewarding in itself, and to have played as a professional, which was a real bonus. There would been have many ex-players turning over in their graves if they knew what had been exposed. The thought of being bribed to throw matches, or to not give your best, was never part of my philosophy, and in fact the thought never entered my mind. Surely, a chance of victory would always outweigh any financial reward for throwing a game.

I would hate to think that some of New Zealand's great victories may have been influenced by opposition players or captains not giving their best in any given situation! New Zealand may not have been considered as one of the great cricketing nations but we fought hard for our successes in every game we won. To my knowledge no New Zealand player or team had contemplated the unthinkable.

I was delighted and very impressed to hear Stephen Fleming, the New Zealand captain, say that he was approached on a tour and immediately advised management and NZC that he had received an approach to influence a game. Well done.

There was a lot of talk and media coverage of Shane Warne and Mark Waugh, who admitted to accepting money for giving a bookmaker information about the weather and pitch conditions. This was hushed up by the Australian Cricket Board and dealt with internally by fining both players, but the public and players around the world were not aware of these events until some time later. This did not sit well with many people. In fact, there were people who thought both players should be banned for a period of time, if not for life.

When a player accepts money for this kind of information, he must know that the information given has some value to other people. There is obviously a motive for the financial inducement. For Warne and Waugh to then turn around and say publicly that they were naive and stupid does not sit comfortably with the critics or do much for their credibility. It should be pointed out, however, that they were not divulging privileged information but were passing along what was already general knowledge, readily available from pre-match interviews, commentators and from journalists while a match was in progress.

In Asian countries, bookies will take bets on anything and everything to do with cricket. Who will open the batting, who will face the first ball, who will score the first run, who will hit the first boundary, how will a batsman be dismissed, how many balls will it take to score a hundred, who will get the first wicket, who will take most wickets in an innings or the match, and who will score most runs in an innings or a match and so on. From the bookmaker's point of view, inside information as to how the pitch will play or the part the weather may play in the match will influence the odds relating to spread betting. For example, if the pitch is good for batting and not going to break up, the odds on Tendulkar scoring a hundred may be 3/1, but if the bookie has inside information that the pitch is bad for batting, the odds might go out to 10/1. If the weather is going to deteriorate, the end result of the match may be affected and the odds are adjusted accordingly. It is well known that millions of US dollars are gambled daily on a cricket match — to pay a player US$30,000 for information or for changing the course of a match in an attempt to lose it is chickenfeed in comparison to the overall money at stake. And of course it is understandable that a player might be tempted, but it doesn't make it right!

I am comforted by the fact that former and current players are also taking a strong view on match fixing, bribery and corruption. My view is that if a player is found guilty, he must be automatically banned for life, all rights and privileges associated with the game evoked, and his playing record erased from the history books as though he never existed. Tough measures, but players like Cronje and Azharuddin knew what they were doing and they were prepared to take a calculated risk. There is a price to pay for this type of dishonesty, which lets the team, the fans and the country down.

An immediate starting point to toughen up on temptation and to protect the players was to ban all mobile phones from dressing rooms during the hours of play. This was an attempt to make contacting bookies and others seeking information during the day that much more difficult. All players are asked to sign an agreement that they will not be involved in this sordid behaviour.

In the future all players and umpires will come under close scrutiny. They must also be prepared to take a united stance on this subject to ensure that those who participate in such deeds are exposed to the authorities and are punished severely.

The paying public has every right to expect that the games they see are above board — a true contest of skill and legitimate performances. Anything less is unacceptable.

Ball doctoring

The debate about ball doctoring has gone on for years. The ICC is taking a very strong stance on this situation. The law is very clear that players cannot change the composition of the ball by using artificial means — the ball must deteriorate naturally, although players can use saliva and then polish the ball to enhance its longevity. Adding hair, sun or lip creams, or scratching the ball with fingernails or using bottle tops and so on is against the law and players are punished accordingly. I would venture to say that in the history of the game, sun creams and other substances have mysteriously found their way onto the ball from time to time.

These days, however, players will never get away with this sort of behaviour. In the old days, there may have been two or three television cameras on the ground and a player could try his luck to see if he could get away with it. Nowadays, there are probably 15 cameras watching the game and the players. In some countries a camera is positioned all day on a star player, including the captain, to watch his every move. Everything is exposed to the viewing audience and to the authorities. Umpires are also constantly checking the ball to see whether anything mischievous has happened.

During the 2004 one-day tri-series in Australia, when India played Zimbabwe, Rahul Dravid was seen on television doing something to the ball. It appeared that he was applying a coloured substance to it, which could have changed the characteristic of the ball and its movement in the air, thus giving the bowler an unfair advantage. He denied deliberate ball tampering, but nonetheless was fined half his match fee by the match referee, Clive Lloyd. According to the Indian management it was an innocent mistake, when Dravid unwittingly shined the ball with fragments of an energy sweet that had stuck to his fingers. The use of television and slow motion replays can be very revealing.

In New Zealand there was some criticism of the fine imposed by Lloyd — many thought that Dravid should have been dealt with more severely. Commentators questioned the credibility of Lloyd to enforce the right punishment and said that he probably took a soft option. Nor was Lloyd's reputation in the game entirely spotless. As captain of the West Indies on the 1980 tour of New Zealand he appeared to condone, if not encourage, the poor behaviour of his team — he did nothing to diffuse the situation that lead to Colin Croft barging umpire Fred Goodall and the West Indian team refused to play on for a period in the second test at Christchurch.

The question was raised: 'How can Lloyd be judgmental when he himself had his faults and helped bring the game into disrepute?' The difference, of course, was that Clive was employed to enforce the rules that were made by the ICC — there were set protocols and guidelines. What Clive did in the past should not be eternally held against him and the same goes for any other player, otherwise no former players would be appointed as match referees.

Every player would have had a wee glitch at some stage during their career. Clive was a fine player and a gentleman, and is highly respected around the world. He had a job to do and did what he felt was right to send a message to all players.

During the 2003 one-day tri-series in Sri Lanka, Pakistan fast bowler Shoaib Akhtar was seen on television screens using his fingernail to scratch the ball. The evidence was compelling and he was suspended by the match referee and missed the final of the tournament, eventually won by New Zealand. It was a silly thing to do and backfired on him and his team, which was disadvantaged when he was barred from playing. Players should realise they will be caught if they try it.

Some years ago, I made a tongue in cheek comment about legalising 'ball tampering'. It caused some reaction. My thought was that a cricket ball does all sorts of things when it is new — swing, seam and bounce favouring the bowler. As the ball gets older, it gets softer and the ball bounces lower therefore favouring the batsman. The balance of the contest is thus adjusted all the time. Of course, some pitch conditions mean that the state of the ball is irrelevant — sometimes the pitch is just such that the batsmen will dominate, whereas other times the ball will dominate the bat. Whatever happens, the game is still a duel with both the batsman and bowler trying to outwit and outperform his opponent.

The question I asked was whether it really mattered if the composition of the ball was changed. I am not suggesting for one minute that a bottle top or some other artificial device be used to scratch the ball, but if the fingernail is used on the ball, does it matter? It would mean the ball might begin to do different things, demanding different skills from the bowler, and the batsman would have to develop something in his technique to combat it. We might see more action and a lot more results, and the umpires would not have to police the problem and no one would be accused of cheating. All very positive stuff! In reality, of course, the laws of cricket are unlikely to be changed to allow this to happen, but it would be fun to debate it.

I wonder what happens to the ball when there is reverse swing — some bowlers around the world are masters of this skill. But it seems to me that something must have happened to the ball for this to occur, usually after 40 overs!

The Pakistan cricket team has been involved with ball tampering accusations for years. I was somewhat surprised to see Imran Khan actually demonstrate, in England, on live television, how to scratch a ball with a bottle top. The Pakistani players had vehemently denied any suggestions of 'ball doctoring' but Imran had shown the world how it could be done.

Drugs in sport

I am totally opposed to the use of drugs in sport. Apart from the possible negative long-term side effects of performance-enhancing drugs, such use gives individuals and teams an unfair advantage over their competitors. The stakes may be high and the financial rewards for success excessive, but at the end of the day, it is another form of cheating. Theoretically, sport is about competing on a fair and level playing field. Everyone knows the rules and plays by them — break them and suffer the consequences.

In most sporting events regular testing for drug use ensures that people compete honestly and fairly, rather than risking humiliation and lengthy suspensions and fines. To be labelled a drug cheat will be with that person for life. However, there are occasions where people have unknowingly taken banned substances or taken medication that contained a banned substance for relief from hayfever or colds. Sometimes a sportsperson can be a victim of circumstance through ignorance or because they have been given the wrong advice or medicine from a doctor. It could be argued that if a sportsperson is suffering from a cold, for example, he is already disadvantaged — and taking a substance that gets him into a condition to compete equally with those who are fit and well is simply righting the imbalance. Somehow, I think there is a huge difference between taking something for a cold or illness and taking steroids and other performance-enhancing drugs.

However, even if you think there are some relatively innocuous substances currently declared illicit in the cricket world, there is no excuse for taking one. All international players have access to the list of banned substances and it is their responsibility to ensure they don't take anything on the list. Pleading ignorance doesn't wash. There is an old saying: 'If in doubt, ask.' There is no excuse.

When Shane Warne took a diuretic pill to reduce the amount of water in his body and enhance his appearance, he copped a suspension that kept him out of the game for a year and may have cost him income reportedly in the vicinity of $A1 million. Unfortunately, there was a degree of dishonesty from Warne. He allegedly said that his mother had given him one pill but he later admitted to taking more than one pill — that made his story much more difficult to believe. He had recovered from a dislocated shoulder very quickly and there was a feeling around the cricket world that the diuretic pill may have been a masking agent used to hide other substances that may have been taken. This was never substantiated, nor proven.

Warne made a public statement that: 'I am a victim of the anti-doping hysteria. I have never taken performance-enhancing drugs.' I guess only he knows the real truth. He may be innocent, or he may not, but I believe that each case needs to be viewed and judged separately instead of having one blanket rule for all those who may transgress.

Drug testing does occur in cricket and players are called upon to give samples at random. I was never tested, but had nothing to hide anyway.

The Pakistan cricket team, who as noted above had attracted allegations of ball tampering, were also involved in drug allegations and scandals, particularly on their tour of the West Indies in 1983. Rumour had it that several players were found to be in possession of some sort of drugs on the beach. These so called allegations prompted the humorists to go into action.

'I see the Pakistan cricket team is on a "high" at the moment.'

'Oh yes, they're on a "trip" in the West Indies.'

'Did you know that the customs officials were somewhat suspicious when they noticed that four Pakistani players arrived 20 minutes after the plane had landed?'

'Yes, and Wasim Akram, the Pakistan captain, has summoned Ian Botham to the West Indies to test the "grass"' (Botham had admitted to smoking marijuana in the past).

However, during the 2006 Champions Trophy in India, there was nothing too funny when flamboyant fast bowler 'The Rawalpindi Express' Shoaib Akhtar and team-mate Mohammad Asif were sent home when both tested positive for a banned steroid. Shoaib was banned for two years and Asif for one. The bans prohibited both players from representing Pakistan in any international match; they could not play domestic cricket under the auspices of the Pakistan Cricket Board, nor could they receive monetary gains or hold any official posts. Both insisted that they did not knowingly take any banned substance but waived their right to have their 'B samples' tested, which sounded suspicious. Shoaib insisted that he had been on a high protein diet which contained beef, chicken and some dietary supplements and herbal medicines, but could not prove it. On the other hand, Asif had been stopped by the team doctor from taking some banned substances a few months before he was tested.

Months later, both players were controversially exonerated on a technicality, but there will always be suspicion over their actions.

Use of technology and television replays

When television replays were first used to determine a decision or the fate of a batsman, I had grave reservations as to whether this would be good for the game. It seemed to me that the constant stoppages, the devaluing of the umpire's role by taking some decision-making away from him, and the end of the idea of the benefit of doubt going in the favour of the batsman, would not be good for the game.

But I've changed my mind on that. It seems to me that replays have changed the game forever and if the technology can be used to determine the right decision without disrupting the game too much, then it should be used as often as possible. If in doubt, the umpire in the middle of the field can signal the third umpire to view a television replay and help adjudicate the final decision. All the players want is accuracy, consistency and the right decision being made, even if a batsman is in or out by millimetres.

The human eye of an umpire trying to judge something at normal speed may not be able to be 100 per cent correct, but the replay from five different angles, slowed down frame by frame, will get the right answer. The course of the game will change because the element of doubt has gone or at least been greatly reduced.

When replays were first used, adjudication could be given on whether a batsman was stumped or run out. It was then extended to determine whether a fielder had come into contact with the boundary rope or line when the ball was near the boundary, and whether four or six runs were or were not scored. Now it is used to determine whether a catch has been fairly caught. During the ICC Champions Trophy in Sri Lanka in 2002, a trial run was made of using replays for lbw decisions — but at this stage the ICC has not fully accepted this and it was not used at the 2003 or 2007 World Cups. It was felt that the umpires were still in the best position to judge those decisions. In tennis, for instance, a player can challenge the linesman's or umpire's call. A replay of the point under television scrutiny determines whether a decision is upheld or overruled.

During the 2008 test series in New Zealand, the West Indies and New Zealand played under a trial or experimental rule whereby the fielding captain and/or the batsman could challenge an umpire's decision and have it referred to the third umpire. The third umpire would then decide whether the decision made by the on-field umpire was right or wrong. This system has great merit and during the series the on-field umpire's decision was occasionally overruled by the third umpire as conclusive replay evidence determined a mistake had been made. Each team had the right to challenge and refer three appeals per innings. If upheld, three challenges would remain, but if a challenge was declined, the referrals were reduced accordingly. This added some excitement to the game and captains had to employ some tactical nous as to the use of the challenge and referral system, deciding when they thought a mistake *had* been made and that they could benefit from an appeal. There was, though, a feeling from both captains after the series that just one decision should be allowed to be challenged. The ICC has a final decision to make on that one.

Personally, I think it would be better that if an umpire was in doubt, he referred an appeal to the third umpire. Or, if the third umpire saw something that would help the umpire in the middle with a decision, he could advise him. This would do away with the captains challenging 50/50 decisions. The important thing is that the right decision is made and if there is any doubt, the batsman should benefit.

Television commentators have the benefit of the 'snickometer' to determine whether a batsman has nicked the ball to the wicketkeeper and 'hot spot' to determine whether the batsman has hit the ball or whether the ball hit the pad first before hitting the bat. Both are excellent pieces of technology that would give the third umpire great assistance in determining the correct decision. Umpires are not permitted, at this stage, to use this technology and have to rely on their own judgment. If the umpire gets the decision wrong, the commentator will invariably say that it was a bad decision. It makes you wonder who would be an umpire today, when every decision is scrutinised five times in slow motion replay before a commentator announces whether the decision was right or wrong. It is trial by television. Doubtless, umpires will always make some poor decisions, but equally they will get some doubtful ones right. And it is odd how umpires never appear to get too many praises for getting it right but are swiftly castigated for getting it wrong.

There appears to be some reluctance by the ICC to allow the fully professional elite world panel of umpires to use the technical assistance they may need to get the decision right. Brian Aldridge, a former New Zealand test umpire who was the NZC umpiring boss, stated that: 'It was manifestly unfair on match officials as they were forced to make decisions with the naked eye while everyone else used high-tech measuring equipment. The only way out of this, as I see it, is to give the umpires unfettered access to all the technological assistance available. That way, they can get the decision right the first time for the good of everyone. It is just a recipe for hanging officials out to dry and we've got to be concerned about the impact that it might have on the image of the job. It is hard for umpires to engender respect if they're constantly being shown up by technology. When we are talking about a professional sport in the twenty-first century, about people's livelihoods being on the line, and the massive crowd and television audiences, the bottom line is to get as many decisions as possible correct.' I can only agree wholeheartedly with that.

One thing is for sure — the players cannot have the best of both worlds. If a batsman nicks a ball and stands his ground waiting for the umpire to make a decision and he gets away with it, the player has to accept that sooner or later he will be a victim of a poor decision. Technology, provided it is conclusive, should always be used.

One of the disadvantages of replays is that umpires tend to rely too often on technology, instead of making the decision themselves. But who can blame them? After all, they must make a decision on the spot, based on what they see and hear in the moment, with no second chance to reassess what has actually happened. I am sure that often they know what decision they would have made, but they go upstairs to the third umpire so that they do not put themselves in a position of making a possible mistake and being blasted by commentators, the general media and the public.

I've also come to accept that the interruptions to play made by such replays are not all bad, and of course they are here for good now in any case. Television replays on the big screens at the grounds allow the spectators to get involved with the decision-making, to review the play and make up their own minds, and this adds excitement and highlights the action of the game — and, of course, if they have missed part of the action, there is an opportunity to see it replayed. Waiting for the final decision that has to be made in a tight and tense match situation draws out the tension and adds to the drama, if the wait isn't overlong. However, it can be tough for the umpires on the ground. They may see a poor decision repeatedly exposed and that could place them in a difficult and perhaps embarrassing situation.

One big and often neglected advantage of replays is that the players can analyse their own or the opposition's techniques or dismissals. To have the ability to see Shane Warne's or Murali's hand in slow motion and close-up, to work out how the wrist or the fingers work to bowl a certain kind of delivery, allows players to be better prepared when batting against bowlers of that quality.

Fast-bowling injuries

Everywhere I go, I am asked the question about why our fast bowlers are breaking down with injury after injury. Some seem to think it is just something wrong with our bowlers, but that's not the case. Injuries from fast bowling is not just a New Zealand problem but a worldwide problem. Every international team will have had their main strike bowler missing for a game or two each season — and in some cases for a full season. Around the world, careers are often terminated too early because of a serious back stress-fracture or major knee injuries that need surgery. After all, the human body was not designed to repeatedly bowl a cricket ball at 140–150 kph without something snapping. The body has to be trained to handle the pressure, the stresses and the strains.

New Zealand has had its share of injured bowlers and at times that has greatly affected the balance and composition of the team. And, of course, when any team loses its main strike weapon, questions will always be asked. Is it over-use, under-use, poor bowling technique, lack of fitness, the wrong training techniques or too much time preparing in gymnasiums instead of running on the grounds and bowling in the nets or in practice matches? Each case must be assessed on its own merits but there have been some interesting findings regarding what typically contributes to fast bowlers breaking down.

Cricket Australia (CA) released a Cricket Injury Report in 2004. The study covered a period from 1998 to 2003 and found that fast bowlers risked more injury when they bowled more than 20–30 overs a week, and that an average of six elite Australian fast bowlers would be out of action with an injury at any given time. The study also showed that 8.7 per cent of the player base was generally unavailable due to injury but that figure rose to 16.1 per cent for pace bowlers. CA said: 'The research determined that strike bowlers significantly increased their risk of injury when their weekly bowling tally strayed to above 20–30 overs per week. Should a bowler bowl above his threshold, they were well advised to adjust their training schedule accordingly so that stresses and strains of fast bowling are allowed to recover.'

In 2001 Glenn Turner, the former New Zealand opening batsman, captain, coach, commentator and selector, did some research on bowling injuries and workloads that I found very interesting. Glenn has always been very analytical and many of his thoughts make a lot of sense. He raised the question of how many overs a fast or medium-pace bowler needs to bowl in both four- and five-day matches. The general rule is that most bowlers will be asked to bowl about 40–45 overs per match, which could be over a three- to five-day period. Logically, a bowler needs to condition himself to bowl about 25 overs in a day's play, and then be prepared to repeat that workload the next day. He raised the question of whether the human mind and body is capable of performing such a workload. He also wondered whether it was just some and not others who were able to manage it.

History shows that in the 1920s Maurice Tate bowled 1500 overs during an English county season and another 600 overs if he toured with an England team during the winter. In the 1960s Fred Trueman bowled around 1100 overs during a county season. Mike Procter, who played for Gloucestershire in the late 1970s, bowled 800–900 overs in county cricket and batted at number four in the batting order. Think of his workload. Richard Hadlee bowled 1131 overs during the 1981/82 season.

In recent times it is interesting to note that England's faster bowlers had a greater workload than other international bowlers. In the 1998/99 season Andrew Caddick bowled 910 overs and South African Shaun Pollock bowled 515 overs, Australian Glenn McGrath 740 overs, West Indian Courtney Walsh 437 overs, plus 600 overs for Gloucestershire.

During that period the New Zealand seamers who bowled most were

Shayne O'Connor, who bowled 533 overs and Chris Cairns, who bowled 487 overs (both had knee operations during their careers).

To me all this suggests that we shouldn't blame injuries on over-bowling, there is a stronger case to suggest that bowlers are not bowling enough.

Training methods have changed considerably. Nowadays there is more emphasis on gym-based work, for strength and conditioning, with some cardiovascular work. Practice sessions have become less skill specific with more time spent on warm-ups, warm-downs and unrelated group games. There is a lot of time given to group and individual briefings and sports science information. There has been a considerable increase in support staff, and in media coverage, marketing and promotional requirements.

Perceptions that over-use is the root cause of injuries must be causing anxiety amongst bowlers in New Zealand. Perhaps this has created a psychological environment in which the expectation of injury brings an over-cautious approach to preparation. Maybe we need to get back to the simpler methods of yesteryear and stop complicating the uncomplicated. Perhaps we need to get bowlers doing more running to reach the necessary cardiovascular fitness and require bowlers to bowl more in the nets prior to a first-class match or a test match. That way, bowlers would gradually build up to the fitness needed to bowl 25 overs a day without breaking down.

Bowlers need to be fit by the start of a series. Then, once into the playing programme, very little maintenance work is required, with more of an emphasis on rest. The only other additional support needed is a bowler with a big heart, a masseur or a physiotherapist to rub and massage the body.

I agree with many of Glenn's thoughts. I have maintained for many years that a fast bowler needs to do a lot of running, sprinting and exercise to increase flexibility and mobility. The body takes shape through bowling. Obviously, there needs to be a balance in one's preparation, but the more a bowler bowls, the more the body is conditioned to handle the workload.

There is a perception that just because a bowler may have played another sport during the winter, that they are fit to play cricket in the summer. Glenn made the point that two of his Worcester county team-mates played first division soccer during the winter and cricket in the summer: 'During the soccer season they had done a lot of strength work and were very fit. However, after one net session they were stiff and sore. Not for the first time, their example showed that to get fit for bowling you need to bowl.'

Chucking

Law 24.3 was very specific: 'The bowler must bowl the ball and not throw it. A ball is fairly delivered in respect of the arm if, once the bowler's arm has reached the level of the shoulder in the delivery swing, the elbow joint is not straightened partially or completely from that point until the ball has left the hand.' (The Law eventually went through some radical changes to allow bowlers to straighten their arms with a tolerance of 15 degrees).

When I was a selector there was debate over the legitimacy of Kyle Mills's bowling action. As I have said earlier, commentator Ian Smith was very concerned about Kyle's bowling action and he expressed a very strong desire to expose him on television during international matches. Smithy has every right to analyse a bowler's technique and talk about it, but it is unreasonable for him to tell the selectors not to select him on the basis of suspicion. It is not a selector's role to prejudge a player and potentially ruin his career when that same player has not been called by international umpires in the past. Even if he has been called for throwing, there is due process for that player to go through.

What I think is unfair is that slow-motion television replays can be used, frame by frame, to scrutinise a bowler's technique and look at every kink in his arm that may or may not be relevant. It is up to the umpire or match referee to report whether a bowler chucks or not. The umpire gets to see the bowler in action and he has to judge whether a fair or legal delivery has been bowled at normal speed.

I would venture to say that if today's technology had been around

40–50 years ago, a lot of bowlers who looked to have good actions then may have come under closer scrutiny. In my view, a bowler's action needs to be determined at normal speed before making a decision as to whether it is legal or not and then for a process to be followed to determine accurately whether a bowler does deliver the ball legally.

In November 2004 a damning article was released by former England fast bowler Angus Fraser, and subsequently a report by the ICC, that 99 per cent of bowlers had 'chucked' the ball during their career, including me. Naturally enough I was amazed to be singled out along with Imran Khan, Curtly Ambrose, Ian Botham, Fred Trueman, Dennis Lillee and others. It was a bizarre feeling to think that I may have had a slight partial straightening of the arm and 'chucked' the ball according to the old law that was applicable during my playing time. All that practice of trying to perfect my action, which was perceived by many to be as near perfect as possible, was really let down!

Along with Angus Fraser, former test players Michael Holding, Aravinda de Silva, Tim May, Dave Richardson and Tony Lewis formed a panel designated to study the illegal bowling action at a meeting in Dubai. With them were three expert biomechanists: Dr Marc Portus, Professor Bruce Elliott and Dr Paul Hurrion. It was their job to look at this most controversial and complicated issue and make recommendations of what should be regarded as a legal delivery. On a screen in front of them they were watching the likes of Glenn McGrath, Shaun Pollock, Allan Donald and Steve Harmison. All these bowlers had been admired by many, but their actions, although perfect to the naked eye, had a bowling arm that partially straightened and which therefore meant that they were bowling illegally.

When players like Muttiah Muralitharan, Brett Lee and Shoaib Akhtar and others had their actions cleared by the ICC, the ICC brought in a new law allowing bowlers a degree of tolerance with the partial straightening of the arm — a spin bowler was allowed 5 degrees, a medium-pace bowler was allowed 7-and-a-half degrees and a fast bowler 10 degrees. The panel recommended to the ICC that all bowlers should be allowed a uniform

15 degree tolerance. This would therefore allow Muralitharan to bowl his banned 'doosra' (where the ball turns from leg to off) because that delivery was at a 14 degree allowance, 9 degrees more tolerance than previously allowed. Cynics would say that the new ruling would allow for no more suspicion on Murali's controversial bowling action and that every delivery he would bowl from now on would be deemed legal — after all, he had captured 532 test wickets at that time.

John F. Reid was NZC's delegate at the conference. The *Press* cricket writer Geoff Longley stated in his article dated 17 November: 'With the benefit of the latest biomechanical technology, Reid acknowledged that Muralitharan's regular bowling style was within the game's laws. Reid said: "Effectively his arm starts bent and stays bent and barely straightens, which is legal. He is not contravening any law and he is not gaining any advantage, because he is not straightening the arm. If you allow bowlers with classic actions who have an 8 degree to 12 degree bend to play, you must also allow Muralitharan." '

The article also stated that fast bowlers whose actions fell in the 8 to 12 degree category included Glenn McGrath, Shaun Pollock, Steve Harmison and Allan Donald. Reid also said: 'The action of Shoaib Akhtar was different again from Muralitharan because he hyper-extended his elbow and gained an advantage, but it was an involuntary movement caused by being double-jointed.'

These findings and the proposed recommendations set by the panel to the ICC for implementation in 2005 caused some debate around the world. General opinions were reflected in the following quotes. My former team-mate, wicketkeeper-batsman Ian Smith, was very critical of the ICC's allegations that Dennis Lillee, Imran Khan and I threw the ball during our careers: 'It is grossly insulting and degrading to the history of cricket — the trio would be utterly shocked with such allegations.' Allan Border, the former Australian captain, said: 'I'm a bit from the old school — throwing is throwing. If you straighten your arm it is a throw.' Ricky Ponting, the Australian captain, added: 'How does an umpire tell if it is 12 degrees, 10 degrees, 9, 13, 14, whatever it is, when it happens like that?

If you can't bowl with a straight arm you should get another job.' Terry Jenner, the former Australian leg spin bowler and Shane Warne's mentor, said: 'I just think we've opened a huge can of worms and it's something we may pay the price for later on.' Geoff Boycott, the former England opening batsman, said: 'It is a sad day for cricket.'

One of the big problems I see is that bowlers all over the world will now be coached to bowl like the controversial modern day bowlers, Muralitharan, Shoaib Akhtar and others. What happens if their arm flexes 15.2 degrees or 16 degrees? Will the ICC move to ban those bowlers or move the tolerance level out a few more degrees? There is a danger that this new tolerance level is encouraging bowlers to chuck. We all know that when a player gets into a bad habit it is very difficult for him to correct it.

If a bowler is now deemed to be suspect, he will be reported by the umpires and the match referee and the bowler would need to attend a laboratory for testing as soon as possible and then undertake remedial work to correct the action.

Politics in sport

In an ideal world it would be nice to think that sport and politics are two separate issues. The reality is that this will never be and that both are well and truly integrated. When governments put funding into sport the door is open for them to have a say and make recommendations and try to influence sporting bodies and convince the public of their rationale and decisions.

The main areas of concern are when security problems in some countries become an issue or sportspeople are compromised. In fact I would welcome governments suggesting to sporting bodies that, based on information received, it would be in the safety interests of the players not to tour a certain country.

What I do have an issue with is when a government says that a team should not tour another country because they do not believe in the politics of that country. They are opposed to the methods by which that country is run, often because of human atrocities afflicted on the people in that country. Surely, whether they want to tour or not then becomes a conscience issue for each player.

Zimbabwe is a prime example. The regime of Robert Mugabe is repugnant and severely disliked, especially by the Western world. In 2002/03 the Zimbabwean Government decreed that white farmers had to give up their land and when some did not do that, those people were forcibly evicted and some were murdered. In 2005 the Mugabe regime had a massive 'clean up' and destroyed the homes of many thousands of black inhabitants, mainly squatters, some of whom died during the exercise. Over a six week period it was estimated that one million people were left homeless in 'Operation Murambatsvina' (murambatsvina translates as 'drive the filth out'). It was also suggested that some of those people who opposed the Mugabe regime at the elections were the victims of this oppressive act and were herded into what were, effectively, concentration camps.

Visual images of the devastation was very concerning, with houses bulldozed, people left homeless, people frozen to death in sub-zero winter conditions at night, and food and general shelter scarce. This was clearly not a great environment for anyone to be placed in, let alone a sports team.

The New Zealand cricket team was placed in a delicate situation when the New Zealand Government severely opposed them touring Zimbabwe in August 2005. Public opinion was against the tour, with a public poll indicating that 90 per cent of those polled thought the tour should be cancelled. NZC and the players were placed in a no-win situation — cancel the tour and NZC would be fined by the ICC because they were in breach of contract, go on the tour and be hounded by the government, media and the public for lacking compassion for those being persecuted in Zimbabwe.

The ICC had determined a Future Tours programme and under their guidelines, which are strictly enforced, the New Zealand cricket team was scheduled to tour Zimbabwe. The ICC said the tour would go ahead because the ICC's responsibility is to world cricket and their decisions were not political — there are over 80,000 youngsters, black and white, playing the game in Zimbabwe. Martin Snedden said the tour would go ahead as scheduled as he had a responsibility to honour the ICC contractual obligation — not to do so would entail ICC fines that would have a severe negative financial impact on cricket in New Zealand. Interestingly enough, India was also going to tour Zimbabwe at the same time as our players, but there was no negative feeling towards that. England and other countries had also honoured their commitment by touring Zimbabwe in recent times — now it was New Zealand's turn. Additonally, while the Black Caps were to be in Zimbabwe, our athletes would be competing against Zimbabwean athletes at the World Championships with no fuss or bans — and that smacked of further hypocrisy to me.

The selectors had picked the team and every player was available. As far as I was concerned they were going there to play cricket, and not for political reasons, or to shake hands with Mugabe, or do a public relations exercise with the Zimbabwean Government.

A slight twist was then introduced into the argument as two separate issues developed — first there was the matter of the New Zealand team going to Zimbabwe in August and second there was the proposed Zimbabwe tour of New Zealand in December. The New Zealand Government took a strong stance against the tour going ahead, saying that the New Zealand team should not tour Zimbabwe but that they could not stop them from going. However they would not issue visas to the Zimbabwe players for the return tour to New Zealand. If the government did not offer visas to the Zimbabwe team and that tour was cancelled it would undermine and effectively destroy New Zealand's ability to co-host the 2011 World Cup with Australia. The ICC would take a strong view against NZC who had reneged on one of its members, even if it was not their fault.

Interestingly enough, the government had previously given a guaranteed entry to all nations that qualified for the 2011 Rugby World Cup should New Zealand win the right to host the event. Zimbabwe contested the 1987 World Cup in New Zealand. It didn't seem fair for rugby to operate under one set of rules and cricket under another. The New Zealand Government's Foreign Affairs Minister, Labour's Phil Goff, was so outraged with the ICC's stance that the New Zealanders would tour Zimbabwe that he sought support from his counterparts in Australia and England to petition the ICC to try to stop the tour. But to no avail, and planning for the tour progressed.

The Green Party, a minnow of New Zealand politics, began pressuring the government, NZC and the players to stop the tour. Green co-leader Rod Donald drafted a Bill to make it illegal for sporting teams to tour Zimbabwe. He also believed that this would provide a loophole that would allow NZC off the hook as far as paying the fine to the ICC was concerned. The ICC confirmed that if the government legislated to make the tour illegal, NZC would not have to pay the fine. However, the government dismissed the idea as it would be in breach of New Zealanders' civil rights. Donald continued his campaign to pressure the government and NZC, and to convince the public that the tour to Zimbabwe should be cancelled. The Greens went to the extreme measure of financing a visit to New Zealand by exiled former Zimbabwe cricketer and political activist Henry Olonga.

Goff also said that if the tour to Zimbabwe was cancelled, the government would not use New Zealand taxpayers' money to pay the $2.8 million fine imposed by the ICC on NZC, so NZC would have the burden of a big financial loss, which they could not afford. Goff's belief was that the money from the fine would go to the Zimbabwe Cricket Union, and guess who the patron is. The money would, therefore, probably end up with Robert Mugabe. In a political twist, prior to the upcoming election, the leader of the opposition, Don Brash, said that the National Party would pay the fine if the tour did not go ahead if they were in government. A nice gesture of good faith!

The New Zealand Government had spoken but everything reeked of double standards. Sure, we would all agree that the situation in Zimbabwe was grim, but what about other parts of the world? To take a stand against

Zimbabwe when the government was actively pursuing free-trade agreements with China, who have a terrible human rights abuse record, was hypocritical. Would the New Zealand Government take a stance and stop our Olympic athletes from going to China to participate in the 2008 Olympics? Unlikely! What about the illegal regime of General Pervez Musharraf in Pakistan? The New Zealand Government welcomed the General in New Zealand to discuss closer ties. In the past, New Zealand cricket teams have toured Sri Lanka without interference when that nation was still experiencing political upheaval as the Tamils tried to establish a free and independent state. New Zealand teams have toured the West Indies and played in Guyana with no problems in spite of a brutal police state in that nation. The government also opposed the decision by the USA and Great Britain to invade Iraq and rid Iraq of the sadistic Sadam Hussein, yet we still have close ties with both countries and trade with them when perhaps we should boycott both. It seems that double standards are rife, but then, of course, politics has always been about expediency more than morality.

Various other New Zealand sporting teams have ventured into countries that have poor human rights records without an eyelid being batted: the New Zealand Breakers basketball team went to China, New Zealand fencers to Cuba, New Zealand's best squash players compete in Egypt annually, the New Zealand Davis Cup tennis team have been to Kazakhstan and Uzbekistan, New Zealand golfers to Myanmar and the New Zealand hockey and tennis teams have been to Pakistan to play their sports. Is it fair for cricket to be singled out over other sports? In a touch of irony, as the Black Caps departed for the Zimbabwe tour, our swimming team was competing in the world swimming champs and one of our swimmers contested the final against a Zimbabwean swimmer who won the gold medal — there was resounding silence on that issue.

If the government was going to make a protest against Mugabe by stopping Zimbabwe cricketers from coming to New Zealand, would they stop Zimbabwean tourists from enjoying our hospitality? Probably not. But preventing the Zimbabwe cricketers from playing in New Zealand would have huge ramifications. There would be a substantial loss of revenue for the players (about $25,000 each) and for NZC, with a potential downgrading of sponsorship deals and loss of television rights. NZC stood to lose $3m if that tour were cancelled and, potentially, millions of other dollars would also be lost. Hotels, airlines, restaurants and all those associated with hosting a tour would suffer. The same would happen in Zimbabwe if the New Zealand tour there were cancelled.

The public might argue that that is the sacrifice our cricketers have to make to take a stance against human rights abuses, but invariably those people are not the ones taking a financial hit when mortgages and bills still have to be paid. It is easy for people who are not facing a potential loss of income to pontificate against our cricketers. Are those same people prepared to contribute $25,000 of their own hard-earned money to help the people in Zimbabwe to try and change the Mugabe regime's thinking? We live in a free world — that is the beauty of a liberal democracy like New Zealand — and although people can attempt to influence others to make a particular decision, we have an individual choice that we have to live with.

Will trying to stop a cricket tour from going ahead bring about change in Zimbabwe? I don't think so. It took South Africa a long time to accept change and even today there are still issues that are difficult to accept. South Africa went through a period of isolation for 20 years because of the government's policy of apartheid. This meant that sporting teams were not selected on merit but on race. There was no equal opportunity. Today in South Africa there still appears to be a race-based quota system in the selection of South African cricket (and rugby) teams with at least five black or coloured players having to be selected in a touring team. This appears to be a directive from the South African Government. This may mean that the best team never takes the field. Can this be right and still be accepted by others in the world? This is political interference and should not be tolerated.

In 2004 a similar situation appeared to be happening in Zimbabwe. Different reports suggested that team selection was being influenced from some higher authority than the Zimbabwe Cricket Union. Some players were being selected because they were black and not necessarily because they were the best players. Fifteen of the team's top players (white players) went on strike because they had issues with their cricket administration, including the selection policy and the sacking of Heath Streak as captain with Tatenda Tabu taking over. The grievances went on for some time and Zimbabwe had to field an under-strength team — on each occasion they were soundly beaten and it became embarrassing. In agreement with the Zimbabwe Cricket Union, the ICC had no alternative but to suspend Zimbabwe's test status for a year, although they could still play one-day international cricket. Will Zimbabwe cricket ever recover?

It was ironic that, following the coup in Fiji in December 2006 (which was deemed to be an illegal act and attracted sanctions against Fiji from Commonwealth countries) that the New Zealand Government was still happy to allow the Fiji sevens rugby team to come to New Zealand to compete in the IRB's sevens world tournament in Wellington. Here was another set of double standards — Zimbabwe cricketers were denied access to New Zealand but the Fijian rugby team was allowed to come and play. The rationale to allow the Fijian team to play was based on two thoughts — if they were banned the IRB may have taken the tournament away from New Zealand and millions of dollars would have been lost to the Wellington area and therefore New Zealanders would have been unfairly punished. Fair enough, but what about the cricket public and businesses who were denied having international cricket? It appeared that there was one rule for rugby, our national game, and another rule for cricket, our summer game. Surely there needs to be more consistency in decision-making.

Twenty20 cricket

Is this the new evolution of the game's development? Are fans and people in general becoming bored with the traditional 50-over game? Are 50-over cricket matches becoming too predictable and is there a need to bring on a new game to satisfy the customers? These are the questions that need to be answered.

I have always believed that real cricket is test cricket, and that view will never change. However, I am realistic enough to say that one-day cricket has been and is still vital for the game's survival and new skills have developed. When Twenty20 cricket was first introduced into English county cricket in 2003, crowds flocked to the grounds in their thousands. In some cases, grounds were sold out. It is a game that is designed to be played in the late afternoon or early evening, allowing spectators — including all the family — to come to the ground after work and relax in a friendly atmosphere. They are entertained by the stars as everyone de-stresses for the day — except, perhaps, for the players, who are under pressure to perform and take risks when batting!

It is a game that is all over within three hours, with exhilarating stroke play, plenty of boundaries and players buzzing like bees around a hive. It is a fast and furious, exciting game and people go home happy that they have got real value for money instead of sitting through seven hours of a traditional one-day game, which has its slow phases.

The whole idea of the game is to attract a new breed of spectator and get bums on seats and it has worked in England and in South Africa. In Australia an exhibition match took place at the WACA in Perth when Western Australia defeated Victoria in front of a sell-out crowd of 20,000 people. An Australian A team attracted good numbers against Pakistan in 2005 and Cricket Australia and NZC have since introduced a domestic competition.

The game was introduced to New Zealand on 17 February 2005. It was a marketer's dream — 30,000 people packed into Eden Park (15,000 more than expected) to watch the one-day world champion Australians take on the Black Caps. The game had an added flavour to it with the Black Caps going 'back to the future' by wearing the old beige uniforms that the 1981 team had worn so successfully. There were a few interesting hairdos, moustaches and beards, white headbands and the white floppy hat as well. Australia won the game but that did not really matter as everyone entered into the spirit of the occasion. What came through loud and clear was that there was more cricket played and entertainment in a Twenty20 match than in a traditional one-day match. In 40 overs 384 runs were scored with 32 fours and 17 sixes hit. In a normal 50-over innings a typical score would be 250–280. The most interesting statistic was that no one bowled a no ball even though a few wides were still bowled. Moreover, this was done with 20 overs having to be bowled in 75 minutes. Michael Clarke, bowling slow left-arm spin, completed one of his overs in 90 seconds. That proves that bowlers can quicken the pace of the game if they really want to! In theory the more Twenty20 cricket is played the better the player skills will be and it is conceivable that scores in the traditional 50-over game will increase.

In 2006 the Black Caps and the West Indies attracted 27,000 people to Eden Park and the match was a tie (126 each) and a 'bowl-out' was played to decide the result of the match — each team nominated five bowlers to bowl two balls each, with the team that hit the stumps the most being declared the winner. This attracted a lot of interest and added excitement as bowlers from both teams kept missing the stumps — until Shane Bond and Scott Styris won the 'shoot out' for the Black Caps.

Such was the popularity of Twenty20 cricket all over the world that NZC decided a provincial tournament should be played in 2006. Average crowds of 2–3000 people were turning up for games, which in most cases was more than typically attended 50-over games.

With the ICC proposing a Twenty20 World Cup concept, most world captains were concerned that this concept of cricket was a fad and may not last and advised administrators that they should not get too carried away with it. There was a place for this form of cricket, especially at international level as a tour-opener match only. If this was to happen, our players needed to be exposed to more and more of this form of cricket at domestic level to prepare them so they could comes to terms with the vagaries of the game.

The first official Twenty20 World Championship took place in South Africa in 2007, with India winning the tournament and New Zealand again exiting at the semi-final stages. However, it was a very successful concept, with some big upsets and tight matches. The beauty of this format is that the shorter and quicker the game, the closer the teams are to each other. A predicted result in a 50-over match could almost be determined at the halfway point, but in this format, the course of a match can be changed in a matter of balls. I enjoyed the spectacle more than the traditional 50-over World Cup — it was more entertaining.

Proposed changes to the traditional 50-over one-day game

Sunil Gavaskar chaired an ICC Cricket Committee meeting and made some recommendations to the ICC for a proposed revamp of the one-day format. The Cricket Committee suggested three new ideas that would revolutionise the game.

He suggested that fielding restrictions should apply for the first 10 overs of every innings and two additional blocks of five overs called 'power plays' would be applied over the course of the innings. The fielding captain would decide when these two blocks would be used. The thought was that this new format would enliven the game by adding an element of unpredictability throughout the course of a match. There is now a rule with the power plays that the fielding side has the first 10 overs as mandatory and then both the fielding and batting sides have five overs of power plays to use at their discretion. Interesting tactics can be applied by either captain which adds to the spectacle and makes the game less predictable.

The second innovation was for the introduction of a soccer-style substitute rule that would allow a player struggling for form to be replaced, although he would not be able to return to the match.

The third area was much greater use of technology to assist the umpires in correct decision-making. The umpires would be allowed to consult on any aspect of any decision.

All three concepts were trialled in the Super test and one-day series when the World played Australia in October 2005, with mixed results.

All three aspects have merit. I have no problem with visual aids assisting umpires with decision-making to ensure the final decision is correct. The idea of tampering with the field restrictions is novel and allows for greater tactical awareness by captains, especially when they have to decide during the innings to declare their interest in using the two five-over 'power play' blocks, which can potentially change the course of the match.

The substitute concept is, however, fraught with danger. I can only imagine what will be going through a player's mind if he is pulled from the field — frustration, negativity, self-doubt and the feeling that such a move could perhaps be career-ending. If a batsman is struggling to come to terms with pitch conditions, or a certain type of bowler, or is scoring his runs too slowly, the coach can replace him with another player who may do better. Or if a bowler is having an off day with the ball by conceding too many runs or bowling too many wides and no balls he too can be replaced. If a player is struggling for form it sounds reasonable that he should be replaced, but it almost certainly means the end for that player when the next game is played. All sports are based around player performance or failure. That is the beauty, the mystery and uncertainty of any game. No one player will be on top of his game all the time but a failure in one game could send the player to the scrap heap. Will a coach be strong enough to pull his captain or star player from the field if they are struggling or will it always be a lesser player who is used as a scapegoat?

I have always felt that if a player is genuinely injured and could take no further part in the game that he should be replaced so that neither team is advantaged or disadvantaged. I can see some common sense applying in that situation but I guess there is always a chance that some teams or players would breach the rules and 'fake' an injury to get a better player on the field to suit a certain match situation.

The super sub rule lasted only a few months before it was abandoned by the ICC. Teams had to declare their super sub player before the toss, which effectively disadvantaged the team who lost the toss. It was a double blow for the losing captain because in losing the toss he was exposed to the conditions that prevailed on the day and the strengths of the opposition, and the winning captain could play his sub out of the game. All it needed to make the contests fairer was for the ICC to legislate the declaration of the super sub player after the toss. However, they were reluctant to do that.

The introduction of the one bouncer per over rule to the one-day game is a great concept. It gives the bowler a chance to dictate the game a little more and it takes away the predictability of a bowler and puts some doubt in the mind of the batsman. Fast bowlers have used the bouncer to good effect, not only to unsettle the batsman, but also to get them out by inducing false shots and it has been used effectively as a run-saving or dot ball. It also means that front foot play has diminished a little and batsmen need to be more of a complete player to be successful. Batsmen need to be more aware of survival and be better prepared technically.

Perhaps one aspect of the 50-over game that could be modified to avoid the predictability of some games and too many one-sided results would be to have two 25-over innings, allowing the top batsmen in both teams to bat twice. In tournament play, a bonus point could be awarded for a first-innings lead, which would make teams get as close as possible to each other — perhaps then there may be closer games and a better spectacle!

Nonetheless, the game has moved on considerably since my era. It is a better spectacle now, with more runs being scored and batsmen having a greater ability to power hit the ball to and over the boundary. Bowlers have also developed more skills with the ball, which makes the games a good contest.

Zimbabwe and Bangladesh playing international cricket

The debate over including both Zimbabwe and Bangladesh in international cricket will go on for years. The detractors would have both teams banned because they struggle to compete and invariably lose by big margins. The playing spectacle is diminished and often public interest is non-existent. There is no doubt that the quality of bowling from those countries is weak, which helps the batting averages of other international players. Bowling averages and strike rates are also enhanced and this can make assessing the real quality of other international players a little difficult.

In the 1980s and 1990s batsmen had to compete and survive against Lillee and Thomson, Holding and Marshall, Waqar and Wasim, Ambrose and Walsh, Donald and Pollock. When Matthew Hayden was first introduced to international cricket he struggled, averaging around 20, and was dropped. On his return he had great success against India in 2001 and averaged over 60 and later went on to score a world record individual score against Zimbabwe to beat Brian Lara's record of 385.

However, I believe that the ICC should be applauded for trying to make the game more global and giving countries a chance to play at the highest level. To put things in perspective, it took New Zealand nearly 26 years to win our first test. Maybe in time both Zimbabwe and Bangladesh will challenge other teams and cause the odd upset in both forms of the game.

The ICL versus the IPL

The Indian Cricket League was established in 2007 by a television guru who owns the Indian channel Zee TV. The idea was to contract many of the world's best cricketers and play several tournaments, which would include a number of Indian international and promising Indian players. Zee TV were keen to enter the television race for broadcasting rights of all Indian cricket, but had been denied by Indian officials (the BCCI) for years. This was their way of breaking into the Indian, and perhaps world, market. Once the ICL was declared as a concept, the BCCI decided to form the Indian Premier League, which was sanctioned by the ICC in direct opposition to the ICL, which was unsanctioned and gained the tag of being a 'rebel' league. Now, the ICC stipulated that any player who signed with the rebel league would be forfeiting their international careers. Some of the players who were going to sign for the ICL decided instead to join the IPL, for, probably, less money.

The question was now whether both leagues could survive. As it turned out many retired international players took up contracts with the ICL. Who could blame the players if they were offered anything from US$200,000 to $1 million for a few weeks' work for two or three years? It would be quite appealing to bowl only four overs, have a slog and pick up a giant pay cheque to help secure a financial future.

Christmas 2008 was a very different and very special time for me. I spent time with my family in New Zealand. For the first time in 36 years I did not have to prepare to go away to play, watch or think about cricket. I was not even at a cricket ground on Boxing Day. Old habits die hard, though, and I did employ the television remote to watch some of the Boxing Day test between Australia and South Africa from the Melbourne Cricket Ground (not to mention the T20 match at Auckland between New Zealand and the West Indies). Maybe in time there will be another role to play within the game.

Statistics

Compiled by Peter Marriott

TEST MATCH CAREER RECORDS

		Batting & Fielding										Bowling						
		M	I	NO	Runs	Ave	HS	100	50	Ct	O	M	R	W	Ave	BB	5wl	10wM
1972-73	v Pakistan	1	1	0	46	46.00	46	-	-	2	25†	0	112	2	56.00	2-84	-	-
1973	in England	1	2	1	4	4.00	4*	-	-	-	45	8	143	1	143.00	1-79	-	-
1973-74	in Australia	3	6	0	68	11.33	20	-	-	2	66.7†	9	255	7	36.42	4-33	-	-
1973-74	v Australia	2	3	0	37	12.33	23	-	-	1	50.4†	7	225	10	22.50	4-71	-	-
1975-76	v India	2	2	0	45	22.50	33	-	-	-	48.3†	4	197	12	16.41	7-23	1	1
1976-77	in Pakistan	3	6	2	214	53.50	87	-	1	2	75.2†	2	447	10	44.70	5-121	1	-
1976-77	in India	3	6	0	60	10.00	21	-	-	1	127	18	437	13	33.61	4-95	-	-
1976-77	v Australia	2	4	0	143	35.75	81	-	1	2	72†	7	354	6	59.00	3-155	-	-
1977-78	v England	3	6	1	80	16.00	39	-	-	-	121.3†	26	371	15	24.73	6-26	1	1
1978	in England	3	6	0	32	5.33	11	-	-	3	121.1	31	270	13	20.76	5-84	1	-
1978-79	v Pakistan	3	5	1	115	28.75	53*	-	1	1	117.6†	13	414	18	23.00	5-62	2	-
1979-80	v West Indies	3	4	0	178	44.50	103	1	1	1	161.3	50	361	19	19.00	6-68	2	1
1980-81	in Australia	3	6	2	98	24.50	51*	-	1	1	147.3	35	364	19	19.15	6-57	2	-
1980-81	v India	3	4	0	29	7.25	20	-	-	2	119.3	37	288	10	28.80	5-47	1	-
1981-82	v Australia	3	5	1	92	23.00	40	-	-	2	91.5	25	226	14	16.14	6-100	2	-
1982-83	v Sri Lanka	2	3	1	59	29.50	30	-	-	1	77.3	27	141	10	14.10	4-33	-	-
1983	in England	4	8	2	301	50.16	92*	-	3	1	232	65	559	21	26.61	6-53	2	-
1983-84	v England	3	4	0	144	36.00	99	-	1	3	109.5	33	232	12	19.33	5-28	1	-
1983-84	in Sri Lanka	3	4	0	75	18.75	29	-	-	3	117.5	48	230	23	10.00	5-29	2	1
1984-85	v Pakistan	3	4	0	131	32.75	89	-	1	-	118.5	29	306	16	19.12	6-51	1	-
1984-85	in West Indies	4	7	1	137	22.83	39*	-	-	1	143	33	409	15	27.26	4-53	-	-
1985-86	in Australia	3	4	0	111	27.75	54	-	1	2	169.3	42	401	33	12.15	9-52	5	2
1985-86	v Australia	3	3	1	105	52.50	72*	-	1	2	157.5	36	387	16	24.18	7-116	1	-
1986	in England	3	3	0	93	31.00	68	-	1	-	153.5	42	390	19	20.52	6-80	2	1
1986-87	v West Indies	3	4	2	74	37.00	35*	-	-	2	113.1	20	354	17	20.82	6-50	2	-
1986-87	in Sri Lanka	1	1	1	151	-	151*	1	-	1	38.5	10	102	4	25.50	4-102	-	-
1987-88	in Australia	3	6	1	111	22.20	36	-	-	-	156	44	353	18	19.61	5-67	3	1
1987-88	v England	1	1	0	37	37.00	37	-	-	-	18	3	50	0	-	-	-	-
1988-89	in India	3	6	1	61	12.20	31	-	-	1	100.5	25	252	18	14.00	6-49	2	1
1988-89	v Pakistan	2	3	1	53	26.50	32	-	-	-	82	21	169	5	33.80	4-101	-	-
1989-90	v India	3	2	0	115	57.50	87	-	1	-	105.5	24	319	12	26.58	4-69	-	-
1989-90	v Australia	1	1	0	18	18.00	18	-	-	-	41.2	8	109	7	15.57	5-39	1	-
1990	in England	3	4	0	107	26.75	86	-	1	2	133.5	24	384	16	24.00	5-53	1	-
Total		**86**	**134**	**19**	**3124**	**27.16**	**151***	**2**	**15**	**39**	**21918**	**806**	**9611**	**431**	**22.29**	**9-52**	**36**	**9**

‡577.1 8-ball (†) plus 2883.3 6-ball overs   balls‡

AGAINST EACH COUNTRY

	M	I	NO	Runs	Ave	HS	100	50	Ct	Balls	R	W	Ave	BB	5wl	10wM
Australia	23	38	5	783	23.72	81	-	4	12	6099	2674	130	20.56	9-52	14	3
England	21	34	4	798	26.60	99	-	6	9	5853	2399	97	24.73	6-26	8	2
India	14	20	1	310	16.31	87	-	1	4	3106	1493	65	22.96	7-23	4	2
Pakistan	12	19	4	559	37.26	89	-	3	5	2949	1448	51	28.39	6-51	4	-
Sri Lanka	6	8	2	285	47.50	151*	1	-	5	1405	473	37	12.78	5-29	2	1
West Indies	10	15	3	389	32.41	103	1	1	4	2506	1124	51	22.03	6-50	4	1
Total	86	134	19	3124	27.16	151*	2	15	39	21918	9611	431	22.29	9-52	36	9

	M	I	NO	Runs	Ave	HS	100	50	Ct
Australia	12	22	3	388	20.42	54	-	2	5
England	14	23	3	537	26.85	92*	-	5	6
India	6	12	1	121	11.00	31	-	-	2
New Zealand	43	59	8	1501	29.43	103	1	7	19
Pakistan	3	6	2	214	53.50	87	-	1	2
Sri Lanka	4	5	1	226	56.50	151*	1	-	4
West Indies	4	7	1	137	22.83	39*	-	-	1
Total	86	134	19	3124	27.16	151*	2	15	39

Balls	R	W	Ave	BB	5wl	10wM
3373	1373	77	17.83	9-52	10	3
4115	1746	70	24.94	6-53	6	1
1367	689	31	22.22	6-49	2	1
10663	4615	201	22.96	7-23	15	3
602	447	10	44.70	5-121	1	-
940	332	27	12.29	5-29	2	1
858	409	15	27.26	4-53	-	-
21918	9611	431	22.29	9-52	36	9

	M	I	NO	Runs	Ave	HS	100	50	Ct
Home	43	59	8	1501	29.43	103	1	7	19
Away	43	75	11	1623	25.35	151*	1	8	20
Total	86	134	19	3124	27.16	151*	2	15	39

Balls	R	W	Ave	BB	5wl	10wM
10663	4615	201	22.96	7-23	15	3
11255	4996	230	21.72	9-52	21	6
21918	9611	431	22.29	9-52	36	9

COLLABORATORS IN THE FIELD

43	I.D.S. Smith
27	J.V. Coney
24	W.K. Lees
20	M.D. Crowe
12	J.G.Bracewell
11	M.G. Burgess
10	B.L. Cairns, J.J. Crowe, G.P. Howarth
9	J.G. Wright
7	K.J. Wadsworth
6	substitutes
5	B.A. Edgar, J.M. Parker
4	S.L. Boock, B.E. Congdon
3	E.J. Chatfield, M.J. Greatbatch, A.H. Jones, A.C. Parore, J.F. Reid, G.M. Turner
2	T.J. Franklin, J.F.M. Morrison, D.R. O'Sullivan, N.M. Parker, K.R. Rutherford
1	B. Andrews, V.R. Brown, G.N. Edwards, E.J. Gray, H.J. Howarth, C.M. Kuggeleijn, P.E. McEwan, P.J. Petherick, A.D.G. Roberts, D.A Stirling, G.B. Troup

SUMMARY OF TEST WICKETS TAKEN

Batsman No.	Wkts
1	55
2	56
3	47
4	31
5	37
6	36
7	40
8	43
9	36
10	30
11	20

Batsmen 1 and 2 (111) represent 25.75% of the total.
Batsmen 1 to 7 (302) represent 70.07% of the total.
Batsmen 8 to 11 (129) represent 29.93% of the total.

SUMMARY OF HOW TEST WICKETS TAKEN

	Wkts	%
Bowled	94	21.81
Leg before wicket	81	18.79
Caught	246	57.08
Caught and bowled	10	2.32

TEST VICTIMS
Number of times dismissed

Australia (47)

9	D.C. Boon
8	G.R.J. Matthews
7	G.R. Marsh
6	A.R. Border, G.S. Chappell, G.M. Wood
5	I.C. Davis, K.J. Hughes, R.W. Marsh
4	D.R. Gilbert, C.J. McDermott, G.M. Ritchie
3	R.G. Holland, D.M. Jones, G.F. Lawson, K.J. O'Keeffe, W.B. Phillips, K.R. Stackpole, J.R. Thomson, S.R. Waugh, B. Yardley
2	I.M. Chappell, G.C. Dyer, A.M.J. Hilditch, R.B. Kerr, D.K. Lillee, A.A. Mallett, P.R. Sleep, K.D. Walters
1	T.M. Alderman, R.J. Bright, G.D. Campbell, G.J. Cosier, S.P. Davis, A.I.C. Dodemaide, G.J. Gilmour, J.D. Higgs, R.M. Hogg, B.M. Laird, I.R. Redpath, B.A. Reid, M.A. Taylor, P.L. Taylor, M.R.J. Veletta, M.H.N. Walker, K.C. Wessels, T.J. Zoehrer

England (35)

9   D.W. Randall
6   P.H. Edmonds, G.A. Gooch, R.W. Taylor
5   R.G.D. Willis
4   D.I. Gower, M.D. Moxon, C.T. Radley
3   I.T. Botham, N.G Cowans, N.A. Foster, M.W. Gatting, E.E. Hemmings, C.M. Old, G.R.J. Roope, C.J. Tavare
2   C.W.J. Athey, G. Boycott, J.E. Emburey, G. Fowler, A.J. Lamb, D.E. Malcolm, R.C. Russell, G.C. Small, C.L Smith, A.J. Stewart
1   J.M. Brearley, G.R. Dilley, M. Hendrick, C.C. Lewis, V.J. Marks, G. Miller, R.A. Smith, J.A. Snow, J.G. Thomas

India (32)

5   Kapil Dev
4   Arun Lal, S.M. Gavaskar, W.V. Raman, D.B. Vengsarkar, G.R. Viswanath
3   M.B. Amarnath, K. Srikkanth
2   S. Amarnath, Arshad Ayub, M. Azharuddin, B.S. Bedi, C.P.S. Chauhan, A.D. Gaekwad, S.M.H. Kirmani, S.V. Manjrekar, K.S. More, R. Patel
1   K.V.B.J. Azad, B.S. Chandrasekhar, K.D. Ghavri, N.D. Hirwani, U.S. Madan Lal, A.V. Mankad, B.P. Patel, S.M. Patil, M. Prabhakar, E.A.S. Prasanna, R.J. Shastri, S. Venkataraghavan, Yashpal Sharma, Yograj Singh

Pakistan (25)

6   Mushtaq Mohammad
5   Talat Ali
4   Imran Khan, Javed Miandad
3   Asif Iqbal, Mohsin Khan, Mudassar Nazar, Sadiq Mohammad
2   Salim Malik, Sarfraz Nawaz, Zaheer Abbas
1   Abdul Qadir, Anil Dalpat, Azeem Hafeez, Haroon Rashid, Intikhab Alam, Majid Khan, Rashid Khan, Rizwan-Uz-Zaman, Saleem Yousuf, Shoaib Mohammad, Sikander Bakht, Tahir Naqqash, Wasim Akram, Wasim Raja

Sri Lanka (14)

6   S. Wettimuny
4   L.R.D. Mendis, J.R. Ratnayake
3   R.G. de Alwis, D.S. de Silva, E.R.N.S. Fernando, S.M.S. Kaluperuma, R.S. Madugalle, R.J. Ratnayake
1   A.M.J.G. Amerasinghe, R.L. Dias, A.P. Gurusinghe, V.B. John, S.A.R. Silva

West Indies (20)

7   D.L. Haynes
6   C.G. Greenidge
5   A.L. Logie
4   J. Garner, M.A. Holding
3   H.A. Gomes, I.V.A. Richards, R.B. Richardson
2   P.J.L. Dujon, C.H. Lloyd, D.L. Murray, L.G. Rowe
1   C.G. Butts, C.E.H. Croft, A.H. Gray, A.I. Kallicharan, C.L. King, M.D. Marshall, D.R. Parry, C.A. Walsh

COMPLETE TEST BOWLING FIGURES BY GROUND

			First Innings				Second Innings			
			O	M	R	W	O	M	R	W
1972-73	v Pakistan	Basin Reserve	18	0	84	2	7	0	28	0
1973	in England	Trent Bridge	26	5	64	0	19	3	79	1
1973-74	in Australia	Melbourne Cricket Ground	25	4	104	0				
		Sydney Cricket Ground	9.4	2	33	4	4.3	0	16	2
		Adelaide Oval	28	3	102	1				
1973-74	v Australia	Lancaster Park	14	2	59	3	18.4	3	71	4
		Eden Park	9	1	45	1	9	1	50	2
1975-76	v India	Lancaster Park	12	1	75	0	14	2	64	1
		Basin Reserve	14	1	35	4	8.3	0	23	7
1976-77	in Pakistan	Gaddafi Stadium	19	0	121	5	5	0	36	0
		Niaz Stadium	19	1	77	1				
		National Stadium	20.2	1	138	4	12	0	75	0
1976-77	in India	Wankhede Stadium	29	5	95	4	16	0	76	1
		Green Park	29	2	121	1	15	1	56	2
		Chepauk	21	7	37	3	17	3	52	2
1976-77	v Australia	Lancaster Park	29	1	155	3	13	4	41	1
		Eden Park	28	2	147	2	2	0	11	0
1977-78	v England	Basin Reserve	28	5	74	4	13.3	4	26	6
		Lancaster Park	43	10	147	4	6	1	17	0
		Eden Park	31	6	107	1				

Season	Opponent	Venue	O	M	R	W	O	M	R	W
1978	in England	The Oval	21.5	6	43	2	11.3	3	18	0
		Trent Bridge	42	11	94	4				
		Lord's	32	9	84	5	13.5	2	31	2
1978-79	v Pakistan	Lancaster Park	25	2	62	5	26	4	83	3
		McLean Park	25	3	101	4	14	1	56	1
		Eden Park	27	3	104	5	0.6	0	8	0
1979-80	v West Indies	Carisbrook	20	9	34	5	36	13	68	6
		Lancaster Park	23.3	5	58	3	22	7	64	0
		Eden Park	31	8	75	4	29	8	62	1
1980-81	in Australia	Brisbane Cricket Ground	37	8	83	3	6	0	28	0
		WACA Ground	27	8	87	5	11.1	4	20	2
		Melbourne Cricket Ground	39	8	89	3	27.2	7	57	6
1980-81	v India	Basin Reserve	16	4	62	0	22.3	7	65	4
		Lancaster Park	33	12	47	5				
		Eden Park	27	11	49	1	21	3	65	0
1981-82	v Australia	Basin Reserve	7	2	15	0				
		Eden Park	20	7	38	2	28	9	63	5
		Lancaster Park	28.5	5	100	6	8	2	10	1
1982-83	v Sri Lanka	Lancaster Park	13.3	1	33	4	22	12	27	0
		Basin Reserve	25	9	47	2	17	5	34	4
1983	in England	The Oval	23.4	6	53	6	37.2	7	99	2
		Headingley	21	9	44	0	26	9	45	0
		Lord's	40	15	93	5	26	7	42	3
		Trent Bridge	30	7	98	1	28	5	85	4
1983-84	v England	Basin Reserve	31.5	6	97	2				
		Lancaster Park	17	9	16	3	18	6	28	5
		Eden Park	43	12	91	2				
1983-84	in Sri Lanka	Asgiriya Stadium	20.5	7	35	4	7	4	8	4
		Sinhalese SCG	22	12	27	2	30	14	58	3
		Colombo CCG	22	4	73	5	16	7	29	5
1984-85	v Pakistan	Basin Reserve	32	11	70	2				
		Eden Park	19.5	3	60	4	17	1	66	2
		Carisbrook	24	5	51	6	26	9	59	2
1984-85	in West Indies	Queen's Park Oval	24.3	6	82	4	17	2	58	0
		Bourda Oval	25.5	5	83	2	16	3	32	2
		Kensington Oval	26	5	86	3				
		Sabina Park	28.4	11	53	4	5	1	15	0
1985-86	in Australia	Brisbane Cricket Ground	23.4	4	52	9	28.5	9	71	6
		Sydney Cricket Ground	24	2	65	5	27.1	10	58	2
		WACA Ground	26.5	6	65	5	39	11	90	6
1985-86	v Australia	Basin Reserve	37.1	5	116	3				
		Lancaster Park	44.4	8	116	7	25	4	47	2
		Eden Park	31	12	60	3	20	7	48	1
1986	in England	Lord's	37.5	11	80	6	27	3	78	1
		Trent Bridge	32	7	80	6	33.1	15	60	4
		The Oval	23.5	6	92	2				
1986-87	v West Indies	Basin Reserve	31	9	77	2	4	0	12	0
		Eden Park	41.4	7	105	6	1	0	9	0
		Lancaster Park	12.3	2	50	6	23	2	101	3
1986-87	in Sri Lanka	Colombo CCG	38.5	10	102	4				
1987-88	in Australia	Brisbane Cricket Ground	31	5	95	3	8	3	14	0
		Adelaide Oval	42	16	68	5				
		Melbourne Cricket Ground	44	11	109	5	31	9	67	5
1987-88	v England	Lancaster Park	18	3	50	0				
1988-89	in India	M Chinnaswamy Stadium	30	10	65	5				
		Wankhede Stadium	20.5	5	49	6	16	3	39	4
		Lal Bahadur Shastri Stadium	34	7	99	3				
1988-89	v Pakistan	Basin Reserve	54	14	101	4				
		Eden Park	28	7	68	1				
1989-90	v India	Lancaster Park	14	1	45	3	22.5	3	69	4
		McLean Park	35	11	73	3				
		Eden Park	30	8	123	2	4	1	9	0
1989-90	v Australia	Basin Reserve	16.2	5	39	5	25	3	70	2
1990	in England	Trent Bridge	33	6	89	4				
		Lord's	29	5	113	3	13	2	32	1
		Edgbaston	37.5	8	97	3	21	3	53	5

HOW WICKETS TAKEN BY GROUNDS

In Australia (5)	M	Balls	R	W	Ave	BB	5w	10w		B	LBW	C	C&B
Adelaide Oval	2	476	170	6	28.33	5-68	1	-		1	2	3	-
Brisbane Cricket Ground	3	807	343	21	16.33	9-52	2	1		6	2	12	1
Melbourne Cricket Ground	3	1048	426	19	22.42	6-57	3	1		4	6	9	-
Sydney Cricket Ground	2	418	172	13	13.23	5-65	1	-		-	6	7	-
WACA Ground	2	624	262	18	14.55	6-90	3	1		5	1	11	1
Total	**12**	**3373**	**1373**	**77**	**17.83**	**9-52**	**10**	**3**		**16**	**17**	**42**	**2**

In England (5)	M	Balls	R	W	Ave	BB	5w	10w		B	LBW	C	C&B
Edgbaston	1	353	150	8	18.75	5-53	1	-		3	-	4	1
Headingley	1	282	89	0	-	-	-	-		-	-	-	-
Lord's	4	1312	553	26	21.26	6-80	3	-		7	5	14	-
The Oval	3	709	305	12	25.41	6-53	1	-		3	4	5	-
Trent Bridge	5	1459	649	24	27.04	6-80	1	1		10	5	8	1
Total	**14**	**4115**	**1746**	**70**	**24.94**	**6-53**	**6**	**1**		**23**	**14**	**31**	**2**

In India (5)	M	Balls	R	W	Ave	BB	5w	10w		B	LBW	C	C&B
Chepauk	1	228	89	5	17.80	3-37	-	-		1	-	4	-
M Chinnaswamy Stadium	1	180	65	5	13.00	5-65	1	-		3	-	2	-
Green Park	1	264	177	3	59.00	2-56	-	-		1	-	2	-
Lal Bahadur Shastri Stadium	1	204	99	3	33.00	3-99	-	-		-	-	3	-
Wankhede Stadium	2	491	259	15	17.26	6-49	1	1		2	2	10	1
Total	**6**	**1367**	**689**	**31**	**22.22**	**6-49**	**2**	**1**		**7**	**2**	**21**	**1**

In New Zealand (5)	M	Balls	R	W	Ave	BB	5w	10w		B	LBW	C	C&B
Basin Reserve	12	2623	1075	53	20.28	7-23	3	2		11	7	33	2
Carisbrook	2	636	212	19	11.15	6-51	3	1		1	8	9	1
Eden Park	13	3203	1463	45	32.51	6-105	3	-		6	12	27	-
Lancaster Park	14	3679	1635	76	21.51	7-116	6	-		18	11	46	1
McLean Park	2	522	230	8	28.75	4-101	-	-		2	3	3	-
Total	**43**	**10663**	**4615**	**201**	**22.96**	**7-23**	**15**	**3**		**38**	**41**	**118**	**4**

In Pakistan (3)	M	Balls	R	W	Ave	BB	5w	10w		B	LBW	C	C&B
Gaddafi Stadium	1	192	157	5	31.40	5-121	1	-		2	-	3	-
National Stadium	1	258	213	4	53.25	4-138	-	-		-	-	4	-
Niaz Stadium	1	152	77	1	77.00	1-77	-	-		-	1	-	-
Total	**3**	**602**	**447**	**10**	**44.70**	**5-121**	**1**	**-**		**2**	**1**	**7**	**-**

In Sri Lanka (3)	M	Balls	R	W	Ave	BB	5w	10w		B	LBW	C	C&B
Asgiriya Stadium	1	167	43	8	5.37	4-8	-	-		1	1	6	-
Colombo CCG	2	461	204	14	14.57	5-29	2	1		3	2	9	-
Sinhalese SCG	1	312	85	5	17.00	3-58	-	-		1	1	2	1
Total	**4**	**940**	**332**	**27**	**12.29**	**5-29**	**2**	**1**		**5**	**4**	**17**	**1**

In West Indies (4)	M	Balls	R	W	Ave	BB	5w	10w		B	LBW	C	C&B
Bourda Oval	1	251	115	4	28.75	2-32	-	-		1	-	3	-
Kensington Oval	1	156	86	3	28.66	3-86	-	-		1	-	2	-
Queen's Park Oval	1	249	140	4	35.00	4-82	-	-		1	1	2	-
Sabina Park	1	202	68	4	17.00	4-53	-	-		-	1	3	-
Total	**4**	**858**	**409**	**15**	**27.26**	**4-53**	**-**	**-**		**3**	**2**	**10**	**-**

FIRST-CLASS CAREER RECORDS

		Batting & Fielding									Bowling							
		M	I	NO	Runs	Ave	HS	100	50	Ct	O	M	R	W	Ave	BB	5wI	10wM
1971-72	Canterbury	3	3	1	16	8.00	11	-	-	2	55†	9	194	10	19.40	4-42	-	-
1972-73	Canterbury	5	7	1	80	13.33	50	-	1	5	119†	18	438	28	15.64	4-25	-	-
	NZ in Australia	1	1	0	9	9.00	9	-	-	-	26†	3	80	1	80.00	1-32	-	-
	NZ in NZ	1	1	0	46	46.00	46	-	-	2	25†	0	112	2	56.00	2-84	-	-
1973	NZ in England	12	7	2	74	14.80	30	-	-	-	355	72	1058	38	27.84	5-56	1	-
1973-74	NZ in Australia	7	11	0	197	17.90	49	-	-	3	175.7†	18	728	16	45.50	4-33	-	-
	Canterbury	1	2	1	34	34.00	25	-	-	-	29†	4	115	6	19.16	4-64	-	-
	NZ in NZ	2	3	0	37	12.33	23	-	-	1	50.4†	7	225	10	22.50	4-71	-	-
1974-75	Canterbury	1	2	1	47	47.00	33	-	-	1	27†	6	82	3	27.33	2-32	-	-
1975-76	Canterbury	7	10	3	155	22.14	53*	-	1	3	174.4†	27	554	28	19.78	5-53	1	-
	NZ in NZ	2	2	0	45	22.50	33	-	-	-	48.3†	4	197	12	16.41	7-23	1	1
1976-77	NZ in Pakistan	5	8	2	224	37.33	87	-	1	2	109.5†	3	610	18	33.88	5-47	2	-
	NZ in India	3	6	0	60	10.00	21	-	-	1	127	18	437	13	33.61	4-95	-	-
	Canterbury	5	7	1	185	30.83	53	-	1	2	109.5†	13	366	12	30.50	3-21	-	-
	NZ in NZ	2	4	0	143	35.75	81	-	1	2	72†	7	354	6	59.00	3-155	-	-
1977-78	Canterbury	7	14	3	266	24.18	77	-	2	2	144.6†	30	489	27	18.11	5-28	2	-
	NZ in NZ	3	6	1	80	16.00	39	-	-	-	121.3†	26	371	15	24.73	6-26	1	1
1978	Nottinghamshire	7	8	4	193	48.25	101*	1	-	1	216.3	48	555	37	15.00	6-39	4	1
	NZ in England	10	13	0	149	11.46	40	-	-	9	280.4	72	714	41	17.41	7-77	2	1
1978-79	Canterbury	7	11	3	214	26.75	79*	-	2	2	181.3†	43	495	32	15.46	6-28	2	-
	NZ in NZ	3	5	1	115	28.75	53*	-	1	1	117.6†	13	414	18	23.00	5-62	2	-
1979	Nottinghamshire	12	16	4	193	16.08	41	-	-	5	317	103	753	47	16.02	7-23	2	-
1979-80	Tasmania	6	10	3	160	22.85	33*	-	-	4	173.2	36	477	13	36.69	5-55	1	-
	NZ in NZ	3	4	0	178	44.50	103	1	1	1	161.3	50	361	19	19.00	6-68	2	1
1980	Nottinghamshire	8	9	1	231	28.87	68	-	1	4	222.1	82	410	29	14.13	5-32	1	-
1980-81	NZ in Australia	5	8	2	249	41.50	103	1	1	2	229.3	52	567	27	21.00	6-57	3	-
	NZ in NZ	3	4	0	29	7.25	20	-	-	2	119.3	37	288	10	28.80	5-47	1	-
1981	Nottinghamshire	21	26	3	745	32.39	142*	1	3	14	708.4	231	1564	105	14.89	7-25	4	-
1981-82	Canterbury	7	13	2	408	37.09	83*	-	3	3	332.3	106	642	45	14.26	6-26	5	-
	NZ in NZ	3	5	1	92	23.00	40	-	-	2	91.5	25	226	14	16.14	6-100	2	-
1982	Nottinghamshire	18	28	2	807	31.03	131	2	4	16	403.5	122	889	61	14.57	7-25	4	-
1982-83	Canterbury	2	4	0	112	28.00	46	-	-	4	75.2	25	136	13	10.46	6-43	1	1
	NZ in NZ	2	3	1	59	29.50	30	-	-	1	77.3	27	141	10	14.10	4-33	-	-
1983	Nottinghamshire	5	4	0	119	29.75	103	1	-	3	86.2	28	210	13	16.15	5-72	1	-
	NZ in England	8	11	2	477	53.00	92*	-	5	3	345.1	95	855	36	23.75	6-53	2	-
1983-84	Canterbury	3	5	1	161	40.25	93	-	1	4	72	29	97	12	8.08	4-14	-	-
	NZ in NZ	3	4	0	144	36.00	99	-	1	3	109.5	33	232	12	19.33	5-28	1	-
	NZ in Sri Lanka	4	4	0	75	18.75	29	-	-	3	128.5	50	258	24	10.75	5-29	2	1
1984	Nottinghamshire	24	31	8	1179	51.26	210*	2	7	23	772.2	245	1645	117	14.05	7-35	6	1
1984-85	Canterbury	5	8	2	90	15.00	30*	-	-	-	168.4	57	346	22	15.72	5-46	2	-
	NZ in NZ	3	4	0	131	32.75	89	-	1	-	118.5	29	306	16	19.12	6-51	1	-
	NZ in West Indies	4	7	1	137	22.83	39*	-	-	1	143	33	409	15	27.26	4-53	-	-
1985	Nottinghamshire	19	29	11	592	32.88	73*	-	5	17	473.5	136	1026	59	17.38	8-41	2	-
1985-86	NZ in Australia	5	6	0	151	25.16	54	-	1	3	241.3	65	537	37	14.51	9-52	5	2
	NZ in NZ	3	3	1	105	52.50	72*	-	1	2	157.5	36	387	16	24.18	7-116	1	-
1986	Nottinghamshire	14	18	5	720	55.38	129*	2	3	6	393.4	108	825	57	14.47	6-31	5	1
	NZ in England	3	3	0	93	31.00	68	-	1	-	153.5	42	390	19	20.52	6-80	2	1
1986-87	Canterbury	8	13	3	207	20.70	50*	-	1	7	294.1	86	581	45	12.91	7-49	6	1
	NZ in NZ	3	4	2	74	37.00	35*	-	-	2	113.1	20	354	17	20.82	6-50	2	-
	NZ in Sri Lanka	1	1	1	151	-	151*	1	-	1	38.5	10	102	4	25.50	4-102	-	-
1987	Nottinghamshire	20	27	7	1075	53.75	133*	2	6	16	568	186	1154	97	11.89	6-20	9	2
	MCC	1	1	0	36	36.00	36	-	-	-	23	3	73	0	-	-	-	-
1987-88	NZ in Australia	5	8	3	151	30.20	36	-	-	1	237.4	63	564	29	19.44	5-30	5	2
	NZ in NZ	1	1	0	37	37.00	37	-	-	-	18	3	50	0	-	-	-	-
1988-89	NZ in India	4	7	2	88	17.60	31	-	-	2	124.5	30	307	27	11.37	9-55	3	1
	Canterbury	1	1	0	37	37.00	37	-	-	-	31	11	65	2	32.50	1-25	-	-
	NZ in NZ	2	3	1	53	26.50	32	-	-	-	82	21	169	5	33.80	4-101	-	-
1989-90	NZ in NZ	4	3	0	133	44.33	87	-	1	-	147.1	32	428	19	22.52	5-39	1	-
1990	NZ in England	5	6	0	204	34.00	90	-	2	4	201.5	39	586	24	24.41	5-27	2	-
	Total	**342**	**473**	**93**	**12052**	**31.71**	**210**	* **14**	**59**	**198**	**67517**	**2827**	**26998**	**1490**	**18.11**	**9-52**	**102**	**18**

**1586.6 8-ball(†) plus 9137.1 6-ball overs

balls**

SUMMARY

	M	I	NO	Runs	Ave	HS	100	50	Ct		Balls	R	W	Ave	BB	5wI	10wM
Canterbury	62	100	22	2012	25.79	93	-	12	35		12564	4600	285	16.14	7-49	19	2
MCC	1	1	0	36	36.00	36	-	-	-		138	73	0	-	-	-	-
NZ in NZ	43	59	8	1501	29.43	103	1	7	19		10663	4615	201	22.96	7-23	15	3
NZ Overseas	82	107	15	2489	27.05	151*	2	11	35		18138	8202	369	22.22	9-52	29	8
Nottinghamshire	148	196	45	5854	38.76	210*	11	29	105		24974	9031	622	14.51	8-41	38	5
Tasmania	6	10	3	160	22.85	33*	-	-	4		1040	477	13	36.69	5-55	1	-
Total	**342**	**473**	**93**	**12052**	**31.71**	**210***	**14**	**59**	**198**		**67517**	**26998**	**1490**	**18.11**	**9-52**	**102**	**18**

IN EACH COUNTRY

	M	I	NO	Runs	Ave	HS	100	50	Ct		Balls	R	W	Ave	BB	5wI	10wM
Australia	29	44	8	917	25.47	103	1	2	13		6907	2953	123	24.00	9-52	14	4
England	187	237	49	6887	36.63	210*	11	37	121		33131	12707	780	16.29	8-41	47	7
India	7	13	2	148	13.45	31	-	-	3		1511	744	40	18.60	9-55	3	1
New Zealand	105	159	30	3513	27.23	103	1	19	54		23227	9215	486	18.96	7-23	34	5
Pakistan	5	8	2	224	37.33	87	-	1	2		877	610	18	33.88	5-47	2	-
Sri Lanka	5	5	1	226	56.50	151*	1	-	4		1006	360	28	12.85	5-29	2	1
West Indies	4	7	1	137	22.83	39*	-	-	1		858	409	15	27.26	4-53	-	-
Total	**342**	**473**	**93**	**12052**	**31.71**	**210***	**14**	**59**	**198**		**67517**	**26998**	**1490**	**18.11**	**9-52**	**102**	**18**

SUMMARY OF HOW FIRST-CLASS WICKETS TAKEN

	Wkts	%
Bowled	349	23.42
Leg before wicket	306	20.54
Caught	802	53.83
Caught and bowled	27	1.81
Hit wicket	6	0.40

TEN WICKETS IN A MATCH
(18)

11-58 **New Zealand v India**	Wellington	1975-76
10-100 **New Zealand v England**	Wellington	1977-78
11-141 Nottinghamshire v Yorkshire	Worksop	1978
11-116 New Zealanders v Warwickshire	Birmingham	1978
11-102 **New Zealand v West Indies**	Dunedin	1979-80
10-83 Canterbury v Central Districts	Christchurch	1982-83
10-102 **New Zealand v Sri Lanka**	Colombo (CCG)	1983-84
11-76 Nottinghamshire v Gloucestershire	Nottingham	1984
15-123 **New Zealand v Australia**	Brisbane	1985-86
11-155 **New Zealand v Australia**	Perth	1985-86
10-72 Nottinghamshire v Surrey	Nottingham	1986
10-140 **New Zealand v England**	Nottingham	1986
12-81 Canterbury v Northern Districts	Christchurch	1986-87
12-83 Nottinghamshire v Somerset	Nottingham	1987
10-46 Nottinghamshire v Sussex	Nottingham	1987
10-67 New Zealanders v Western Australia	Perth	1987-88
10-176 **New Zealand v Australia**	Melbourne	1987-88
10-88 **New Zealand v India**	Bombay	1988-89

FIVE WICKETS IN AN INNINGS
(102)

5-56 New Zealanders v Lancashire	Manchester	1973
7-23 **New Zealand v India**	Wellington	1975-76
5-53 Canterbury v Wellington	Christchurch	1975-76
5-47 New Zealanders v Prime Minister's XI	Rawalpindi	1976-77
5-121 **New Zealand v Pakistan**	Lahore	1976-77
5-28 Canterbury v Auckland	Christchurch	1977-78
5-50 Canterbury v England XI	Christchurch	1977-78
6-26 **New Zealand v England**	Wellington	1977-78
5-25 Nottinghamshire v Derbyshire	Nottingham	1978
6-39 Nottinghamshire v Yorkshire	Worksop	1978
5-102 Nottinghamshire v Yorkshire	Worksop	1978
5-29 Nottinghamshire v Warwickshire	Nottingham	1978
7-77 New Zealanders v Warwickshire	Birmingham	1978
5-84 **New Zealand v England**	Lord's	1978
6-28 Canterbury v Central Districts	Christchurch	1978-79
5-50 Canterbury v Auckland	Christchurch	1978-79
5-62 **New Zealand v Pakistan**	Christchurch	1978-79
5-104 **New Zealand v Pakistan**	Auckland	1978-79
7-28 Nottinghamshire v Glamorgan	Nottingham	1979
7-23 Nottinghamshire v Sussex	Nottingham	1979

5-55 Tasmania v Queensland	Hobart	1979-80	9-52 **New Zealand v Australia**	Brisbane	1985-86
5-34 **New Zealand v West Indies**	Dunedin	1979-80	6-71 **New Zealand v Australia**	Brisbane	1985-86
6-68 **New Zealand v West Indies**	Dunedin	1979-80	5-65 **New Zealand v Australia**	Sydney	1985-86
5-32 Nottinghamshire v Hampshire	Nottingham	1980	5-65 **New Zealand v Australia**	Perth	1985-86
5-61 New Zealanders v Queensland	Brisbane	1980-81	6-90 **New Zealand v Australia**	Perth	1985-86
5-87 **New Zealand v Australia**	Perth	1980-81	7-116 **New Zealand v Australia**	Christchurch	1985-86
6-57 **New Zealand v Australia**	Melbourne	1980-81	5-41 Nottinghamshire v Leicestershire	Nottingham	1986
5-47 **New Zealand v India**	Christchurch	1980-81	6-31 Nottinghamshire v Derbyshire	Derby	1986
7-25 Nottinghamshire v Lancashire	Liverpool	1981	6-33 Nottinghamshire v Surrey	Nottingham	1986
6-60 Nottinghamshire v Essex	Chelmsford	1981	6-42 Nottinghamshire v Warwickshire	Nottingham	1986
5-47 Nottinghamshire v Lancashire	Nottingham	1981	6-80 **New Zealand v England**	Lord's	1986
5-34 Nottinghamshire v Northamptonshire	Cleethorps	1981	6-80 **New Zealand v England**	Nottingham	1986
5-81 Canterbury v Wellington	Wellington	1981-82	6-51 Nottinghamshire v Essex	Nottingham	1986
5-49 Canterbury v Northern Districts	Christchurch	1981-82	5-39 Canterbury v Auckland	Auckland	1986-87
6-26 Canterbury v Auckland	Christchurch	1981-82	5-44 Canterbury v Northern Districts	Gisborne	1986-87
6-40 Canterbury v Central Districts	Palmerston Nth	1981-82	5-28 Canterbury v Otago	Alexandra	1986-87
5-35 Canterbury v Wellington	Christchurch	1981-82	7-49 Canterbury v Northern Districts	Christchurch	1986-87
5-63 **New Zealand v Australia**	Auckland	1981-82	5-32 Canterbury v Northern Districts	Christchurch	1986-87
6-100 **New Zealand v Australia**	Christchurch	1981-82	5-32 Canterbury v Auckland	Rangiora	1986-87
6-65 Nottinghamshire v Lancashire	Manchester	1982	6-105 **New Zealand v West Indies**	Auckland	1986-87
7-25 Nottinghamshire v Hampshire	Nottingham	1982	6-50 **New Zealand v West Indies**	Christchurch	1986-87
5-64 Nottingamshire v Derbyshire	Chesterfield	1982	6-44 Nottinghamshire v Kent	Canterbury	1987
5-21 Nottinghamshire v Sussex	Hove	1982	5-29 Nottinghamshire v Leicestershire	Nottingham	1987
6-43 Canterbury v Central Districts	Christchurch	1982-83	6-53 Nottinghamshire v Sussex	Eastbourne	1987
6-53 **New Zealand v England**	The Oval	1983	5-39 Nottinghamshire v Warwickshire	Worksop	1987
5-93 **New Zealand v England**	Lord's	1983	6-42 Nottinghamshire v Somerset	Nottingham	1987
5-72 Nottinghamshire v Middlesex	Nottingham	1983	6-41 Nottinghamshire v Somerset	Nottingham	1987
5-28 **New Zealand v England**	Christchurch	1983-84	6-60 Nottinghamshire v Northamptonshire	Nottingham	1987
5-73 **New Zealand v Sri Lanka**	Colombo (CCC)	1983-84	6-20 Nottinghamshire v Sussex	Nottingham	1987
5-29 **New Zealand v Sri Lanka**	Colombo (CCC)	1983-84	6-38 Nottinghamshire v Glamorgan	Nottingham	1987
6-52 Nottinghamshire v Essex	Chelmsford	1984	5-37 New Zealanders v Western Australia	Perth	1987-88
5-35 Nottinghamshire v Hampshire	Bournemouth	1984	5-30 New Zealanders v Western Australia	Perth	1987-88
7-35 Nottinghamshire v Gloucestershire	Nottingham	1984	5-68 **New Zealand v Australia**	Adelaide	1987-88
5-61 Nottinghamshire v Worcestershire	Nottingham	1984	5-109 **New Zealand v Australia**	Melbourne	1987-88
5-40 Nottinghamshire v Lancashire	Blackpool	1984	5-67 **New Zealand v Australia**	Melbourne	1987-88
6-55 Nottinghamshire v Warwickshire	Nottingham	1984	9-55 New Zealanders v Western Zone	Rajkot	1988-89
5-46 Canterbury v Wellington	Rangiora	1984-85	5-65 **New Zealand v India**	Bangalore	1988-89
5-74 Canterbury v Auckland	Auckland	1984-85	6-49 **New Zealand v India**	Bombay	1988-89
6-51 **New Zealand v Pakistan**	Dunedin	1984-85	5-39 **New Zealand v Australia**	Wellington	1989-90
7-34 Nottinghamshire v Middlesex	Lord's	1985	5-27 New Zealanders v Worcestershire	Worcester	1990
8-41 Nottinghamshire v Lancashire	Nottingham	1985	5-53 **New Zealand v England**	Birmingham	1990

HAT TRICKS

(2)

Canterbury v Central Districts	Nelson	1971-72
Nottinghamshire v Kent	Canterbury	1987

CENTURIES

(14)

101* Nottinghamshire v Derbyshire	Nottingham	1978	100* Nottinghamshire v Hampshire	Bournemouth	1984
103 **New Zealand v West Indies**	Christchurch	1979-80	210* Nottinghamshire v Middlesex	Lord's	1984
103 New Zealanders v Queensland	Brisbane	1980-81	105* Nottinghamshire v Surrey	The Oval	1986
142* Nottinghamshire v Yorkshire	Bradford	1981	129* Nottinghamshire v Somerset	Nottingham	1986
131 Nottinghamshire v Surrey	The Oval	1982	151* **New Zealand v Sri Lanka**	Colombo (CCC)	1986-87
100* Nottinghamshire v Worcestershire	Worcester	1982	133* Nottinghamshire v Somerset	Taunton	1987
103 Nottinghamshire v Sussex	Hove	1983	101 Nottinghamshire v Somerset	Nottingham	1987

ONE-DAY INTERNATIONAL CAREER RECORDS

		Batting & Fielding							Bowling						
		M	I	NO	Runs	Ave	HS	Ct	Balls	R	W	Ave	BB	4w	B/W
1972-73	Pakistan in NZ	1	1	1	21	-	21 *	-	40	37	0	-	-	-	-
1973	England in England	2	1	0	28	28.00	28	1	114	58	2	29.00	2-23	-	57
1973-74	Australia in NZ	1	1	0	3	3.00	3	-	48	35	0	-	-	-	-
1974-75	England in NZ	2	1	1	6	-	6 *	1	64	25	2	12.50	2-21	-	32
1975(1)	East Africa in England	1	1	1	6	-	6 *	-	72	10	0	-	-	-	-
	England in England	1	1	0	0	0.00	0	-	72	66	1	66.00	1-66	-	72
	India in England	1	1	0	15	15.00	15	1	72	48	2	24.00	2-48	-	36
1975-76	India in NZ	2	1	0	0	0.00	0	1	104	63	1	63.00	1-35	-	104
1978	England in England	2	2	0	2	1.00	1	-	132	92	3	30.66	2-22	-	44
1979 (1)	Sri Lanka in England	1	-	-	-	-	-	-	72	24	1	24.00	1-24	-	72
	India in England	1	-	-	-	-	-	-	60	20	2	10.00	2-20	-	30
	West Indies in England	1	1	0	42	42.00	42	-	66	41	1	41.00	1-41	-	66
	England in England	1	1	0	15	15.00	15	-	72	32	1	32.00	1-32	-	72
1979-80	West Indies in NZ	1	1	0	41	41.00	41	-	60	28	2	14.00	2-28	-	30
1980-81(2)	Australia in Australia	9	8	1	117	16.71	39	3	511	323	11	29.36	5-26	1	46
	India in Australia	5	4	0	56	14.00	32	1	276	125	6	20.83	5-32	1	46
1980-81	India in NZ	2	2	0	45	22.50	23	1	84	33	3	11.00	2-27	-	28
1981-82	Australia in NZ	3	3	0	36	12.00	18	-	153	64	3	21.33	2-24	-	51
1982-83(2)	Australia in Australia	5	5	0	63	12.60	24	4	229	98	5	19.60	2-15	-	45
	England in Australia	5	4	0	139	34.75	79	-	282	169	7	24.14	3-15	-	40
1982-83	Sri Lanka in NZ	3	2	0	20	10.00	11	2	150	49	3	16.33	3-9	-	50
1982-83(3)	Australia in Australia	1	1	0	0	0.00	0	-	42	15	1	15.00	1-15	-	42
1983(1)	England in England	2	2	0	32	16.00	31	-	132	58	4	14.50	3-32	-	33
	Pakistan in England	2	2	0	24	12.00	13	-	126	81	4	20.25	3-20	-	31
	Sri Lanka in England	2	1	0	15	15.00	15	2	133	41	6	6.83	5-25	1	22
1983-84	England in NZ	3	2	0	44	22.00	23	-	180	114	8	14.25	5-32	1	22
1983-84	Sri Lanka in Sri Lanka	3	3	0	28	9.33	13	2	135	68	7	9.71	3-19	-	19
1984-85	Pakistan in NZ	4	3	2	56	56.00	34 *	1	221	132	6	22.00	3-32	-	36
1984-85(4)	West Indies in Australia	2	1	0	11	11.00	11	-	60	23	3	7.66	3-23	-	20
	Sri Lanka in Australia	1	1	0	9	9.00	9	2	36	23	2	11.50	2-23	-	18
	India in Australia	1	1	0	3	3.00	3	-	51	50	1	50.00	1-50	-	51
1984-85	West Indies in West Indies	5	4	1	75	25.00	41	-	210	119	3	39.66	2-29	-	70
1985-86(2)	Australia in Australia	5	5	2	95	31.66	30 *	-	205	127	9	14.11	3-14	-	22
	India in Australia	5	5	1	104	26.00	71	-	288	155	6	25.83	2-16	-	48
1985-86	Australia in NZ	4	4	1	79	26.33	40	-	224	112	9	12.44	4-15	1	24
1986	England in England	2	2	1	29	29.00	18 *	-	122	63	2	31.50	2-29	-	61
1986-87	West Indies in NZ	3	3	0	53	17.66	24	2	138	96	2	48.00	2-46	-	69
1987-88(2)	Australia in Australia	5	5	0	108	27.00	34	-	256	163	5	32.60	3-35	-	51
	Sri Lanka in Australia	4	3	1	98	49.00	52	1	228	94	5	18.80	3-35	-	45
1987-88	England in NZ	1	1	1	33	-	33 *	-	60	43	0	-	-	-	-
1987-88(5)	India in Sharjah	2	2	1	38	38.00	35 *	1	120	103	4	25.75	3-54	-	30
	Sri Lanka in Sharjah	1	1	0	14	14.00	14	-	60	25	1	25.00	1-25	-	60
1988-89	Pakistan in NZ	1	-	-	-	-	-	-	60	38	5	7.60	5-38	1	12
1989-90(6)	Australia in NZ	3	2	0	81	40.50	79	1	174	117	3	39.00	2-43	-	58
	India in NZ	1	1	0	46	46.00	46	-	56	27	2	13.50	2-27	-	28
1990	England in England	2	2	1	21	21.00	12	-	132	80	4	20.00	2-34	-	33
	Total	**115**	**98**	**17**	**1751**	**21.61**	**79**	**27**	**6182**	**3407**	**158**	**21.56**	**5-25**	**6**	**39**

(1) World Cup
(2) World Series Cup
(3) Bushfire Appeal Match
(4) World Championship of Cricket
(5) Sharjah Cup
(6) Rothman's Cup

FIFTIES
(4)

79	New Zealand v England	Adelaide	1982-83
71	New Zealand v India	Adelaide	1985-86
52	New Zealand v Sri Lanka	Hobart	1987-88
79	New Zealand v Australia	Auckland	1989-90

FOUR WICKETS IN AN INNINGS
(6)

5-32	New Zealand v India	Perth	1980-81
5-26	New Zealand v Australia	Sydney	
5-25	New Zealand v Sri Lanka	Bristol	1983
5-32	New Zealand v England	Christchurch	1983-84
4-15	New Zealand v Australia	Dunedin	1985-86
5-38	New Zealand v Pakistan	Dunedin	1988-89

SUMMARY

	M	I	NO	Runs	Ave	HS	Ct		Balls	R	W	Ave	BB	4w	B/W
Rothman's Cup	4	3	0	127	42.33	79	1		230	144	5	28.80	2-27	-	46
World Cup	13	10	1	149	16.55	42	3		877	421	22	19.13	5-25	1	39
World Series Cup	43	39	6	780	23.63	79	9		2275	1254	54	23.22	5-26	2	42
World Championship of Cricket	4	3	0	23	7.66	11	2		147	96	6	16.00	3-23	-	24
Sharjah	3	3	1	52	26.00	35*	1		180	128	5	25.60	3-54	-	36
Others	48	40	9	620	20.00	41	11		2473	1364	66	20.66	5-32	3	37
Totals	**115**	**98**	**17**	**1751**	**21.61**	**79**	**27**		**6182**	**3407**	**158**	**21.56**	**5-25**	**6**	**39**

BY COUNTRY

	M	I	NO	Runs	Ave	HS	Ct		Balls	R	W	Ave	BB	4w	B/W
Australia	36	34	5	582	20.06	79	8		1842	1054	46	22.91	5-26	2	40
East Africa	1	1	1	6	-	6*	-		72	10	0	-	-	-	-
England	23	19	4	349	23.26	79	2		1362	800	34	23.52	5-32	1	40
India	20	17	2	307	20.46	71	5		1111	624	27	23.11	5-32	1	41
Pakistan	8	6	3	101	33.66	34*	1		447	288	15	19.20	5-38	1	29
Sri Lanka	15	11	1	184	18.40	52	9		814	324	25	12.96	5-25	1	32
West Indies	12	10	1	222	24.66	42	2		534	307	11	27.90	3-23	-	48
Totals	**115**	**98**	**17**	**1751**	**21.61**	**79**	**27**		**6182**	**3407**	**158**	**21.56**	**5-25**	**6**	**39**